Brand Protection and the Global Risk of Product Counterfeits

This book is dedicated to the practitioners who, every day, work tirelessly to fight brand infringement.

Brand Protection and the Global Risk of Product Counterfeits

A Total Business Solution Approach

Edited by

Jeremy M. Wilson

Professor, School of Criminal Justice, Michigan State University, USA

Edward Elgar
PUBLISHING

Cheltenham, UK • Northampton, MA, USA

Published by
Edward Elgar Publishing Limited
The Lypiatts
15 Lansdown Road
Cheltenham
Glos GL50 2JA
UK

Edward Elgar Publishing, Inc.
William Pratt House
9 Dewey Court
Northampton
Massachusetts 01060
USA

Paperback edition 2023

A catalogue record for this book
is available from the British Library

Library of Congress Control Number: 2022937611

This book is available electronically in the **Elgar**online
Business subject collection
http://dx.doi.org/10.4337/9781839105821

ISBN 978 1 83910 581 4 (cased)
ISBN 978 1 83910 582 1 (eBook)
ISBN 978 1 0353 2208 4 (paperback)

Printed and bound by CPI Group (UK) Ltd, Croydon, CR0 4YY

Contents

Figures

Tables

Boxes

Contributors

John Carriero is the Senior Director of Brand Protection for Under Armour, Inc. John created, designed, and currently works to enhance the global program for one of the world's most valuable sports brands. John's extensive experience includes military intelligence, private sector security, K-9 security, loss prevention, corporate security, and brand protection, with global assignments. John holds two BA degrees from The Ohio State University.

Peggy E. Chaudhry, PhD, is an Associate Professor at the Villanova School of Business (VSB), Villanova, Pennsylvania. She received her PhD in International Business with minors in International Economics and Marketing at the University of Wisconsin at Madison. Her expertise and publications center on managerial tactics to curb counterfeit trade, consumer complicity with counterfeit goods, and gray markets.

B. William Demeré, PhD, is an Assistant Professor and the RubinBrown Faculty Scholar in the School of Accountancy at the University of Missouri. His PhD is from Michigan State University, and he previously worked at Deloitte and taught at Virginia Tech. His research focuses on measurement issues in accounting and corporate governance, and he currently teaches advanced auditing and data analytics.

Clifford A. Grammich, PhD, is Director of Birdhill Research and Communications, LLC, providing research and communication services for public and private clients. His work includes brand protection, industrial base, criminal justice, national security, police organization, public opinion, education, social policy, and demographic issues. His recent peer-reviewed publications include several works on product counterfeiting and brand protection as well as on police administration.

Warren MacInnis oversees the Global Brand Protection program for Underwriters Laboratories (UL) and has been with UL since 2007. Prior to joining UL, Warren served with the Royal Canadian Mounted Police for nearly 22 years and spent his last 10 years in the Greater Toronto Area of Ontario, Canada, investigating intellectual property crime offenses and leading a team of anti-counterfeiting investigators.

Sean O'Hearen is a Managing Consultant for Excellis Health Solutions and leads their Brand Protection practice. In this role, Sean provides consulting services and solutions to businesses primarily in the pharmaceutical, medical devices, and consumer health and personal care industries. His expertise and areas of focus include strategy, risk assessment, planning, operations, technology, communication, and cross-functional collaboration for brand protection.

Ashley Paintsil, MA, is a doctoral student in the Department of Communication, University of Delaware. Her research focuses on organizational communication and media psychology with a specific interest in brand social media communication. She received her MS in Fashion and Apparel Studies from the University of Delaware. She has ten years of industry experience as an editorial director at fashion and technology publications.

John Reiners is Managing Editor at Oxford Economics covering the EMEA region, overseeing business research programs based on large-scale primary research, with many quantifying the impact of technology adoption on businesses, economies, and wider society. After graduating in Economics, he worked as a financial manager and management consultant, advising businesses and public officials across sectors and internationally.

Karen L. Sedatole, PhD, is the Asa Griggs Candler Professor of Accounting at Emory University's Goizueta Business School. Her research focuses on the design and effectiveness of performance measurement and reward systems, the role of forecasting and budgetary systems within organizations, and control in inter-organizational collaborations. Her PhD is from the University of Michigan.

Kami J. Silk, PhD, is the Edward F. and Elizabeth Goodman Rosenberg Professor of Communication and Chairperson of the Department of Communication, University of Delaware. She oversees academic programs in communication, including the Strategic Communication Master's Program, maintains an active and externally funded program of health and risk communication research, and teaches courses in organizational communication, persuasion, and research.

Chanterelle Sung is a former Director of Compliance at Pfizer and was previously the Director of Strategic Planning and Operations for Pfizer Global Security. Prior to working at Pfizer, she served as an Assistant District Attorney for New York County, an Inspector General for New York City, and Director of Monitoring and Compliance/Senior Counsel for New York State's Office of Storm Recovery. She received her JD from Boston College Law School and BA from Princeton University.

Brandon D.H. Thomas, MA, is a doctoral candidate in the Department of Communication at Michigan State University. Brandon's research interests assess how individuals communicate and process health and risk information relating to environmental contamination. Currently a public health researcher, Brandon uses communication theory to guide public health practices.

Vivian Vassallo, Senior Director, IP Protection and Enforcement at Dolby, has been working in the fields of compliance, gray market, supply chain integrity, and anti-counterfeiting for more than 25 years. She is a driving force in developing global brand protection strategies while considering complex business issues in resolving disputes, meeting corporate business compliance, and intellectual property protection enforcement goals. Prior to Dolby, Vivian worked for 3Com Corporation as Business Compliance lead.

Jeremy M. Wilson, PhD, is a Professor of Criminal Justice at Michigan State University where he founded and directed for ten years the Center for Anti-Counterfeiting and Product Protection. As a scholar, educator, technical assistance provider, advisor, and consultant, he has spent decades working hand-in-hand with industry, law enforcement, government, and other institutions to bring science to the development, implementation, and evaluation of strategies to bolster brand protection, protect intellectual property, and promote public safety. His partnerships have resulted in over 150 publications, more than $11M in sponsored projects, and honors from industry, law enforcement, and academia.

Foreword

When I first came to brand protection, I found most organizations started in law or security and relied on enforcement. At Johnson & Johnson, we started upstream, in the supply chain. We sought how to be more preventive than reactive, but, in reality, most of our work was reactive.

In my first 100 days, I interviewed senior leaders on their perspective and to learn what was keeping them up at night. I found that while we were doing excellent work, most of it was in response to brand protection incidents rather than a more preventative approach. So I looked at our best practices and started a series of formal and informal benchmarking to better understand what other brand protection organizations were doing, and how we could embark on our journey from a response-based organization to a prevention-based one.

Early on, I brought Jeremy Wilson into my work. Jeremy was my go-to subject matter expert, and a safe haven for any questions I had, no matter how simple or complex. Jeremy helped me discover the best practices and what we needed to become the best brand protection organization. He helped me learn how to borrow from others and how to organize for what we needed to do.

Jeremy's research with Rod Kinghorn and Cliff Grammich at Michigan State University on developing a total business solution to brand protection helped point the way for me and others. Their research has helped us identify how to build up our capabilities, to be high-touch with our global stakeholders, and to convey subject matter expertise. When we identify risks, we apply the total business solution against those risks. We can't always prevent bad things, but the total business solution helps us address them when they occur.

The total business solution helps us in ongoing program management as well. In program reviews we go through our projects: where they are going, what we need to do, what we continue to do, and what to do going forward. We forecast our return on investment. The principles of the total business solution guide us in doing so and help us to identify what to convey in making our case to senior leaders.

Brand protection and the total business solution can be applied to all businesses. The bigger your brand, the bigger your market share, the more vulnerable you are to counterfeiters, and the more you need to protect your brand. Small businesses as well can benefit from a total business solution as they seek to grow. Indeed, small businesses are likely to find it easier to put in place a total business solution and embed it in all its processes.

No matter where you are in your brand protection work, a total business solution has something for you. The first steps in a total business solution need not be expensive. Among low-cost steps to implementing brand protection are building a network, including brand protection language in agreements, recording trademarks, and putting no-cost brand protection features in your packaging. From there, this volume, through its discussion of elements of the total business solution and its case studies, can help you identify where to expand.

Whatever you need to put in place for brand protection, you will find guidance on it here. This volume can help you:

- Assess the risk of counterfeiting. This includes measurement approaches, assessing enterprise risk, and understanding consumer motivations.
- Mitigate the risk of counterfeiting. This includes coordinating tactics and functions, identifying and prioritizing new tactics, and communicating the value of brand protection.
- Allocate resources and measure the value of your programs. This includes measuring performance, determining program value, and determining tradeoffs in anti-counterfeiting efforts.
- Build a brand protection team that is best suited to your organization, its culture, and the specific elements of your brand protection strategy.
- Learn from others. This includes case studies of five leading brand protection programs across a variety of industries and what they have learned over time.

Jeremy Wilson has been a trusted source on these issues for more than a decade. He has given brand protection programs access to each other and to wider areas of expertise. He has helped foster efforts that give brand owners, law enforcement, government agencies, and academic researchers the opportunity to access and to learn from each other.

His work has helped us move from prevention to proactive engagement with the end-to-end value chain in the fight against counterfeits. He has helped us leverage networks and, with the total business solution, map our efforts into our organizations, and address brand protection challenges as they evolve.

This volume invites you to learn from and join in this collaboration. While product counterfeiting is a large and evolving problem, all parts of the firm can help combat it. This work will show you how to start or improve. As counterfeiting continues to grow, so will the need for a total business solution. With the lessons in this volume, you can stay ahead of this evolving challenge and position your brand at the forefront in protecting your value and customers.

Richard Kaeser
Vice President of Global Brand Protection
Johnson & Johnson

Preface

In fall of 2008, I was formally introduced to the problems of counterfeit products and intellectual property violations. A new professor at Michigan State University (MSU), I had just arrived from the RAND Corporation, where I led and developed platforms of research and centers on policing, gun violence prevention, and internal security. My dean invited me to a meeting with Johnson & Johnson, General Motors, a representative from the insurance industry, and a few other university representatives. Our guests spoke about the enormous global problem with intellectual property infringements generally and product counterfeits specifically. They discussed the importance of the problem and its various detrimental consequences, noting that the field is fragmented and that there was little strategic guidance in the fight against product counterfeits. They argued that the university, as an academic institution with a land-grant mission to support research and related activities for the public good, coupled with highly ranked programs in the disciplines associated with protecting intellectual property (e.g., criminal justice, business, engineering, law, communications), was uniquely positioned to rally key stakeholders and develop the science to form the basis of effective anti-counterfeit strategy, and they encouraged us to do so.

Shortly thereafter, my dean, who had just recruited me to MSU to help establish platforms of interdisciplinary, externally funded research, asked me to lead the university's response to this problem. I was told this wouldn't take too much of my time and that they just needed someone to steer the ship—true story! With the support of many, I founded and directed for a decade the Center for Anti-Counterfeiting and Product Protection, the first academic hub integrating interdisciplinary research, education, and outreach aimed at uniting stakeholders and science to combat product counterfeiting.

I decided to return to full-time faculty in the fall of 2018, which enabled me to spend more time developing and leading innovative anti-counterfeiting and brand protection research. This transition also allowed me to work even more extensively with firms, law enforcement agencies, and others to translate my research into lessons they can apply to improve their overall resource allocation, strategy formulation, and performance.

This book is an extension of one of the major platforms of research I have developed in partnership with and for the benefit of firms. It depicts and helps to flesh out a total business solution approach to brand protection.

Writing on the basic principles of the total business solution originally with Rod Kinghorn, retired Global Security Director for General Motors, and then expanding upon them with Clifford Grammich, Director of Birdhill Research and Communications, the basic notion is that to maximize the performance and efficiency of brand protection programs, firms need to be as strategic, data-driven, proactive, and comprehensive as possible. While simple to say and perhaps obvious to read, my experience suggests these ideals are incredibly difficult to operationalize in practice and many firms struggle to achieve them, if they prioritize them at all.

Building on many studies conducted in partnership with firms across virtually all industries, this edited volume seeks to introduce the concept of the total business solution, further develop and explore its features, and share examples of it working in the field. Its aim is to help firms bolster their brand protection efforts, either by establishing new programs or further advancing those underway. This book will also be helpful for anyone, including industry practitioners, policymakers, scholars, law enforcement officials, and students, looking to understand the complexities of brand protection, the nature of and response to counterfeit risk, and organizational development. Helping to expand its comprehensiveness, relevancy, and utility, a wide array of experts contributed to this volume, including a unique blend of academics and scholars from criminal justice, accounting, political science, international business, and communications, as well as practitioners from the pharmaceutical and healthcare, apparel, electronics, and safety certification industries.

Jeremy M. Wilson
Okemos, Michigan, USA

Acknowledgments

This book represents a journey of inspiration, discovery, and partnership. Its completion would not have been possible without the support of countless individuals and institutions. Its production is a symbol of the camaraderie among the brand protection community, and that community's desire to continue to innovate and find better ways to protect consumers, society, and firms from the dangers of infringers. I would like to acknowledge several of those who have helped support the development of this book and its insights.

Since I began studying brand protection, hundreds of firms across every industry have welcomed, or at least tolerated (!), my endless inquiries and requests. Those representing these firms have generously shared their time, experience, and resources in numerous ways, ranging from supporting and serving as case studies in research projects to joining me in professional gatherings to simply having constructive conversations. These interactions and collaborations have simultaneously inspired my interest in this topic and offered a means to explore it. The total business solution is a direct product of diverse field work with these partners. Without them, this body of work would not have been possible. Thank you all for your continued support. It is a distinct honor and privilege to work with you. My greatest hope is that you find this volume valuable, and a good investment of your time, as I know that is your most precious resource.

There are three individuals I'd like to call out for their specific support in the development of the total business solution. Rod Kinghorn was instrumental in shaping my early thoughts about the total business solution. His practical, field-based perspective inspired me to think of brand protection as an organic system, and to always be asking if and how my work was "relevant" and provided "value" to the brand protection community. Rich Kaeser saw the "relevance" and "value" of the work Rod and I began developing. His support and partnership fueled the next phase of the total business solution's development, enabling Cliff Grammich and me to begin fleshing it out, defining and illustrating various principles, and creating and sharing lessons on it. Cliff brought organization to our varied and, in some ways, massive undertakings, and identified key connections among our body of work. Moreover, his ability to focus ensured we executed on key deliverables. Gentlemen, I cannot thank you enough for your partnership and support of the total business solution, but most importantly for your friendship.

This volume represents the collective work of brilliant thinkers, executors, and "needle-movers." Fittingly, scholars from numerous academic disciplines share their work alongside practitioners from varied industries. This inter-disciplinary compilation of thought-leaders is ground-breaking and results in a product that advances both the science and practice of brand protection. Together, the contributors effectively explore various nooks and crannies of the total business solution, offering useful lessons for applying the approach and identifying where future research might focus. Fellow contributors, you have my sincerest appreciation for all your efforts in supporting this project, and for sharing your expertise for the benefit of all.

When it comes to advancing science and developing quality publications, few processes are as instrumental as peer review. Having outside experts review content is one of the greatest ways to help ensure products meet rig-orous industry standards. Peer review is also one of the most time-consuming and thankless parts of the production process. I am profoundly grateful to the wide array of esteemed experts who graciously offered their time to support this project by reviewing chapters and providing their comments. To promote overall quality and applicability, each contribution was reviewed by several experts, with at least one each from academia and industry. For their assis-tance in reviewing chapters, I'd like to extend special gratitude to Christina Alataris, John Carriero, Paul Cassano, Peggy Chaudhry, Harry Cole, Dustin Cooley, Will Demeré, Lev Fejes, Cliff Grammich, Branislav Hock, Rod Kinghorn, Ahmet Kirca, Maria Lapinski, Greg Lemione, Jeff Mieseler, Tim Mohn, Mahesh Nalla, Sean O'Hearen, Joseph Parker, David Shepherd, Kami Silk, DJ Smith, Chanterelle Sung, Alan Swayne, Vivian Vassallo, and other anonymous reviewers.

As might be expected for such a large writing project, editing, formatting, and producing this book was no easy task. I'd like to thank the Edward Elgar Publishing staff for their efficient and effective support in all aspects of pro-ducing this book.

My greatest thanks of all are reserved for my girls. My wife, Angie, and my daughter, Alex, inspire me every day. Angie provided ongoing moral support while Alex provided much needed comic relief throughout the many years this project has required. Both have been patient when my work (often) bled into our nights and weekends. Thank you for seeing the big picture of my work, and always being there for me.

My greatest fear in writing an acknowledgments section is failing to mention a specific person who has made a meaningful contribution to this effort. I no doubt have done so—there are so many amazing people who have helped shape this project one way or another. Please forgive me for any unin-tentional oversights.

PART I

Introduction to *Brand Protection and the Global Risk of Product Counterfeits*

1. The brand protector's dilemma and the total business solution

Jeremy M. Wilson

What keeps you up at night? This is a question I've asked countless practitioners responsible for protecting the integrity of their brand(s). Interestingly, their responses tend to be similar regardless of their industry or functional focus (e.g., legal, security, quality). Broadly speaking, the primary concerns of those focused on thwarting brand infringements can be summarized as:

- What is the nature of our risk?
- How large is our problem?
- How do I articulate the need for resources from senior leadership?
- How do I most effectively allocate resources and build an effective brand protection program?
- How do I demonstrate and communicate the value of our brand protection program?

These questions form the basis of what I call the "brand protector's dilemma." I consider them a dilemma not just because addressing them requires a great deal of effort, but also because in some ways they are never truly answered as circumstances continually change. Both those leading the most advanced brand protection programs and those just realizing they are at risk for infringement and must do something about it continually struggle to answer these questions. The total business solution has been developed precisely to help firms address these and other fundamental questions in light of changing risks, needs, and circumstances.

Industry and law enforcement practitioners recognize that society will never arrest or litigate its way out of the problems associated with intellectual property infringement. This suggests enforcement of intellectual property rights is necessary but not sufficient for brand protection. Moreover, firms are intimately familiar with infringement problems. While victims, they can also influence opportunity structures that can facilitate or impede the illicit behavior. As a result, it is imperative that firms determine how best to mitigate intellectual property and brand risks. The total business solution approach to brand protection helps firms help themselves and others by providing a guiding framework for answering key questions that help establish the foundation of a comprehensive, balanced, and efficient brand protection program.

WHAT IS BRAND PROTECTION?

What falls under the umbrella of brand protection for different firms varies almost as much as the firms themselves. Firms build their brand protection programs around their specific types of brand risk, which varies in form and complexity from one company to another. As the total business solution is meant to be comprehensive yet adaptable, the definition of brand protection that guides its foundation and is used throughout this book is equally broad and field-driven: *brand protection is the effort, in any form, scope, or scale, undertaken by firms to protect the value, image, and reputation of its brand(s).* Of course, this necessitates defining "brand," which is equally difficult. Again, for the purposes of the total business solution it is most helpful to conceptualize the term broadly: *a brand is the collection of elements that identifies or is unique to a company or its products or services.* This encompasses trademarks, logos, slogans, and similar identifiers, but much more as well. A firm's brand is the complete perception consumers and clients have of what the firm does. This includes everything from what it produces and provides to the social and political decisions it makes. As such, the "brand" is arguably a company's most important and valuable asset.

There are many forms of illicit or otherwise fraudulent behaviors that affect brands and that firms seek to mitigate. Frequently involving intellectual property violations, these can include both criminal and civil violations, such as those concerning trade secrets, trade dress, product overruns, simulations, and knockoffs. Formal brand protection programs tend to focus on product counterfeits (trademark violations), copyright and patent infringement, diverted product (gray or parallel markets where genuine product is sold in unauthorized channels), and the adulteration, tampering, and theft of product, with product counterfeits and diversion representing perhaps the greatest risks on which most concentrate.

There are differences of opinion on the types of infringements that brand protection efforts should address, and firms tend to build brand protection programs around the elements they define as most important to protecting their brand. Nonetheless, trademark violations are generally a core concern among firms that manufacture products, so many illustrations of the total business solution throughout this book highlight scenarios involving counterfeits. Yet, it is important to remember that the total business solution is meant to be a broad philosophy and framework that can be applied to mitigate virtually all forms of brand risk.

WHY FIRMS (AND OTHERS) SHOULD CARE ABOUT BRAND PROTECTION

Brand infringements represent a major risk to firms, but also to many others. According to the Organisation for Economic Co-operation and Development (2021), in 2019, counterfeited and pirated products alone represented as much as 2.5 percent ($461B) of world trade, including 5.8 percent ($134B) of imports in Europe. Counterfeit goods extend to every industry and type of product. In 2020, the most frequently seized goods by US Customs and Border Protection (2021) included handbags/wallets, apparel/accessories, footwear, watches/jewelry, consumer electronics, consumer products, pharmaceuticals, automotive/transportation, and sporting goods.

The consequences of brand infringements are considerable. For example, those associated with counterfeiting include harms to individuals, businesses, and society. Individual consumers who purchase counterfeit goods are, especially if they believe they are purchasing legitimate goods, denied the use of safe, genuine products. Counterfeit harms can also be more direct and evolve over time with, for example counterfeit face masks, test kits, and medications becoming prevalent during the COVID-19 pandemic (US Customs and Border Protection, 2020). In addition to direct loss of sales, legitimate businesses may suffer loss of reputation from poorly performing counterfeit goods that illegitimately bear their trademark, and even warranty, liability, and legal costs for them. Counterfeiters undermine the investments that firms make in research, development, and for meeting production and safety standards, while essentially using a firm's reputation to compete against it. Businesses and other institutions can also be unwitting purchasers of counterfeit goods and suffer harms from the poor performance of such goods; this has included military contractors who purchased counterfeit goods from suppliers (Sullivan and Wilson, 2017). Finally, larger entities such as governments, economies, and societies may all suffer from product counterfeiting. Governments suffer loss of tax revenue and must spend to thwart counterfeiting and related crimes. Economies are deprived of jobs and innovation when legitimate manufacturers are unable to overcome the losses they suffer from counterfeiting. Societies may suffer risks to public safety and national security through the links of counterfeiting to transnational organized crime, extremism, human trafficking, supply chain infiltration, and still other crimes (EUIPO, 2020; US Department of Homeland Security, 2020; United Nations Office on Drugs and Crime, 2019; Sullivan et al., 2014; Heinonen and Wilson, 2012).

BRAND PROTECTION AS A FUNCTION OF OPPORTUNITY

A foundational principle underpinning the total business solution is that brand infringements generally, and product counterfeiting specifically, are functions of opportunity. Two related theories helpful for explaining opportunity-based crimes are rational choice and routine activities. Originating from principles of deterrence (Beccaria, 1764) and utilitarianism (Bentham, 1789), rational choice theory considers crime from the perspective of a hedonistic individual. It views crime as a function of rational actors weighing the perceived risks and rewards of engaging in illicit behavior (Becker, 1968). In the context of brand protection, an individual may choose to counterfeit products if they see doing so will result in considerable profit while the risk of being caught is low or, if caught, the penalty is minor.

Routine activities theory, as originally defined by Cohen and Felson (1979), posits that the structure of activity patterns, such as those associated with daily life (e.g., working, traveling, socializing with friends, surfing the internet, attending school, shopping, relaxing on vacation), influences criminal opportunity. It is this opportunity that gives rise to predatory crime. More concretely, crime is affected by the convergence in space and time of a motivated offender, a suitable target, and an absence of capable guardians. These elements form the chemistry of the crime (Felson, 1998). A motivated offender is anyone with criminal inclinations and the ability to carry them out. In the context of product counterfeiting, a target could be a branded product that is in high demand or where a counterfeit could be created or sold easily or with a high profit margin. A capable guardian is any person whose simple presence could discourage crime. Altogether, routine activities theory suggests that crime is likely where there is a motivated offender, a suitable target, and an absence of a capable guardian. Conversely, crime is less likely without a motivated offender, a suitable target, or in the presence of a capable guardian.

A critical principle of opportunity theories is that crime can be prevented by reducing structures conducive for it (Felson and Clarke, 1998). A key development here is situational crime prevention (Clarke, 1995), defined as

> opportunity-reducing measures that are (1) directed at highly specific forms of crime (2) that involve the management, design or manipulation of the immediate environment in as systematic and permanent way as possible (3) so as to increase the effort and risks of crime and reduce the rewards as perceived by a wide range of offenders. (Clarke, 1992, p. 4)

Importantly, this body of work has evolved into developing situational prevention techniques for reducing crime, which can be classified into five broad
categories that can influence offender decision making:

- Increasing the effort needed to complete the crime.
- Increasing the risks in completing the crime.
- Reducing the rewards expected from the crime.
- Reducing provocations that may encourage offenders to commit criminal
  acts.
- Removing excuses that may "rationalize" or justify offender actions
  (Cornish and Clarke, 2003).

These techniques help provide a roadmap for preventing crime and are instrumental for considering ways to mitigate the risk of brand infringement.

In summary, the total business solution to brand protection is predicated on
a foundation of established criminal justice theory. It considers brand infringements as a function of opportunity, influenced by routine activities, and
would-be, utilitarian-seeking offenders who consider each opportunity based
on a calculation of the perceived costs and benefits of committing the crime.
Importantly, brands can protect themselves and prevent such illicit behaviors
by understanding and purposefully affecting the opportunity structures that
give rise to them.

PRINCIPLES OF THE TOTAL BUSINESS SOLUTION

Grounded in opportunity theory and significant industry outreach, experience,
and practice, the total business solution originated from a series of papers
I developed with Rod Kinghorn (Wilson and Kinghorn, 2014; Kinghorn and
Wilson, 2013) and then began to flesh out more fully with Cliff Grammich
(Wilson and Grammich, 2020a; 2020b), after several of its concepts could
be explored through various benchmarking projects and additional collaboration and outreach with industry partners. These works spoke of the risk that
virtually all brands (and other stakeholders) face with respect to counterfeits,
and the primarily reactive and frequently piecemeal approach most firms
take to address the problem. We argued for a more thoughtful approach to
maximize brand protection performance. We attempted to outline basic tenets
of a total business solution approach that could help form both a philosophy
and a framework for building effective brand protection programs. Our efforts
led us to six basic principles of a total business solution for brand protection.
These were to:

1. *Identify the infringer as the unseen competitor.* Brand infringers use
   a firm's own intellectual property against it. They leverage a firm's invest-

ments in product development, marketing, and reputation to compete against the firm. While not as visible as legitimate competitors, infringers nonetheless exercise strategy and capitalize on opportunity in executing their schemes. Just as firms assess the strategies and processes of their legitimate competitors so too should they systematically study and examine the operations of the illicit actors they are competing against. Doing so can help firms understand the processes and systems that create counterfeiting and other brand infringement opportunities, and thereby enable the development of informed responses to reduce them.

2. *Prioritize prevention, proactivity, and strategy.* For a variety of practical reasons (not the least of which is the difficulty of measuring the risk and therefore allocating resources toward it), firms traditionally have taken a reactive stance, typically centered on enforcement activities, in dealing with brand infringements. This is inefficient as it results in the well-known "whack-a-mole" cycle of incident–response–incident–response, without ever addressing the underlying conditions that give rise to the problems. As noted earlier, many industry and law enforcement practitioners claim society will never arrest or litigate its way out of these problems. A more efficient solution is to be more strategic and proactive, aiming to craft and implement purposeful actions that can minimize or prevent opportunities for brand infringements. Such prevention can reduce the need for a reactive response as well as the cost and damage to the firm resulting from infringements. When reaction is necessary, a well-thought-out, comprehensive, and pre-planned strategy can address the issue more efficiently.

3. *Integrate controls and mechanisms for detecting and responding to infringements.* If a firm isn't aware of infringements when they occur, it can't respond to them, let alone learn from and formulate strategies to prevent them. Firms should implement as part of their business culture mechanisms across the enterprise and throughout the entire value chain, from product development through distribution, to alert it to instances that create risk to the brand. While many of these will necessarily be internal, they can be based on external information as well.

    Such information is also useful for gauging the mitigation of risk over time and across locations. Beyond providing the firm insight on the nature and prevalence of risks, controls can also provide clear and consistent directives for the most appropriate response to specific problems. These ensure problems are uniformly and effectively addressed as they occur.

4. *Maximize data, metrics, and analysis to assess and mitigate risk and gauge performance.* Moving away from business as usual, gut feelings, and the implementation of actions with little reflection, firms should draw upon evidence and systematic analysis to assess the nature of their risk, drive the development and implementation of specific and coordinated

activities, assess the effectiveness of their strategies, and evaluate the overall performance and value of their brand protection programs. This includes not just employing productivity measures that gauge how much a program does, but outcome-based performance metrics that assess what a program accomplishes. It is important for firms to integrate a data-driven focus as part of their brand protection culture and to incorporate metrics and analysis throughout the entire business process.

5.   *Formulate and execute a holistic approach that integrates and coordinates all parts of the firm for brand protection.* Brand protection programs, if they exist at all in a firm, are typically implemented in a rather narrow or siloed fashion as part of a single or few functions, such as security or legal. However, virtually every part of the firm can play a role in brand protection. Maximizing brand protection requires understanding that risk is interdisciplinary, and mitigating it requires a similar multi-faceted approach. A total business solution requires firms to integrate as many functions as possible in a comprehensive and purposeful way to protect the brand.

6.   *Create and promote a culture of continuous improvement.* Brand infringers continuously learn and find new opportunities on which to capitalize—so too should firms as they seek to protect their brands. Firms should never be complacent. They need to engender a culture of brand protection that promotes the ongoing search for understanding, innovation, and improvement. In other words, brand protection programs need to become learning organizations (Senge, 1990; Senge et al., 1999; Ortenblad, 2019). Senge defines learning organizations as "organizations where people continually expand their capacity to create the results they truly desire, where new and expansive patterns of thinking are nurtured, where collective aspiration is set free, and where people are continually learning how to learn together" (1990, p. 3). He posits that vital dimensions of these organizations are systems thinking, personal mastery, mental models (assumptions and generalizations that influence how people understand and respond to the world), building shared vision, and team learning. Garvin (1993, p. 80) defines a learning organization more simply as "an organization skilled at creating, acquiring, and transferring knowledge, and at modifying its behavior to reflect new knowledge and insights." He characterizes the practices or processes of a learning organization as problem-solving, experimenting, learning from others, learning from experience, and transferring knowledge. Watkins and Marsick (1993; Marsick and Watkins, 1999) offer yet another interpretation of learning organizations, citing features such as creating continuous learning opportunities, promoting inquiry and dialogue, encouraging collaboration and team learning, establishing systems to capture and share learning, empowering people toward

a collective vision, connecting the organization to its environment, and providing strategic leadership for learning. In short, firms need to recognize the circular nature of brand protection in that they must continuously leverage information from their experience and translate it into lessons for establishing an ever-innovating brand protection program that effectively adapts to changing risks and circumstances.

Based on science and field experience, these principles collectively form the foundation of the total business solution approach to maximizing brand protection. While constructive, these principles are broad and can be operationalized in many ways based on firm risk, ethos, values, interpretations, resources, experience, constraints, and still other factors. To help establish a science of brand protection, the remainder of this book explores various elements of the framework and approaches to its implementation.

OUTLINE OF THE BOOK

Part I: Introduction

This chapter constitutes Part I, serving as an introduction for the book. The discussion of the brand protector's dilemma and foundations of the total business solution are meant to offer useful context and set the stage for the substantive content to follow.

Part II: Assessing the Nature of Product Counterfeit Risk

Part II focuses on various approaches for assessing and understanding brand infringement risk and its components. The three chapters that constitute this part examine risk from very different perspectives. Together, they demonstrate the need to consider various aspects of risk, different perspectives for examining brand protection risk, systematic approaches to establishing a risk-based brand protection program, and the adaptability of the total business solution.

In Chapter 2, "Building and optimizing a brand protection program: a total business solution model," Grammich and I build on over a decade of field research to lay out the building blocks of establishing a brand protection program that is grounded in the total business solution philosophy. We note that while brands are among their most valuable assets, firms may have little in place for brand protection. Those that do have brand protection programs in place often rely on reactive actions rather than including strategies for prevention as well. This chapter introduces the elements of a total business solution program model, describing a proactive solution that goes beyond initial reaction to a brand protection problem. Its elements include problem recognition, risk assessment, strategy development, strategy implementation, performance measurement, and assessment. In assessing risks, it focuses on where the threat, vulnerability, and consequence of counterfeiting are greatest for a firm. Each element of the total business solution program model builds on and informs the others. No element of the program is by itself sufficient. Together, however, they can help reduce the opportunity for infringers.

Sean O'Hearen turns the risk discussion to the relevance of standards. In "Risk management and risk assessment for brand protection" (Chapter 3), he explains there have been few systematic approaches to brand protection, but the risk management standards of the International Organization for Standardization (ISO) offer practical guidance for brand protection professionals. He contends that ISO 31000 has elements which can apply to each of the tenets of the total business solution to brand protection. These include risk identification for identifying the infringer as the unseen competitor; leadership and commitment for emphasizing prevention, proactivity, and security; defining risk criteria and preparing and implementing risk treatment plans for setting performance metrics and data; establishing principles and undertaking risk analysis for highlighting the value of internal and external controls; and establishing principles for creating a culture of continuous improvement and learning and promoting a holistic approach to brand protection. This chapter describes applications of these elements as well as how to conduct risk analysis at the levels of the product, brand, and value chain.

Finally, in "Combatting illicit trade: understanding consumer motivations" (Chapter 4), Peggy Chaudhry and John Reiners consider risk from the perspective of consumer attitudes and behaviors. Their chapter provides a synopsis of an Oxford Economics research study that examined fundamental concerns of combatting illicit trade. This study analyzed 37,000 survey respondents across 37 European countries and provides a comprehensive picture of consumer attitudes and behaviors regarding illicit trade. Specifically, the study evaluated five product categories with high excise duties (cigarettes and alcoholic drinks) and other goods subject to infringement of intellectual property rights (films, music, and games; clothing and accessories; and medicines) to better understand consumer motivations to obtain illicit goods. They find that consumers' reasons for buying illicit goods are highly nuanced. Though many seek out illicit products to get a better price, other factors such as quality, reliability, and availability also stimulate the purchase decision. The research stemming from the Oxford Economic study proposes a new way of analyzing consumer motivations through novel illicit trade matrices to inform brand owners and other stakeholders in targeting strategies to combat illicit trade.

Part III: Mitigating the Risk of Counterfeit Products

Translating analysis and understanding of risk into responses, Part III dives into approaches for reducing the risk of brand infringement. In Chapters 5 and 6, Grammich and I look closely at strategies and tactics firms can use for mitigating risk. In "Brand protection and organizational silos: integrating tactics and firm functions in the fight against counterfeits" (Chapter 5), we argue that previous research offers few integrative approaches to address product counterfeiting. Many current approaches are "siloed," with little interaction across functions. We explain that a total business solution for brand protection promotes a holistic approach that integrates and coordinates all parts of the firm for brand protection. To better understand the tactics that firms may use in a total business solution to brand protection, we asked 42 subject matter experts to identify the tactics that a firm would ideally use in brand protection and the functions that should use these tactics. We then categorized these tactics to identify all dimensions of an enterprise-wide approach to brand protection. We find that many of the most important actions that firms can take to protect their brands are proactive. The functions and categories we identify with large numbers of tactics can indicate where to launch or expand brand protection programs.

Complementing the unique insight we gathered from the subject matter experts in Chapter 5, in "Options for mitigating the risk of product counterfeits: lessons from research and practice" (Chapter 6), Grammich and I look deeper into academic research on brand protection tactics. We discuss the degree to which research on product counterfeiting is disjointed and sporadic. It focuses on topics such as prevalence and not on tactics for reducing counterfeiting. Nevertheless, academic research on tactics can offer insights to practitioners. Such research is likely to be more independent, comprehensive, and rigorous than what practitioners can do for themselves. We review academic research on anti-counterfeiting tactics that businesses may use. We compare the distribution of researcher-suggested tactics by category with those that practitioners offer. While practitioner-suggested tactics may give the best insight of current tactics used, researcher-suggested tactics can provide additional context and detail. Our examination reveals that firms may wish to rely on practitioner-suggested tactics in launching a program, and researcher-suggested tactics for expanding it.

In Chapter 7, "Communicating the value of brand protection through a persuasive internal communications approach," Kami Silk, Brandon Thomas, Ashley Paintsil, and I turn to the critical issue of communicating internally about the important role of brand protection and what the enterprise must do to protect itself from counterfeits. We discuss the importance of using communication effectively to create an organizational culture that values and elevates brand protection across all levels of the organization. Focusing on persuasive communication techniques and opportunities, we review organizational functions and tactics that brand protection experts recommend and offer suggestions for maximizing internal communications strategies to increase the value of brand protection among organizational members.

Part IV: Resource Allocation for and Measuring the Value of Brand Protection Programs

Resourcing and measuring the performance of any business program is crucial, and brand protection is no exception. In fact, my research and outreach with brand protection practitioners indicates many are under increasing pressure to measure and demonstrate their program's return on investment (ROI) and value to the firm. The ability to illustrate success is paramount when practitioners must request funding to help protect their firm against brand risks. Part IV seeks to offer approaches and lessons for considering how best to allocate resources for and gauge the performance of brand protection programs.

In "Counterfeiting and anti-counterfeiting costs: an application of cost of quality concepts" (Chapter 8), Will Demeré, Karen Sedatole, and I apply concepts from the Cost of Quality (CoQ) literature to provide insights into the nature of anti-counterfeiting investments and the returns to these investments. We start by describing the evolution of the CoQ model and contribute further to this model by incorporating additional cost characteristics. We then apply CoQ concepts to counterfeiting to better understand how firms can invest in anti-counterfeiting and dynamically assess their return to such investments. Based on interviews with brand protection professionals, we also provide insights into how firms are allocating resources relative to this framework. While there are substantial measurement challenges in assessing returns to anti-counterfeiting investments, we show how the CoQ model can help to highlight important cost–benefit tradeoffs and dynamic effects over time, as well as the limitations of metrics in fully capturing difficult-to-measure costs and returns.

O'Hearen explores in Chapter 9 how brand protection practitioners may adopt a balanced scorecard to demonstrate the value of their work. In "Performance measurement for brand protection: a strategic scorecard approach," he explains that just as balanced scorecards have helped profit center managers demonstrate how their work contributes to the firm's bottom line, so too may they help brand protection practitioners shed their "cost center" image and demonstrate how their work supports it. This approach considers design elements such as target audience, link to strategy, benefits, program and operational perspectives, data measures and management, and engagement. It also considers components such as total program value recovery, the number of consumers protected, sales loss exposure, trends in incidents, monitoring of offline and online markets, defensive actions such as partner audits and customs recordals, and integration of best practices. Above all, he finds that scorecards offer a means for practitioners to standardize their efforts and learn from each other.

As brand owners deploy resources for brand protection, they seek to understand their ROI and how to make their investments more effective. In Chapter 10, "Determining the value of brand protection programs: identifying and assessing performance metrics in brand protection," Grammich, Demeré, Sedatole, and I investigate how firms measure their ROI in brand protection and consider alternatives to ROI that they might use. We interviewed brand protection professionals from ten firms in three broad industry categories: microelectronics and computer products; food, agricultural, and pharmaceutical products; and apparel, consumer, and luxury products. Because previous research on this topic is lacking, we identified firms' metrics for activities, outcomes, and valuation. We also sought to identify the context of implementation for their metrics. We found firms most often measure their activities rather than assess activity outcomes or value. We summarize and classify the metrics that respondents reported using and offer recommendations for improving brand protection metrics. We explain that understanding current metrics and their context, as well as metrics firms might use, can contribute to the practice of brand protection measurement and the success of brand protection programs.

Part V: The Total Business Solution in Practice

Steeped in both research and practice, the chapters of the first four sections do well to offer systematic and methodical reviews of key components of the total business solution. However, there is also great value in considering case studies of the total business solution that can elucidate the experiences of practitioners implementing aspects of the framework. The purpose of Part V is to offer such illustrative examples.

In "Brand protection: creating an enforcement framework for action" (Chapter 11), Warren MacInnis zeroes in on enforcement, noting that effective brand protection programs should have several components that contribute to it. He explains that an effective enforcement strategy can form a strong foundation for anti-counterfeiting efforts and be an integral part of any total business solution. He provides a guide for the design, implementation, and operation of an effective enforcement function. In his view, one of the most critical components of any enforcement function is investigations, the thorough and systematic process to gather evidence and determine the facts of an incident. Investigations should address the who, what, when, where, why, and how of an incident, and give attention to the questions of what is known, how it is known, and why it matters. He notes that effective intelligence gathering and analysis capabilities also provide value by identifying and targeting counterfeiting operations, prioritizing investigative efforts, focusing resources on repeat or serious offenders, and helping rights holders increase the effectiveness and efficiency of their security efforts. He points out that product authentication forms yet another key component of enforcement programs.

Chanterelle Sung explores the total business solution through the lens of patient safety in her chapter "Product integrity for patient safety: a Pfizer case study" (Chapter 12). Noting that counterfeit medicines, and efforts to combat them, have been a reality for many years, she discusses how one major pharmaceutical manufacturer, Pfizer, addressed the problem through application of the total business solution to brand protection. As she characterizes it, Pfizer's product integrity function is based primarily within the Pfizer Global Security team, which works across the enterprise and its functions and regions to protect patients from counterfeit medicine. Pfizer has sought to reduce demand through education of the public, advocacy with policymakers, and training of law enforcement officials and healthcare professionals. It has sought to reduce supply through proactive enforcement, made possible by a data-driven risk mitigation strategy, including self-assessment and visualization of risk priorities through dashboards and metrics. The outcomes-focused initiative helped stimulate new thinking on how to address counterfeits, required working with other functions across the enterprise, and demonstrated the value of brand protection efforts.

Focusing on the demonstration of value, John Carriero, in his chapter "Calculating brand protection impact" (Chapter 13), contends that among the first things that executives want to know about a brand protection program is the impact it is having. He argues that calculating the brand protection impact (BPI) can help demonstrate the impact a program is having and its change over time. He presents a framework establishing that BPI should consider units seized through ground enforcement work, units seized through factory raids, marketplace and auction site enforcement, website and domain enforcement, and restitution. This chapter illustrates how brand protection professionals can calculate values in demonstrating the conservative effect of their efforts. It also discusses non-quantitative programs, such as trainings, that can have a positive impact on brand protection programs. Finally, it provides an example of technology (smart tags) that can have an impact across a company, engaging other functions in brand protection efforts while supporting the work of those functions as well.

In the final case example, Vivian Vassallo establishes in "The never-ending brand protection conundrum" (Chapter 14) that there is no single set of rules that organizations should pursue in brand protection. Rather, different organizations may require different skills, and brand protection practitioners may also learn from each other over time. Within an organization, she explains, brand protection teams should position themselves to make brand protection everyone's problem to address. Brand protection practitioners may also find they need to balance enforcement efforts, focusing on areas where they are more likely to have success. While noting that brand protection processes are important, she warns against relying too heavily on them as they can force brand protection teams to miss outlying cases. She highlights how brand protection practitioners can develop insights about brand protection issues and cases by relying on other functions of the firm and by performing data analysis over time.

Part VI: Tenets of the Total Business Solution

In the final chapter, "Implementation of a total business solution for brand protection: core principles in theory and practice" (Chapter 15), the only one in Part VI, I attempt to take stock of key lessons the contributors provide in relation to the total business solution. The six primary principles, or tenets, of the total business solution are revisited: identify the infringer as the unseen competitor; prioritize prevention, proactivity, and strategy; integrate controls and mechanisms for detecting and responding to infringements; maximize data, metrics, and analysis to assess and mitigate risk and gauge performance; formulate and execute a holistic approach that integrates and coordinates all parts of the firm for brand protection; and create and promote a culture of continuous improvement. For each of these tenets, I synthesize the information and context that the contributors offered, trying to further flesh out and operationalize key aspects of each primary tenet of the total business solution. The review illustrates the significant interconnectedness of all the total business solution tenets.

REFERENCES

Beccaria, C. (1764), *An Essay on Crimes and Punishment*, https://www.thefederalistpapers.org/wp-content/uploads/2013/01/Cesare-Beccaria-On-Crimes-and-Punishment.pdf.

Becker, G. (1968), 'Crime and punishment: an economic approach', *Journal of Political Economy*, **76**, 169–217.

Bentham, J. (1789), *An Introduction to the Principle of Morals and Legislation*, London: Oxford at the Clarendon Press, https://oll-resources.s3.us-east-2.amazonaws.com/oll3/store/titles/278/0175_Bk.pdf.

Clarke, R. (1992), *Situational Crime Prevention: Successful Case Studies*, New York: Harrow and Heston.

Clarke, R. (1995), 'Building a safer society: strategic approaches to crime prevention', *Crime and Justice*, **19**, 91–150.

Cohen, L. E., and Felson, M. (1979), 'Social change and crime rate trends: a routine activity approach', *American Sociological Review*, **44**, 588–608.

Cornish, D., and Clarke, R. (2003), 'Opportunities, precipitators and criminal decisions: a reply to Wortley's critique of situational crime prevention', *Crime Prevention Studies*, **16**, 41–96.

EUIPO (2020), *IP Crime and Its Link to Other Serious Crimes: Focus on Poly-Criminality*, European Union Intellectual Property Office, https://euipo.europa .eu/tunnel-web/secure/webdav/guest/document_library/observatory/documents/ reports/2020_IP_crime_and_its_link_to_other_serious_crimes/2020_IP_crime_and _its_link_to_other_serious_crimes_Full.pdf.

Felson, M. (1998), *Crime and Everyday Life*, 2nd Ed., Thousand Oaks, CA: Pine Forge Press.

Felson, M., and Clarke, R. V. (1998), *Opportunity Makes the Thief*, Crime Detection and Prevention Series, Paper 98, Police Research Group. London: Home Office.

Garvin, D. (1993), 'Building a learning organization', *Harvard Business Review*, **71**(4), 78–91.

Heinonen, J., and Wilson, J. M. (2012), 'Product counterfeiting at the state level: a risk assessment of Michigan-related incidents', *International Journal of Comparative and Applied Criminal Justice*, **36**(4), 273–290.

Kinghorn, R., and Wilson, J. M. (2013), *Anti-Counterfeit Strategy for Brand Owners*, East Lansing, MI: Michigan State University Center for Anti-Counterfeiting and Product Protection, https://jeremywilson.org/2013/11/18/anti-counterfeit-strategy -for-brand-owners/.

Marsick, V., and Watkins, K. (1999), *Facilitating Learning Organizations: Making Learning Count*, London: Gower Press.

Organisation for Economic Co-operation and Development (2021), *Global Trade in Fakes: A Worrying Threat*, https://euipo.europa.eu/ohimportal/en/web/observatory/ report-on-trade-in-fakes.

Ortenblad, A. (2019), *The Learning Organization*, Oxford: Oxford University Press.

Senge, P. M. (1990), *The Fifth Discipline: The Art and Practice of the Learning Organization*, New York: Doubleday.

Senge, P. M., Kleiner, A., Roberts, C., Ross, R., Roth, G., and Smith, B. (1999), *The Dance of Change: The Challenges to Sustaining Momentum in Learning Organizations*, New York: Doubleday.

Sullivan, B. A., Chermak, S., Wilson, J. M., and Freilich, J. D. (2014), 'The nexus between terrorism and product counterfeiting in the United States', *Global Crime*, **15**(3–4), 357–378.

Sullivan, B. A., and Wilson, J. M. (2017), 'An empirical examination of product counterfeiting crime impacting the U.S. military', *Trends in Organized Crime*, **20**(3–4), 316–337. https://doi.org/10.1007/s12117-017-9306-7.

United Nations Office on Drugs and Crime (2019), *The Illicit Trafficking of Counterfeit Goods and Transnational Organized Crime*, https://www.unodc.org/documents/ counterfeit/FocusSheet/Counterfeit_focussheet_EN_HIRES.pdf.

US Customs and Border Protection (2020, October 7), 'CBP Baltimore field office seizes nearly 59,000 counterfeit COVID-19 facemasks and other test kits and medications', https://www.cbp.gov/newsroom/local-media-release/cbp-baltimore-field -office-seizes-nearly-59000-counterfeit-covid-19.

US Customs and Border Protection (2021), *Intellectual Property Rights Seizure Statistics: Fiscal Year 2020*, https://www.cbp.gov/document/report/fy-2020-ipr -seizure-statistics.

US Department of Homeland Security (2020), *Combating Trafficking in Counterfeit and Pirated Goods: Report to the President of the United States*, https://www.dhs.gov/sites/default/files/publications/20_0124_plcy_counterfeit-pirated-goods-report_01.pdf.

Watkins, K., and Marsick, V. (1993), *Sculpting the Learning Organization: Lessons in the Art and Science of Systematic Change*, San Francisco, CA: Jossey-Bass.

Wilson, J. M., and Grammich, C. (2020a), 'Brand protection across the enterprise: toward a total business solution', *Business Horizons*, **63**(3), 363–376.

Wilson, J. M., and Grammich, C. (2020b), 'Protecting brands from counterfeiting risks: tactics of a total business solution', *Journal of Risk Research*, DOI: 10.1080/13669877.2020.1806908.

Wilson, J. M., and Kinghorn, R. (2014). *Brand Protection as a Total Business Solution*, East Lansing, MI: Michigan State University Center for Anti-Counterfeiting and Product Protection, https://jeremywilson.org/2014/11/17/brand-protection-as-a-total-business-solution/.

PART II

Assessing the nature of product counterfeit risk

2. Building and optimizing a brand protection program: a total business solution model[1]

Jeremy M. Wilson and Clifford A. Grammich

COUNTERFEITING AS A FUNCTION OF OPPORTUNITY

Though the value of their brands is among their most valuable assets, firms may have little in place for brand protection. This is particularly true for protection against counterfeit products, that is, goods or packaging bearing a trademark that is virtually the same as one registered to an authorized owner. Brand management strategies targeting counterfeit risks are typically reactive and arise only when a firm suspects lost sales, detects significant quality issues from customer returns or complaints, or receives a third-party tip (Wilson et al., 2016; Wilson and Kinghorn, 2014).

Such an approach might be most effective if product counterfeiting were a random occurrence. But, like other crimes, it is not random. Rather, product counterfeiting is more likely to occur where a suitable target is available, there is the lack of a guardian to prevent the crime from happening, and a motivated offender is present (Cohen and Felson, 1979; Arizona State University Center for Problem-Oriented Policing, 2021a; Hollis et al., 2015). In other words, crime is based on opportunity structures. Systematic assessment can help illuminate the criminal opportunity and, in turn, inform strategy to reduce it. The most effective crime interventions are those that are data-driven and comprehensive. They seek to shrink the opportunity for crime by increasing the effort needed to commit the crime, increasing the risk of being caught committing the crime, and reducing the rewards for the crime by reducing the provocations and excuses for committing it.

There are many contributors to the opportunity for product counterfeiting. Perhaps foremost among these is the expansion of the global economy. Consumerism, that is, the insatiable desire of many consumers for goods they cannot afford, also provides opportunities for counterfeiters (Schornstein,

2013). Counterfeiters typically make their products where manufacturing is cheap and governments have little interest in enforcing intellectual property laws (Macolini, 2019). E-commerce further complicates the problem of product counterfeiting (Grammich, 2021). In addition to using legitimate platforms such as Amazon, eBay, or Alibaba, counterfeiters may use less visible virtual marketplaces, including the dark web.

At the same time, firms are increasingly using technology to combat counterfeiting. Security experts, for example, are seeking to integrate anti-counterfeit and product-authentication solutions to reduce vulnerability to counterfeiting (Wilson, 2017). Firms may also seek to minimize other supply chain vulnerabilities and seek inclusion and enforcement of anti-counterfeiting clauses in contracts to help minimize opportunities for counterfeiting.

In short, there is a wide array of factors that both expand and shrink the opportunity for counterfeiting to occur. It is important for brands to understand these dynamics, and to build into their programs efforts to minimize counterfeit opportunity. Over time, brands have learned that they can never seize, arrest, or litigate their way out of the counterfeit problem. Rather, effective strategies will require a proactive approach, including coordination and collaboration among multiple partners, both within and outside a firm. Such an approach can begin most effectively by involving as many functions as possible within a firm, and having these engage their relevant outside partners as well. Consistent with the total business solution framework, this proactive approach is the most efficient way to ultimately reduce the risk of counterfeiting.

INITIAL RESPONSES TO COUNTERFEITING

Because of the limited knowledge they have of product counterfeiting, firms commonly address the problem only after discovering they have been victimized (Post and Post, 2007; see also Daniels, 2016, on one firm learning of infringements of its trademark for a service it had not previously offered). Upon discovery, firms may seek monetary damages and injunctions against counterfeiters (Hoecht and Trott, 2014). Businesses that see legal actions as an effective deterrent may seek partnerships with customs and law enforcement agencies. Crackdown operations involving undercover informants, raids, and seizures can deter counterfeiting if conducted in ways to maximize loss to counterfeiters. Firms may also gather and organize evidence for law enforcement officials (Foucart, 2016).

Firms may seek to minimize supply chain vulnerabilities to product diversion or embezzlement, using both physical and virtual strategies (Stevenson and Busby, 2015). Similarly, firms may rely on contractual agreements, including penalties for nonconformance, and employee background checks as well as periodic field audits (Hoecht and Trott, 2014). Organizations may use anti-counterfeiting labeling and packaging and track-and-trace technology to follow a product through its life cycle (Stumpf et al., 2011). Vertically integrating supply chains can provide the most direct control over them and minimize risks to counterfeiting (Stevenson and Busby, 2015).

Still other approaches to product counterfeiting may involve raising awareness among consumers and collaborating with competitors to identify sources of counterfeit trade (Hoecht and Trott, 2014). Internal education and awareness can also help firms minimize the threat of counterfeiting (Wilson and Kinghorn, 2014). Such efforts may include aligning brand protection with performance objectives and incorporating brand protection values into daily operations (Post and Post, 2007).

Altogether, previous work suggests several common strategies that firms may use to address product counterfeiting but few systematic approaches to doing so. Firms may hire a risk officer or specialist to address counterfeiting issues, but often their approach is reactive, addressing the problem only after it occurs. Furthermore, many approaches are siloed, with little interaction among those in different organizational functions addressing the problem (Wilcock and Boys, 2014). Firms may seek to quantify risks as best they can (Wilson, 2017), but how well they address problems before they occur, or how well organized they are to do so, is unclear.

There are few, if any, frameworks to guide brand managers seeking to protect their brands from infringement. Most previous strategies focused on consumer attitudes and corporate actions, with little known about their effectiveness (Yang and Sonmez, 2017). Some anti-counterfeiting methods may have limited application (Lancaster, 2017). For example, track-and-trace technologies are helpful, but only for monitoring the legitimate supply chain. Public efforts to curb counterfeiting must be multifaceted (Betti, 2017). Legislative approaches, for example, can be effective but time-consuming, while law enforcement operations may react fastest but only address part of the problem.

TOWARD A TOTAL BUSINESS SOLUTION PROGRAM MODEL

When firms launch brand protection programs, they will often shape the program to respond to immediate problems so that they can jump to action. As time progresses, firms may give more thought to what constitutes a robust program and what are all the actions it should take to address the problem.

This chapter seeks to provide a comprehensive guide to how firms can organize for brand protection. It is grounded in and helps to operationalize a total business solution to brand protection. To implement a total business solution, firms must be strategic, evidence-based, proactive, always learning, and comprehensive in their approach to mitigating counterfeit risk (Wilson and Grammich, 2020a; 2020b). We provide a model for identifying and assessing risks and provide details on how to most effectively organize to address them.

To our knowledge, there is no previously existing comprehensive and pro-active model for addressing brand protection. Accordingly, we developed this model from the tenets of the total business solution, from what we learned on what works well for others, from relevant principles of research on policing and organizations, and from our own field work and benchmarking studies over time. Our model provides a road map for firms to use as they develop and shape a brand protection program for their own specific needs. It seeks to guide firms in their response to product counterfeiting while helping them increase the risks that counterfeiters face and reduce the opportunities counterfeiters may find.

Our total business solution program model has six elements, each of which we describe below. These elements correspond to tenets of the total business solution for brand protection, discussed elsewhere in this volume. As shown in Figure 2.1, these elements, and their correspondence to the tenets of the total business solution for brand protection, are:

- *Problem recognition.* This supports efforts to identify the infringer as the unseen competitor. The first step is to ask what the problem is, how to address it, and how to get action on it. This includes the decision to move forward with assessment and to determine who is responsible for address-ing the problem, the first step in setting policy on the problem.
- *Risk assessment.* This supports efforts to emphasize prevention, proactiv-ity, and strategy in brand protection. It does so by considering simultane-ously the threat of product counterfeiting, the vulnerability of a firm to product counterfeiting, and the consequences of a specific threat.
- *Strategy development.* Strategies should create and rely on performance metrics and use data and analysis to assess and mitigate risk. Strategies should work through the stages of analyzing and implementing the response to the problem, as well as consider ways to determine that a program has been implemented and is performing properly.
- *Strategy implementation.* In implementing strategies, firms should high-light the value of internal and external controls and mechanisms for detecting and responding to infringements. This should include not only the steps to take to prevent counterfeiting but also the steps to take when counterfeiting occurs, including pre-crisis planning, steps to minimize any crises that arise, and post-crisis learning and improvement.
- *Performance measurement.* This can help create a culture of continuous improvement and embracing learning. Performance measures can help

assess how well brand protection teams are meeting their goals and whether they're adding value to the organization, as well as point to learning opportunities for the brand protection team.

* *Assessment.* Assessments can help promote a holistic approach that integrates and coordinates all parts of the firm for brand protection. Indeed, assessment ultimately informs every other element of the model. Assessments can show whether firms accomplished what they wanted to accomplish in their brand protection programs. Ideally, assessments would also show what return on investment firms have received from their brand protection programs.

All these elements build on and inform each other. Problem recognition, for example, is necessary before risk assessment, while the final assessment stage can help refine each preceding step. Below we review each of these elements and how firms can implement them.

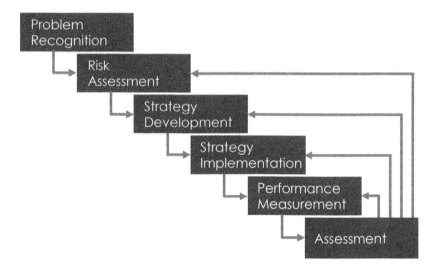

Figure 2.1   Total business solution program model

PROBLEM RECOGNITION

Many brand owners who claim not to have a product counterfeiting problem have likely never looked for it (Wilson and Kinghorn, 2014). Indeed, virtually any product can be counterfeited. The critical first step in protecting the brand is therefore to recognize the risk to the brand (Hopkins et al., 2003). Someone within the firm must determine a problem exists and that the firm will respond, beginning by assessing the extent of the problem. Internal partners such as a risk management team may have a role to play here.

Assessing the risk of counterfeits will require firms to develop a general awareness of counterfeits in the marketplace. Just as firms assess the strategies and activities of their legitimate competitors, so they should assess the strategies and activities of those infringing their intellectual property (Staake and Fleisch, 2008). Counterfeiters compete with authentic brands, so brands should treat them as competitors and analyze their nature and operations in order to reduce infringers' opportunities.

A general awareness of counterfeits in the marketplace should lead to identifying and understanding specific incidents of product counterfeiting. Firms may face new and evolving counterfeiting threats. The rapidly increasing popularity of self-balancing scooters, for example, led counterfeiters not only to produce counterfeit scooters but to affix counterfeit safety certification labels to them when the victimized firm did not yet offer such a certification program (Daniels, 2016). Brand owners may also find that by tweaking online search terms they can identify myriad counterfeits of their products in virtual marketplaces (Love, 2016).

Counterfeiters reduce a firm's market share through competition and by diminishing a brand's reputation. Hence, one of the measures that brands may wish to monitor is their changing market share in regions where counterfeiters are operating. More generally, firms may wish to assess the threat counterfeiters may pose, the vulnerability that the firm has to counterfeit products, and the consequences of product counterfeits in developing and implementing its strategy against counterfeits.

The total business solution contends that controls are critical for identifying problems that the firm must ultimately acknowledge (Wilson and Grammich, 2020a; 2020b). Spikes in warranty claims or consumer complaints or sudden dips in sales, for example, might signal counterfeits of a specific product entering a specific market. Managers should establish mechanisms throughout the enterprise and its supply chain to alert the firm of business activities that put the brand at risk (Berman, 2008; Post and Post, 2007). Research on the total business solution has identified 35 specific functions that play a role in brand protection (Wilson and Grammich, 2020a), and these efforts should be coordinated for this purpose.

Integrated as part of the business culture, these mechanisms should be implemented across the enterprise, throughout the supply chain, and across all product stages from conception through distribution to immediately and systematically signal activities that put the firm at risk (Berman, 2008; Post and Post, 2007). Specific mechanisms may include establishing communication channels to ensure all involved in brand protection are informed of issues such as significant changes in sales, substantial quantities of products at discounters or on websites, increased orders for proprietary components, or increased gray-market activity.

Firms should provide consumers and resellers an easy way, such as a complaint website or hotline, to report suspected counterfeit goods and verify genuine products. They should also have effective directives in place to respond to issues as they arise, particularly for assessing risk and even measuring performance in responding to and mitigating risks.

Control measures should also include management of personnel. By one estimate, "85 percent of trade secret thefts are committed by someone ... familiar to the trade secret owner. [Such cases] are generally not a 'whodunnit'" (Mayers and LeMieux, 2018). Due-diligence processes regarding intellectual property protection are necessary for new hires as well as employees who join a firm through merger or acquisition.

Altogether, firms should recognize that problem recognition is not just a function of observing the problem but also one of determining what action to take in response to it. This broadly reflects an issue we will later raise in strategy development, on how strategy requires both addressing the overarching structure a brand protection team should have, with the structure reflecting the general issues a team will address, and a focus on specific procedures to implement in response to a problem. Firms should recognize that controls provide an ongoing source of intelligence to help firms identify problems, and can also be useful in informing risk assessment, specific actions to take, and even performance measurement.

RISK ASSESSMENT

Traditionally, and particularly within criminal justice, security personnel have relied on their own experience in deciding which risks to prioritize and address (Bonta, 1996). Yet such subjective methods can lead to bias and less accurate predictions than more structured quantitative assessments (Brennan et al., 2009). Organizations have therefore sought to use actuarial risk assessments rather than relying on the subjective judgment of employees. Controls can provide specific data points to consider in risk assessment.

A risk assessment seeks to predict the likelihood of occurrence for a specific outcome (Van Voorhis, 2009). Risk assessments should also identify targets for change (Schwalbe, 2008). Interventions can be most effective when they are targeted toward higher-risk cases, rather than applied equally and widely (Lowenkamp et al., 2006).

There are many assessment frameworks that firms may use to investigate risk. In fact, most firms may already have assessment processes in place for other forms of risk that could be adapted to counterfeiting. Given its intuitiveness, flexibility, and demonstration across substantive domains, we propose a risk assessment model originally based on identifying and mitigat-ing risks for crimes with potentially catastrophic consequences (Willis et al., 2005; Wilson et al., 2007). The risk assessment model we propose has three elements: the *threat* of a product counterfeiting incident, the *vulnerability* of a firm to product counterfeiting, and the *consequences* of a specific threat.

The *threat* of product counterfeiting represents the probability than an entity (counterfeiter) has both the intent and the ability to counterfeit a product. High profit margins, high market demand, and product exclusivity all contribute to the likelihood that an entity will develop an intent to counterfeit a product (Wilson and Kinghorn, 2014). In assessing the threat of counterfeiting, brand owners may wish to assess how frequently other products in the same category are counterfeited, the desirability of a product, the difficulty in obtaining a product from an authorized source, the market for non-deceptive coun-terfeits, and access to the equipment, materials, and knowledge needed for counterfeiting (Kennedy et al., 2017).

The *vulnerability* of product counterfeiting is the probability that a firm will be damaged (e.g., through loss of revenues or reputation) given a spe-cific incident of product counterfeiting. It does not reflect the magnitude of damage, that is, the consequences of counterfeiting, but only the susceptibility to damage if a given product is counterfeited. Vulnerability may be increased where there is a lack of capable guardians to observe and prevent illicit activity (Felson, 1995; Hollis and Wilson, 2014). Specific points of vulnerability to counterfeiting may include use of contract manufacturers or contract packag-ers for all or part of a product, use of non-proprietary or non-exclusive compo-nents for a product, and distribution channels (Kennedy et al., 2017). Products manufactured and packaged exclusively within a brand owner's facilities likely have less vulnerability to counterfeiting than those produced elsewhere. Products that use proprietary rather than common components also may be less vulnerable to counterfeiting. Finally, products that are shipped directly to consumers from brand owners may be less vulnerable to counterfeiting than those distributed by other means. Of course, firms must consider several issues in sourcing, producing, and distributing their products. We note these only to help brand owners identify where vulnerabilities to counterfeiting may arise.

The *consequences* are a result of the counterfeiting threat and vulnerabil-ity. Put another way, the consequence is the expected magnitude of damage (e.g., in revenue or reputation) to a brand owner given a specific incident of counterfeiting at a specific time and place. Consequences may vary by inci-dent as well as by the specific circumstances of an incident. A counterfeiting incident occurring at one time or place may not have the same consequences as a counterfeiting incident involving the same product at another time or place. In considering the consequences of counterfeiting, brand owners may wish to consider the likelihood that a counterfeit will affect earnings, the costs of responding to an incident of counterfeiting, and the effect on product reputation (Kennedy et al., 2017). The effect on earnings may vary by whether consumers are purchasing deceptive or non-deceptive counterfeits. A consumer purchasing a deceptive counterfeit luxury item for near the price of the genuine article, for example, is more likely to represent a loss to the brand owner than a customer purchasing a non-deceptive item at a lower price. The costs of responding to incidents of product counterfeiting include those of investigation and enforcement, product recalls, and lawsuits. Response costs can also vary by the type of product counterfeited, particularly if brand owners pay the cost of product returns, replacement, or repair associated with failure of counterfeit goods. The effects on product reputation can be greatest when firms do not thwart the entry of counterfeit products into the market, counterfeit goods intermingle with legitimate product, and consumers are unable to distinguish counterfeit from legitimate product. Such conditions can lead consumers to seek alternative products, harming the legitimate brand owner.

The product of (1) the probability a good will be counterfeited (i.e., the *threat* of counterfeit), (2) the probability that a good, if counterfeited, can lead to any damage to the firm (i.e., the *vulnerability* of a firm to counterfeit), and (3) the estimate of the damage to a firm should a good be counterfeited (i.e., the *consequences* of counterfeiting) is the risk of counterfeiting. That is, risk is the result of *threat*, *vulnerability*, and *consequences*. Although we focus on product risk, this framework can be adapted to gauge counterfeit risk in other forms, such as by region, supply chain component, and vendors and partners. How a firm operationalizes risk will affect how it develops strategy to combat counterfeiting.

STRATEGY DEVELOPMENT

In developing strategy, firms should consider two dimensions. The first is the structural nature of its brand protection program, including the size, nature, and location of its brand protection team. The structure of the brand protection team will shape how a firm will first respond to counterfeiting incidents. The expertise employed by the team will dictate the first tools that the brand protection team can apply to the counterfeiting incident. Different products may have different counterfeiting issues; those for luxury products, for example, are likely to be different, or pose different dangers, than those for pharmaceutical products. Hence, firms producing these different types of products are likely to need different types of expertise, infrastructure, and resources for brand protection, reflecting the most pressing issues each will face when confronting a product counterfeiting issue.

The second dimension that firms should consider in developing brand protection strategy is procedural, that is, the activities that the program will choose to conduct over time. These, too, will vary by firm, the products made, and the nature of firm risk, but there is a difference with the structure: while a firm's brand protection program structure is likely to remain relatively stable over time, its procedures, that is, the activities it conducts, are likely to vary. The feedback loop from program assessment is likely to affect both, but it is more likely to affect activities, or to affect activities more rapidly than it affects program structure.

In addressing counterfeits, firms should consider the threat, vulnerability, and consequences of counterfeiting. Doing so allows firms to compare the risk of different types of goods. Some products may have a high threat of being counterfeited but pose little damage to a firm's reputation. Others may not be likely to be counterfeited but there could be severe damage if they are. Considering the threat, vulnerability, and consequences of counterfeiting together allows firms to determine what products pose the most risk and prioritize efforts accordingly. Defining risk by examining the threat, vulnerability, and consequences of a counterfeit good allows brand owners to map their anti-counterfeiting strategy more precisely. Market surveillance can help identify the goods with the highest threat of being counterfeited. Introducing proprietary components or exerting more control over the supply chain can reduce the vulnerability of a firm to counterfeiting. Managing the consequences by increasing preparation for and the response to counterfeiting incidents can also help reduce the overall risk.

Because not all incidents of counterfeiting can be predicted and prevented, reaction will be a necessary component of a brand protection program. Nevertheless, proactive efforts should seek to reduce opportunities for counterfeiting as much as possible (Davison, 2011; Haelterman, 2013; Hollis and Wilson, 2014). Crime, including product counterfeiting, can be reduced by making it harder to commit, increasing the chance of apprehension, reducing its rewards, and removing provocations or excuses for it (Cornish and Clarke, 2003). Research on the total business solution has identified 12 categories of tactics that can be implemented across the firm to prevent and respond to product counterfeiting (Wilson and Grammich, 2020b). These are:

- analysis
- communications and coordination
- education and awareness
- enforcement
- firm policy and process
- legal
- physical security
- product protection
- public policy

- resources
- strategy
- supplier compliance.

Proactive efforts against counterfeiting can lead to fewer incidents requiring a response, lower overall costs, and less damage to the brand. A preplanned strategy for incidents can further help by providing a more comprehensive and efficient solution than one designed hastily.

Market monitoring can also have a role in brand protection strategy. By identifying where counterfeiters are gaining market share, brand owners can identify where to target their resources. This may include markets where brand owners have not yet sold products but counterfeiters using their name have. Monitoring may also include identifying the authenticity of returned products and tracking excess, obsolete, or scrap material. Prevention may include screening employees and suppliers, using packaging that helps consumers authenticate products, and securing warehouse facilities and supply chains. More generally, proactive strategies emphasize prevention, awareness, education, and partnerships.

Brand protection strategies should consider the goals and values of a firm, as well as how a firm would define success. This will help the firm define the budget it wishes to spend on activities as well as the size of the brand protection team it needs and the skills it wants within that team. Particular strategies may vary by whether a firm wishes to be reactive or proactive, as well as by the immediacy of the dangers that fake products pose to consumers. One analysis of metrics used by firms to assess their brand protection programs, for example, found that microelectronics and computer firms, as well as firms producing food, agricultural, and pharmaceutical products, had more metrics, particularly for those relating to brand protection activities, than those firms dealing in apparel, luxury, and consumer items (see Chapter 10).

Mechanisms for brand protection should be integrated with the business culture to protect the brand from product conception through distribution. Specific actions may include establishing communication channels to ensure all involved in brand protection are informed of issues such as significant changes in sales, substantial quantities of product at discounters or on websites, increased orders for proprietary components, or increased gray-market activity. Firms should also provide consumers and resellers an easy way, such as a complaint website or hotline, to report suspected counterfeit goods and verify genuine products.

STRATEGY IMPLEMENTATION

Strategy implementation involves putting the developed strategy into action. While the work is completed by the brand protection team, external partnerships can offer firms means to leverage resources and to identify new opportunities for advancing brand protection (see Chapter 6). Academic partners can help firms identify the extent of issues that a firm faces, different ways to meet those issues, and means for identifying future issues. Early development of partnerships with law enforcement agencies can help law enforcement officials identify problematic products and make investigations more efficient. Law enforcement partnerships can also help ensure product counterfeiting cases are prosecuted as such rather than as financial crimes such as money laundering.

Over time, partnerships can transform to consider other issues, such as regulation of supply chains or development of new initiatives among competitors to address common issues. Industry associations and share groups can combine individual efforts to better address issues, share relevant information among members, and identify standardized approaches to combat widespread problems.

Strategy implementation should include steps for firms to take when counterfeiting is not prevented and crises could occur. This can include pre-crisis planning, such as identifying signs and signals of a pending crisis and probing to identify if one is developing; crisis planning to contain damage, address a crisis breakout, and recover from the crisis; and post-crisis learning and resolution by identifying what went well, what could be improved, and what can help prevent future crises (Grayson and Evert-Burks, 2016).

Preventing and responding to crises requires organizations to consider their brand protection and strategy. This requires continuous measurement and modification of plans over time. The program implementation priorities that are determined can reflect risk tolerance, anticipated effects, and organizational priorities. In some cases, organizations may need to assign different priorities to different products or have different contingency plans for different products. In one case where a firm was addressing one counterfeit problem for a product grossing more than $1 billion annually and another for a product grossing $2 million annually, the corporate-wide brand protection team taught the team for the second product the tools for responding to a brand protection incident while offering supplementary help as time allowed (De Stefano, 2017).

PERFORMANCE MEASUREMENT

Brand protection programs should include performance metrics for all business activities associated with brand protection and implement data-driven processes to evaluate and reduce risks (Staake and Fleisch, 2008; Underwriters Laboratories, 2017). To measure their performance, firms may collect metrics on brand protection *inputs*, *outputs*, and *outcomes* (see Chapter 10). Controls used to assess risk and indicate approaches for addressing problems can inform measurements of inputs, outputs, and outcomes, and their analysis.

Inputs indicate the investments that are made in brand protection. They might include the number or cost of brand protection personnel and the direct costs of enforcement.

Outputs indicate the activities that firms conduct with the investments (inputs) they make in brand protection. They might include the number of raids, seizure actions, or takedowns.

Outcomes indicate the effectiveness of brand protection activities (outputs). They might include indicators on the prevalence of counterfeit products, the effect that counterfeit products have on brand image or value, sales of counterfeit products and how they affect sales of legitimate products, and market share for counterfeit and legitimate products. Presumably, for example, brand protection activities (outputs) will improve outcomes by reducing the prevalence of counterfeit products and the effect that counterfeit products have on brand image and value. Comparing outcomes to inputs can help illustrate the return on investment for a brand protection program.

Metrics should include all aspects of brand protection. While benchmarks on metrics and their values by industry, firm size, region, and other characteristics may be instructive, firms tend to develop performance metrics frameworks and interpret the information they provide based on their own organization and values (see Chapter 10). Proactive measures are particularly needed where illicit actors gain insights before product distribution. Data collection will remain an evolving process as firms identify and manage the data they need.

Firms may face a challenge in discerning appropriate metrics among the myriad data available to them (Kennedy, 2018). For example, while consumers may be eager to share data after an incident of counterfeiting, their reports may be lacking in quality or accuracy. Still, such data might help identify whether infringing products sold in a particular channel are being reported.

ASSESSMENT

The total business solution suggests that brand protection programs must become learning organizations to maximize performance (Wilson and Grammich, 2020a). As part of a learning organization (Senge, 1990; Ortenblad, 2019), managers should draw from their experience with prior brand risks and integrate the lessons learned into mechanisms designed to prevent a counterfeit issue from recurring. The brand protection process is circular, not linear. Firms should continually seek to strengthen their brand protection efforts.

Consistent with the total business solution philosophy, firm culture should support the notion that the brand protection program must continually innovate and evolve, as counterfeiters do. Such innovation should be of two types. In the short run, firms should adjust their activities as new threats emerge. In the long run, firms should assess and adjust their program structure as necessary, particularly as new products and threats to them evolve.

Once firms have taken steps to mitigate counterfeiting risks, they should use the results to strengthen their processes and controls to prevent an issue from reoccurring (Kinghorn and Wilson, 2013). Firms may wish to take specific steps such as having senior management provide support and direction, conducting ongoing risk assessment of routine operations, and using the results of investigations to educate employees and improve business processes. Many risks that firms need to address are external to their businesses and will require stronger partnerships with suppliers, contractors, distributors, consumers, and law enforcement.

While continuous learning processes will not eliminate brand protection failures, some costs incurred in response to these failures may still deter future infringement (see Chapter 8). For example, legal actions against infringers may signal to others the willingness of a firm to fight infringement and deter future attempts. Firms should account for such effects in planning and revising their responses to counterfeiting.

Ongoing assessment and becoming a learning organization is not just an aspirational goal for brand protection, but an essential one to successfully implement a total business solution. Ongoing assessment allows for continued support of the program and creates a path for continuous improvement. It also ensures the continual flow of intelligence gathering and information sharing with internal partners.

CONCLUSION

The steps suggested in this chapter—problem recognition, risk assessment, strategy development, strategy implementation, performance measurement, and assessment—help create a total business solution to brand protection. None by itself is sufficient. Risk assessment, for example, can identify where risks are greatest, but not what should be done about them.

Much of preventing product counterfeiting follows the principles of situational crime prevention (Cornish and Clarke, 2003; Arizona State University Center for Problem-Oriented Policing, 2021b). These include reducing the opportunity for crime and illicit activity by increasing the effort the offender must make to carry out the crime, increasing the risks the offender must face in completing the crime, reducing the rewards or benefits the offender may expect to reap from the crime, removing excuses that offenders may use to rationalize their crime, and reducing or avoiding provocations to commit the crime.

Product counterfeiters, like other criminal offenders, seize opportunities as they perceive them. Such decisions may be constrained by time and information and can vary by crime or even stage of the crime process (Cornish and Clarke, 2003). Considering product counterfeiting risks from a brand owner's view—or, conversely and to the extent possible, opportunities from a potential counterfeiter's view—can help brand owners address the problem holistically. The framework we present can also help them consider the problem over time, and to adjust their programs as their products, and the opportunities and vulnerabilities that counterfeiters perceive in them, evolve.

NOTE

1.   A previous version of this chapter appeared as Wilson, J. M., and Grammich, C. (2021). *A Strategic Roadmap for Building Brand Protection Programs.* Princeton, NJ: Systech.

REFERENCES

Arizona State University Center for Problem-Oriented Policing (2021a). The problem analysis triangle. https://popcenter.asu.edu/content/problem-analysis-triangle-0.

Arizona State University Center for Problem-Oriented Policing (2021b). Situational crime prevention. https://popcenter.asu.edu/content/situational-crime-prevention-0.

Berman, B. (2008). Strategies to detect and reduce counterfeiting activity. *Business Horizons*, **51** (3), 191–199. https://doi.org/10.1016/j.bushor.2008.01.002.

Betti, S. (2017). Key global enforcement issues on illicit trade in counterfeit goods. In P. E. Chaudry (Ed.), *Handbook of research on counterfeiting and illicit trade* (pp. 30–51). Cheltenham, UK and Northampton, MA, USA: Edward Elgar Publishing.

Bonta, J. (1996). Risk-needs assessment and treatment. In A. T. Harland (Ed.), *Choosing correctional options that work: defining the demand and evaluating the supply* (pp. 18–32). Newbury Park, CA: SAGE Publications.

Brennan, T., Dieterich, W., and Ehret, B. (2009). Evaluating the predictive validity of the COMPAS risk and needs assessment system. *Criminal Justice and Behavior*, **36** (1), 21–40. https://doi.org/10.1177%2F0093854808326545.

Cohen, L. E., and Felson, M. (1979). Social change and crime rate trends: a routine activity approach. *American Sociological Review*, **44** (4), 588–608. http://dx.doi.org/10.2307/2094589.

Cornish, D. B., and Clarke, R. V. (2003). Opportunities, precipitators, and criminal decisions: a reply to Wortley's critique of situational crime prevention. *Crime Prevention Studies*, **16**, 41–96. https://popcenter.asu.edu/sites/default/files/Responses/crime_prevention/PDFs/Cornish&Clarke.pdf.

Daniels, J. (2016). The self-balancing scooter crisis and the enforcement of a certification trademark. *The Brand Protection Professional*, **1** (2), 22–24. https://joom.ag/8AbW/p22.

Davison, M. (2011). *Pharmaceutical anti-counterfeiting: combating the real danger from fake drugs*. Hoboken, NJ: Wiley.

De Stefano, M. (2017). Managing multi-brand brand protection programs. *The Brand Protection Professional*, **2** (1), 22–23. https://joom.ag/nwTW/p22.

Felson, M. (1995). Those who discourage crime. In J. E. Eck and D. Weisburd (Eds.), *Crime and place*, Vol. 4, *Crime prevention studies* (pp. 53–66). Monsey, NY: Criminal Justice Press.

Foucart, B. (2016). How to be a good victim. *The Brand Protection Professional*, **1** (1), 18–19. https://bpp.msu.edu/magazine/how-to-be-a-good-victim/.

Grammich, C. A. (2021). UL World Anti-counterfeiting Virtual Research Symposium 2020. Underwriters Laboratories. https://besafebuyreal.ul.org/sites/default/files/2021-03/Whitepaper%20Symposium%20Summary_interactive_Final.pdf.

Grayson, A., and Evert-Burks, L. (2016). Crisis mitigation through communication in brand protection. *The Brand Protection Professional*, **1** (2), 26–29. https://joom.ag/8AbW/p26.

Haelterman, H. (2013). *Situational crime prevention and supply chain security: theory for best practice*. Alexandria, VA: ASIS Foundation.

Hoecht, A., and Trott, P. (2014). How should firms deal with counterfeiting? A review of the success conditions of anti-counterfeiting strategies. *International Journal of Emerging Markets*, **9** (1), 98–119. https://doi.org/10.1108/IJOEM-02-2011-0014.

Hollis, M. E., Fejes, Z. L., Fenoff, R., and Wilson, J. M. (2015). Routine activities and product counterfeiting: a research note, **39** (3), 257–272. https://doi.org/10.1080/01924036.2014.973055.

Hollis, M. E., and Wilson, J. (2014). Who are the guardians in product counterfeiting? A theoretical application of routine activities theory. *Crime Prevention and Community Safety*, **16** (3), 169–188. https://doi.org/10.1057/cpcs.2014.6.

Hopkins, D. M., Kontnik, L. T., and Turnage, M. T. (2003). *Counterfeiting exposed: protecting your brand and customers*. Hoboken, NJ: Wiley.

Kennedy, J. (2018). Maximizing data value. *The Brand Protection Professional*, **3** (4), 16. https://joom.ag/Tr8a/p16.

Kennedy, J. P., Wilson, J., and Labrecque, R. (2017). Towards a more proactive approach to brand protection: development of the organizational risk assessment for product counterfeiting (ORAPC). *Global Crime*, **18** (4), 329–352. https://doi.org/10.1080/17440572.2017.1313733.

Kinghorn, R., and Wilson, J. M. (2013, October). Anti-counterfeit strategy for brand owners. Michigan State University Center for Anti-Counterfeiting and Product Protection. https://a-capp.msu.edu/wp-content/uploads/2018/05/BACKGROUNDER-Anti-Counterfeit-Strategy-for-Brand-Owners.pdf.

Lancaster, I. (2017). Detecting counterfeits in the supply chain: how to use authentication methods. In P. E. Chaudry (Ed.), *Handbook of research on counterfeiting and illicit trade* (pp. 459–483). Cheltenham, UK and Northampton, MA, USA: Edward Elgar Publishing.

Love, A. (2016). A view from the field: WWE infringer smackdown. *The Brand Protection Professional*, **1** (2), 42–45. https://joom.ag/8AbW/p42.

Lowenkamp, C. T., Latessa, E. J., and Holsinger, A. M. (2006). The risk principle in action: what have we learned from 13,676 offenders and 97 correctional programs? *Crime and Delinquency*, **52** (1), 77–93. https://doi.org/10.1177%2F0011128705281747.

Macolini, C. T. (2019). *Counterfeits: war stories and lessons learned—an investigator's perspective*. Miami, FL: MIC Worldwide.

Mayers, J., and LeMieux, M. (2018). Tilting at windmills: your organization's intellectual property is not cabbage. *The Brand Protection Professional*, **3** (4), 10–13. https://joom.ag/Tr8a/p10.

Ortenblad, A. (2019). *The Oxford handbook of the learning organization*. Oxford: Oxford University Press.

Post, R. S., and Post, P. N. (2007). *Global brand integrity management*. New York: McGraw-Hill.

Schornstein, S. L. (2013). *Criminal enforcement of intellectual property rights: U.S. perspective*. Providence, NJ: Matthew Bender & Co.

Schwalbe, C. S. (2008). Strengthening the integration of actuarial risk assessment with clinical judgment in an evidence based practice framework. *Children and Youth Services Review*, **30** (12), 1458–1464. https://doi.org/10.1016/j.childyouth.2007.11.021.

Senge, P. (1990). *The fifth discipline: the art and practice of the learning organization*. New York: Doubleday.

Staake, T., and Fleisch, E. (2008). *Countering counterfeit trade: illicit market insights, best-practice strategies, and management toolbox*. Berlin: Springer.

Stevenson, M., and Busby, J. (2015). An exploratory analysis of counterfeiting strategies: towards counterfeit-resilient supply chains. *International Journal of Operations and Production Management*, **35** (1), 110–144. https://doi.org/10.1108/IJOPM-04-2012-0174.

Stumpf, S. A., Chaudhry, P. E., and Perretta, L. (2011). Fake: can business stanch the flow of counterfeit products? *Journal of Business Strategy*, **32** (2), 4–12. https://doi.org/10.1108/02756661111109725.

Underwriters Laboratories (2017). Protecting brands from product counterfeiting. https://www.ul.com/insights/protecting-brands-product-counterfeiting.

Van Voorhis, P. (2009). An overview of offender classification systems. In P. Van Voorhis, M. Braswell, and D. Lester (Eds.), *Correctional counseling and rehabilitation* (7th edn., pp. 133–162). Cincinnati, OH: LexisNexis Group.

Wilcock, A. E., and Boys, K. A. (2014). Reduce product counterfeiting: an integrated approach. *Business Horizons*, **57** (2), 279–288. https://doi.org/10.1016/j.bushor.2013.12.001.

Willis, H. H., Morral, A. R., Kelly, T. K., and Medby, J. J. (2005). *Estimating terrorism risk*. Santa Monica, CA: RAND Corporation. https://www.rand.org/pubs/monographs/MG388.html.

Wilson, J. M. (2017). The future of brand protection: responding to the global risk. *Journal of Brand Management*, **24** (3), 271–283. https://doi.org/10.1057/s41262-017-0032-x.

Wilson, J. M., and Grammich, C. A. (2020a). Brand protection across the enterprise: toward a total business solution. *Business Horizons*, **63** (3), 363–376. https://doi.org/10.1016/j.bushor.2020.02.002.

Wilson, J. M., and Grammich, C. A. (2020b). Protecting brands from counterfeiting risks: tactics of a total business solution. *Journal of Risk Research*, online before print. https://doi.org/10.1080/13669877.2020.1806908.

Wilson, J. M., Grammich, C., and Chan, F. (2016). Organizing for brand protection and responding to product counterfeit risk: an analysis of global firms. *Journal of Brand Management*, **23** (3), 345–361. https://doi.org/10.1057/bm.2016.12.

Wilson, J. M., Jackson, B. A., Eisman, M., Steinberg, P., and Riley, K. J. (2007). *Securing America's passenger-rail systems*. Santa Monica, CA: RAND Corporation. https://www.rand.org/pubs/monographs/MG705.html.

Wilson, J. M., and Kinghorn, R. (2014). Brand protection as a total business solution. Michigan State University Center for Anti-Counterfeiting and Product Protection. https://a-capp.msu.edu/wp-content/uploads/2018/05/PAPER-SERIES-Brand-Protec tion-as-a-Total-Business-Solution.pdf.

Yang, D., and Sonmez, M. (2017). Effectiveness against counterfeiting: four decades of strategic inquiry. In P. E. Chaudry (Ed.), *Handbook of research on counterfeiting and illicit trade* (pp. 404–431). Cheltenham, UK and Northampton, MA, USA: Edward Elgar Publishing.

3. Risk management and risk assessment for brand protection

Sean O'Hearen

INTRODUCTION

The renowned Chinese general and strategist, Sun Tzu, said, "If you know the enemy and know yourself, you need not fear the result of a hundred battles." Applied to brand protection, Tzu's guidance tells us we must not only understand how the counterfeiter—our enemy—thinks and works, but also how well we, as brand owners, are prepared to counter his actions through our own thinking and preparedness. We need to understand and anticipate his methods, motivations, and modes of attack. "Think like a bad guy," as one of my colleagues likes to say enthusiastically. The way we do that is through a good battle plan, which for our purposes we can refer to as a risk management plan for brand protection. That is, a well-thought-out and systematic plan designed to manage and mitigate risks related to counterfeiting, unauthorized or illegal diversion, and product tampering (together known as "illicit trade").

This book advances and builds on a "Total Business Solution" ("TBS") approach (Wilson and Grammich, 2020) for brand protection, a new, innovative, research-based paradigm for the discipline. This chapter summarizes how the tenets of a TBS approach dovetail well with standard risk management practices, and how together they constitute a strategic framework and foundational principles that can help brand protection practitioners shift from what has traditionally been a mostly reactive and tactical approach to one that is more strategic, proactive, and preventive—and more effective over the long term.

It will then concentrate on risk assessment practices for brand protection, the cornerstone of effective risk management. Risk assessment is the ongoing and dynamic process that enables our understanding of the enemy and our own strengths and weaknesses. For brand protection, it's important to assess risk for individual products within an organization's portfolio, because each product will have a different risk profile, and to assess risk for the organization's value chain, the overall system which delivers all products to markets and consumers. By looking at illicit trade risk comprehensively in this way, decisions can be made about how to win the battles and the war against counterfeiters in the global marketplace.

That war continues to escalate, impacting virtually every industry and region of the world. One estimate (Frontier Economics Ltd., 2017) forecasts the total value of international and domestic trade in counterfeit and pirated goods will reach $1.95 trillion US by 2022. This growing worldwide trade in counterfeit and illicit products not only puts people's health and lives at risk, but it can also seriously undermine their trust in genuine brands and products, a bedrock of our economy. For these reasons and more, companies around the world must continue to innovate and seek new strategies, practices, processes, and technologies to combat the threat of illicit trade.

RISK LANDSCAPE—THE FRONT LINES OF BRAND PROTECTION

From a brand protection practitioner's perspective, the value chain that ultimately delivers a "brand experience" to an end user is fraught with hazards and potential loss exposure. There are many points along that chain that may be exploited by bad actors in pursuit of profits. They use deception, dirty-dealing, fraud, corruption, theft, or some other illicit means to infiltrate legitimate channels with counterfeit product. Even a company's own employees or supply chain partners may unwittingly or naively do harm or introduce risk by their actions or inaction, due to being unaware of the potential hazards and consequences related to illicit trade. In some cases, insiders may even be in on the illicit scheme.

Infringers may also avoid the legitimate supply chain altogether, choosing to reach consumers directly through other channels, such as the internet or social media, or by targeting markets that are underserved or unserved by a particular brand. Of course, these shadow or parallel supply chains are even harder for brand owners to detect and defeat. They may even use some of the same suppliers, manufacturers, and/or distributors as the legitimate distribution network.

When a brand attack occurs, major corporate investments in brand building over many years can be jeopardized without warning and with no easy recourse or remedy. In today's commercial landscape, as global supply chains become more complex and advancements in technology lower barriers to entry, the opportunities for criminals and the risks for brand owners are both on the rise (Chaudhry, 2017).

Consider just a few real-world scenarios that illustrate potential risk sources in a typical value/supply chain:

1. A hospital purchasing agent under budget pressure is convinced by a seller that the medical devices she's buying at a discount from the secondary market are, in fact, genuine.
2. A packaging supplier finds it strange that they are receiving large orders for the same bottle design that another customer's popular shampoo brand uses, but they don't want to accuse the customer of wrongdoing.
3. A plant manager at a contract manufacturing site decides that the extra cash in his pocket is worth the risk of producing an unauthorized "Sunday run" or two of a top-selling beauty product.

These are just some examples of how illicit and potentially dangerous products can infiltrate legitimate supply chains and reach unsuspecting patients and consumers. Each scenario involves different motivations and root causes, but only the unethical plant manager seems clearly wrong.

The negative outcomes in all three of these scenarios are that legitimate product sales are likely displaced by counterfeit goods and consumers' health and safety are put at risk. As situations like these and others persist, multiply, and grow, an organization's business objectives and hard-won reputation are also put at risk. Business plans falter for a variety of reasons, and leaders may not always suspect illicit trade as a cause, especially if there has not been a history of its occurrence. But in today's business landscape, leaders need to be keenly aware of their illicit trade risk exposure across the entire value chain, and the real possibility of the "unseen competitor" (Wilson and Grammich, 2020).

SHIFT FROM REACTIVE TO PROACTIVE RISK MANAGEMENT

With the prevailing approach to brand protection continuing to be reactive and response driven, by the time a business leader is alerted to the presence of a counterfeit or diverted product, it can be hard to contain the damage—and hopefully no one got hurt! At that point an investigation will likely commence and best efforts will be made to identify root causes and the source of illicit product, which can be time-consuming and expensive. If all goes well, law enforcement gets involved and the process ends with a raid and seizure of infringing goods, and perhaps additional civil or criminal enforcement action against the perpetrator(s). The value of goods seized is tallied and a win is registered for the security/brand protection team. When the next incident occurs, the process rolls again.

This is a simplified view of an investigation and enforcement driven approach—often referred to as "whack-a-mole"—but it serves to make a point. The point is that a "firefighter" mentality and approach will do little to prevent any of the incidents described in the examples, or others, from occurring in the first place or re-occurring. Effective response actions will always be a necessary and valuable component of a brand protection program, but they should not be the primary or only tool. They can promote deterrence, but they do little to fortify or strengthen the resilience of the value chain against illicit trade risks over time. There is a better, more strategic and balanced way.

Breaking out of the mostly reactionary, investigation and enforcement driven mode of brand protection and evolving toward a proactive and preventive approach, as advocated by the TBS philosophy, requires a fundamental shift in thinking and practice. That shift involves recognizing brand protection as a risk management discipline and employing a risk management mindset and framework in the conduct of brand protection operations—as opposed to reacting to the next incident when and if it occurs. A risk management mindset sees creating and protecting value as its primary goals and seeks to provide leaders with information to support decisions about risks that could impact business objectives, either positively or negatively. In addition to helping the organization become better prepared and resilient, it can also improve its agility and ability to respond to brand attacks.

This approach enables answers to the key questions business leaders typically ask of risk management professionals: 1) How much risk do we have due to XYZ? and 2) How much less risk will we have if we invest in your proposed mitigation action plan? As a practitioner, if you cannot come up with reasonably solid answers to these questions, framed in a way that expresses return on investment (ROI) for comparison to other potential investments, then you may have trouble securing resources to advance the set of objectives you've identified as essential for brand protection. Making the business case for brand protection, which has historically been one of the key challenges for practitioners, is explored elsewhere in this volume.

One such risk management standard that can be adopted is ISO 31000:2018, Risk Management—Guidelines, developed by the International Organization for Standardization (ISO). The ISO standard provides a framework and easy-to-follow guidance for risk management principles and processes, which can help establish a systematic and structured approach to brand protection as a risk management discipline. Another widely recognized risk management standard is the COSO (Committee of Sponsoring Organizations of the Treadway Commission) Enterprise Risk Management Framework, but because COSO focuses primarily on financial and compliance risks and associated audit practices, ISO 31000 appears to be a better choice for brand protection. It is universal by design and provides "a common approach to managing any type of risk and is not industry or sector specific" (ISO, 2018, p. 1). An organization may also have its own preferred risk management approach, which a brand protection program may choose to adopt. The important point is to follow a systematic and structured approach that includes a well-developed risk assessment capability, which the next section discusses.

ISO 31000 also dovetails nicely with a TBS approach to brand protection, which addresses a gap that has been identified in the research, namely that "there are few, if any, theories, frameworks, philosophies, or approaches to guide brand managers as they labor to protect their brands from infringers" (Wilson and Grammich, 2020, p. 365). Table 3.1 highlights the ISO's alignment with the six basic tenets of the TBS philosophy.

The ISO standard also explains that "the application of these guidelines can be customized to any organization and its context." It is prescriptive but not overly so, leaving plenty of leeway to construct a robust system within the guidelines to suit an organization's needs. Because ISO is a widely employed international standard, embracing ISO has the added benefit of creating consistency—of language, terms, processes, methods, reporting, and so on—with how risks are managed across the various risk domains that organizations typically must address in today's business environment, for example strategic, operational, financial, reputational, and compliance risks. There is also much that can be learned through collaboration with other risk management functions within the business—especially more mature ones such as cyber security—and much that can be gained by integrating brand protection into an existing enterprise risk management (ERM) framework and system within an organization.

Relatedly, there appears to be movement underway to embrace formal risk management practices within the corporate security realm, the functional area typically responsible for brand protection (Wilson, Grammich, and Chan, 2016). In 2019, ASIS International, the world's largest association of security management professionals, released its Enterprise Security Risk Management (ESRM) Guideline, which is based on ISO 31000:2018 and another standard, ANSI/ASIS/RIMS RA.1—2015, Risk Assessment Standard. The organization bills the standard as "the first strategic security management tool of its kind, elevating the security function by establishing a partnership between security professionals and business leaders to manage security risks" (ASIS International, 2019). So, clearly, ASIS sees the value in shifting away from a task-based, investigation and enforcement type of approach toward one based on proactive and preventive risk management.

There are no known empirical studies that look at the application of standard risk management frameworks, such as ISO 31000, to brand protection practice, but discussions with practitioners and first-hand experience indicate that many, if not most, of the elements of a formal risk management process, as

Table 3.1   *Comparison of tenets of a Total Business Solution to ISO 31000:2018*

Total Business Solution	ISO 31000:2018
Identify the infringer as the unseen competitor	6.4.2 Risk identification The purpose of risk identification is to find, recognize, and describe risks that might help or prevent an organization achieving its objectives.
Brands should emphasize prevention, proactivity, and strategy	5.2 Leadership and commitment Top management … should demonstrate leadership and commitment by: • customizing and implementing all components of the framework; • issuing a statement or policy that establishes a risk management approach, plan or course of action; • ensuring that the necessary resources are allocated to managing risk; • assigning authority, responsibility and accountability at appropriate levels within the organization. This will help the organization to: • align risk management with its objectives, strategy and culture; … … Oversight bodies are often expected or required to: • ensure that risks are adequately considered when setting the organization's objectives; …
Firms should use performance metrics and data analysis to assess and mitigate risk	6.3.4 Defining risk criteria … To set risk criteria, the following should be considered: … • consistency in the use of measurements; … 6.5.3 Preparing and implementing risk treatment plans … The information provided in the treatment plan should include: … • the performance measures; …

Total Business Solution	ISO 31000:2018
Brand managers should highlight the value of internal and external controls and mechanisms for detecting and responding to infringements	4 Principles The purpose of risk management is the creation and protection of value. … The principles … provide guidance on the characteristics of effective and efficient risk management, communicating its value and explaining its intention and purpose. 6.4.3 Risk analysis … Risk analysis should consider factors such as: … • the effectiveness of existing controls; …
Managers should create a culture of continuous improvement and learning	4 Principles … h) Continual improvement Risk management is continually improved through learning and experience. …

Managers should promote a holistic approach that integrates all parts of the firm for brand protection	4 Principles
	…
	  a) Integrated
	Risk management is an integral part of all organizational activities.
	  b) Structured and comprehensive
	A structured and comprehensive approach to risk management contributes to consistent and comparable results.
	…

defined by ISO 31000, have been deployed in some form or fashion for brand protection. However, the standard does not appear to have been formally or widely adopted by the community of practice. Many practitioners may not even be aware of its existence or applicability.

The ISO 31000 guidelines are concise and easy to follow, consisting of "11 principles, a framework, and a process that can to be tailored to fit an organization of any type and of any size" (International Organization for Standardization, 2018, p. v).[1] The principles and framework serve "to assist the organization in integrating risk management into significant activities and functions" (International Organization for Standardization, 2018, p. 4), which is critical for effective brand protection. The remaining discussion of this chapter will focus on applying the ISO Risk Assessment process to the practice of brand protection. This is not to imply that the other aspects of the ISO process or guidelines are less important. On the contrary, the guidelines should be implemented as a whole and in a systematic and structured way to be most effective.

Importantly, establishing "Leadership and Commitment"—as it relates to brand protection—as prescribed in the ISO framework comes first, ahead of risk assessment. Senior management support is critical and "communication and consultation" with relevant stakeholders, internal and external, are essential to the ISO process, as they are to the TBS philosophy.

Once an organization makes a commitment to brand protection, risk assessment then becomes the central mechanism for establishing and maintaining the key cross-functional and value chain relationships that support a proactive and integrative strategy. It creates awareness and understanding of brand protection related risks in each stakeholder's area of responsibility and sets the stage for a collaborative approach to implementing recommended mitigations and controls. In short, risk assessment is the impetus for integration and ownership of brand protection throughout the enterprise, which could be the single most important success factor for the TBS/ISO approach.

RISK MEASUREMENT AND ANALYSIS OVERVIEW

Before delving into details of risk assessment for brand protection, it is important to set the stage with a brief overview of techniques for the analysis part of the process. Analysis of course enables evaluation and subsequent decision making about risk treatment. The challenge for brand protection practitioners, which has been well documented (Kennedy and Wilson, 2017), is that there are many unknowns and a high degree of uncertainty involved with measurement and analysis in this field. This is in fact true of many risk domains. What's important is to do a structured analysis using a consistent methodology that allows you to arrive at a defensible conclusion and recommendation that comports with the decision-making style and needs of stakeholders within your organization.

In terms of methodologies, there are numerous techniques for risk measurement and analysis, ranging from purely subjective expert opinion ("based on my experience I see this as high risk") to sophisticated quantitative statistical analysis ("there is a 5 percent chance of losing $10 million dollars annually due to counterfeiting of brand ABC"). ISO 31000's companion guide and standard, titled IEC 31010, Risk Management—Risk Assessment Techniques, includes a table cataloguing 42 different techniques for risk assessment with varying degrees of complexity, effort, and expertise involved in their application. As advised in the standard (p. 29),

> The choice of technique and the way it is applied should be tailored to the context and use, and provide information of the type and form needed by the stakeholders. In general terms, the number and type of technique selected should be scaled to the

significance of the decision, and take into account constraints on time and other resources, and opportunity costs.

In deciding whether a qualitative or quantitative technique is more appropriate, the main criteria to consider are the form of output of most use to stakeholders and the availability and reliability of data. Quantitative techniques generally require high quality data if they are to provide meaningful results. However, in some cases where data is not sufficient, the rigour needed to apply a quantitative technique can provide an improved understanding of the risk, even though the result of the calculation might be uncertain.

Regardless of the technique or methodology chosen, the output should provide the decision maker with an understanding of the likelihood or probability of a risk event/source actually occurring and the consequences or impact of that occurrence (unmitigated or inherent risk) in relation to the business objectives under consideration in the analysis. This result can then be compared to the current level of preparedness or assurance—that is, due to existing controls, countermeasures, and mitigations (residual risk). If the resulting exposure level is greater than what the organization has defined as acceptable (what ISO calls "risk criteria" but is also commonly referred to as "risk appetite"), then appropriate action can be recommended and/or taken.

In practice, risk indices and risk matrices (e.g., heat maps) appear to be the most commonly used techniques for analysis in brand protection. A risk index breaks down the area of risk under consideration (e.g., risk of illicit trade) into relevant factors and then applies a scoring/rating system to determine relative likelihood, consequence, and preparedness levels. Typically these systems involve a series of questions for each of the factors, the answers to which are assigned a score. Usually Likert-type scales (1–5) or simple high, medium, low ratings are employed in these models. Factors are also often weighted based on their relative perceived importance to the decision output. Depending on the model, the resulting scores are tallied either by multiplication or addition, with higher scores indicating greater levels of risk, relatively speaking, which can then be compared to established risk criteria. Subsequently mapping the scores on a two-dimensional risk "heat map" (color coded: red, yellow, green) is a common way to easily visualize the results and enable decision making.

While risk indices and matrices are widely used and have the benefit of being fairly easy to develop and deploy, practitioners should be aware—and make decision makers aware—of their limitations. For example, inputs to these models are typically a mix of quanititative and qualitative data (i.e., semi-quantitative). Thus, they may rely heavily on the subjective judgment of the person(s) conducting the analyses, which can introduce inconsistencies and variation in scoring. They may also be difficult to validate against real-world data, if such data cannot easily be obtained. Given these limitations, the numerical outputs from a risk index may suggest a degree of accuracy that is not warranted, especially when dealing with high degrees of uncertainty and having little real-world data. Bigger decisions, in terms of risk or investment level, may necessitate a better model, which includes more data and quantitative analysis (Hubbard, 2014). That being said, experienced business people are usually familiar with risk indices and matrices, and as long as any assumptions and caveats are made clear, they serve a useful purpose to advance the practice of brand protection.

The next generation of risk analysis techniques for brand protection involves the use of advanced data and analytics and probabilistic models. These are truly quantitative statistical models that rely on multiple data sets, including actual incident data, to mathematically compute likelihood (at the product or market level) and consequence (e.g., sales loss exposure). Models of this kind require a high level of specialist expertise (e.g., data scientist, econometrician) and investment to build, validate, and maintain, and therefore may not be practicable for many organizations.

RISK ASSESSMENT PRACTICES FOR BRAND PROTECTION

Risk assessment creates understanding, establishes priorities, informs action plans, and drives resource allocation for brand protection risk management. It initiates the process that, when done well, propels value creation by informing decisions that lead to investments to enhance product and value chain security and reduce disruptive illicit trade incidents, thereby protecting patients and consumers, increasing the likelihood of achieving business objectives, and preserving brand trust and reputation. Effective risk assessment enables efficient allocation of resources and provides management with assurance that risks that could potentially impact business objectives are being addressed. It's also the key to "right-sizing" investment in brand protection in proportion to clearly identified and understood risks, both within the product security risk domain and relative to other enterprise risks a company must address.

The ISO process breaks risk assessment down into three steps:

1. risk identification,
2. risk analysis, and
3. risk evaluation.

Essentially, the steps involve considering the following:

1. What are the threats and sources of risk and their causes? What are the assets that require protection? What vulnerabilities could be exploited by a threat actor to damage an asset?

2. What is the likelihood of an identified risk occurring and what are the potential consequences—in terms of achievement of organizational objectives—if it does occur?
3. How do the results of the analysis compare to our established risk criteria and is there cause for further analysis or action (i.e., risk treatment)?

The present discussion of risk assessment and analysis techniques centers on risk from two perspectives: 1) the individual product level, and 2) the value chain level. Value chain refers to all the "interrelated activities a company uses to create a competitive advantage" (Investopedia, 2020). One of the six tenets of the TBS is that "Managers should promote a holistic approach that integrates all parts of the firm for brand protection" (Wilson and Grammich, 2020, p. 368). A value chain view of risk is consistent with and enables this holistic approach. While supply chain (plan, source, make, deliver, use/return), as a subset of value chain, remains a central focus, the research shows there are numerous other functions—links in the value chain—that play a role in brand protection and have risks associated with their activities from a brand protection perspective. These two views of risk are overlapping and reinforcing, of course, since controls or countermeasures put in place even for just one product will likely benefit to some degree all products that originate from and/ or transit that system. The sections that follow give some examples of these risks, discuss how to assess them, and outline how to engage functional business partners in the process.[2]

RISK ASSESSMENT AT THE PRODUCT/BRAND LEVEL

Step one for brand owners is to understand risk at the product/brand level. Infringers are generally driven by profit and, as such, target successful brands that present the fewest hurdles, lowest risk, and greatest reward (Kennedy and McGarrell, 2011). A company may have 50 brands, but perhaps only two ring the bell for the counterfeiters. This is why it's important to screen at the individual product level to prioritize which products in a portfolio are most likely to be targeted, or if there are known counterfeiting issues, to better understand the root causes and circumstances for those products, so that effective mitigations can be undertaken. Consistent with a TBS approach, key stakeholders who are closest to the product (e.g., Commercial, Quality, Packaging, Supply Chain) should be engaged to provide inputs to the assessment.

Prior to considering product-level risk for a portfolio from an infringer's perspective (i.e., likelihood of a product being violated), it can be helpful to first rank products from the company's perspective. This assessment exercise is basically posing the question: How concerned should we, the brand owners, be if product XYZ is targeted by infringers? This generally involves segmenting products into a risk matrix based on a few select factors, such as financial importance to the company (revenue and growth forecast), brand strength/equity, product life cycle, and consumer/patient safety concerns, if applicable. This ranking then provides an initial screen that can be applied for prioritization purposes when/if a product is attacked by an infringer. For example, assume the segmentation exercise categorizes products into level 1, 2, and 3, with level 1 being the most important. In the event of a confirmed incident, a level 1 product will get resources before a level 2 or 3 product does. A level 1 product may also get resources proactively to reduce the likelihood and impact of illicit trade. Another scenario may involve a product scoring high via the product risk assessment model described below, but because it is near the end of its product life cycle, it is classed as a level 3 product in the segmentation model and therefore is not as likely to receive investment for brand protection.

Segmentation is also useful from a strategic standpoint, whereby brand protection program requirements can be specified in advance based on the ranking system. Thus, the level of security and investment required can be planned and tiered ahead of time, in a thoughtful, systematic fashion, rather than on an ad hoc, reactive basis.

Flipping to the infringer's perspective and his reasons for targeting a particular brand, the risk assessment model becomes a bit more complex, taking into account the threat landscape (risk identification) and the variety of factors that influence or contribute to likelihood and consequence (risk analysis) of counterfeiting and illicit trade. As discussed earlier, a structured risk scoring model is useful for this purpose. Researchers (Kennedy and Wilson, 2017; Kennedy and McGarrell, 2011) have developed models of this type that provide a solid foundation for practice in this area. These models offer practitioners an excellent starting or comparative reference point for assessing product-level risk for their brands. They can be tailored and further developed according to an organization's needs and market profile. Practitioners also report the use of similar models and scoring methodologies for their programs (Trent, 2013).

Spink's "Counterfeit Product Risk Model" (Kennedy and McGarrell, 2011) focuses primarily on the likelihood side of the risk equation, but it is instructive in that it breaks the analysis down into five factors or key drivers that either increase or effect the likelihood that a product will be targeted by infringers. Those factors are as follows:

- Counterfeit history—Has the product been counterfeited before, which is the strongest indicator of risk?
- Counterfeit ability—How easy or hard is it to produce a fake that will fool consumers?[3]
- Counterfeit attractiveness—How much profit can be made by the infringer?

- Counterfeit hurdles—What measures has the brand owner put in place to increase the level of difficulty or risk for the infringer or decrease his likelihood of success?
- Market profile—Other key factor having to do with supply chain, market channels, geography, and so on.

As Spink suggests, these five factors can be further broken down into sub-factors with relevant questions assigned for ranking and scoring purposes. In this way, it can serve as an excellent framework for an organization to develop its own risk analysis model. Spink's model also includes consideration of "hurdles" or controls, "whether designed or inherent in a system," that mitigate risk to some degree, which should be a key component of any assessment.

The Organizational Risk Assessment for Product Counterfeiting (ORAPC) model developed by Kennedy and Wilson (2017) follows a similar logic to Spink's five factors, though it is more complete in that it also includes the "consequences" component of the assessment. The ORAPC includes three components:

- Threat of an event (presence of offender with capability to "attack");
- The target's vulnerability (likelihood of damage, given an "attack"); and
- The consequences (nature and scale of damage if "attack" is successful).

In this model, the assessment of "hurdles" or deterrent factors is incorporated into the "vulnerability" portion. In effect, vulnerability and likelihood are reduced when appropriate controls and countermeasures are in place.

Each of the three components of the model includes a series of questions (7–10) with answers selected on a scale of 1–5 according to the threat level, likelihood, or level of impact (consequence). The questions are also weighted according to their relative importance to the decision output. Scores are totaled in each area and then aggregated to give an overall score which represents the relative product counterfeiting risk for the product being analyzed. The model covers all the key questions, is fairly simple to use with some training, and can be tailored to an organization's needs. As such, the ORAPC can be a very useful tool for brand protection practitioners to implement a systematic approach to product-level risk analysis.

Armed with the results of a detailed and systematic analysis, as described above, a practitioner can then confidently begin to evaluate options and formulate recommendations for decision makers, usually with input from the relevant stakeholders. Outputs from the analysis can be evaluated against established risk criteria, thresholds for action, and a leader's appetite for the potential impact to business objectives.

As mentioned earlier with regard to segmentation, outputs (e.g., high, medium, low risk) from product-level assessments are often tied to preset and standardized recommendations for product security features and other controls and mitigations, which improves the efficiency and scaling of a program. Risk treatment, which involves the selection and implementation of those controls and mitigations, is beyond the scope of this chapter (see Part III, Mitigating the Risk of Counterfeit Products), so we'll now broaden our risk assessment aperture and take a systemic view of the overall value chain.

RISK ASSESSMENT AT THE VALUE CHAIN LEVEL

Experience tells us there are many and varied threats, risk sources, and potential modes of failure related to brand protection/product security that exist for a typical enterprise value chain. Some are obvious and potentially significant, such as the risk of an infringer selling counterfeits through e-commerce channels and social media. Others may be less apparent, yet still have a major impact on a company's ability to protect its brands and grow, such as the risk of an infringer registering your trademarks in a foreign jurisdiction before you, the rightful owner, do. Still others may be overlooked or presumed taken care of, such as the risk of a supply chain partner not having adequate physical security measures in place. The complex chain of business activities, transactions, events, and stakeholders required to bring any product to market presents a lot of opportunity for a motivated offender to exploit.

The goal of this value chain assessment exercise is to identify and assess all the present-day, known factors—major, minor, and in between—that may contribute to illicit trade risk across the entire, end-to-end value chain. By systematically identifying and assessing these risks, a brand owner can then implement mitigations and controls that will enhance the security and integrity of the entire system, and for all products manufactured within that system. Every intervention adds strength to the chain. As mentioned earlier, there is overlap between a product-level assessment and a value chain assessment. The difference is that the value chain assessment is much broader and takes a holistic view of the organization, consistent with a TBS approach.

On that point, Wilson and Grammich's (2020) TBS research revealed 35 functions that may play a role in brand protection. Of the unique tactics associated with those functions, the "Analysis" category ranked highest with 121 tactics (tied with "Product Protection"). This finding reinforces the central importance of risk assessment and analysis to the process and highlights the importance of cross-functional collaboration when conducting these assessments. Most of the "Analysis" tactics related to collection of data to support decision making, and 40 percent of them fell under the specific heading of "Analysis—Risks."

Additionally, about 90 percent of the 756 unique tactics cited in Wilson and Grammich's research represent some form of "risk treatment" (i.e., decision point, mitigation, or control) designed to address risks arising from one or more of the value chain areas or business activities identified in Table 3.2. This is not surprising, of course, but it highlights the systemic connection between the assessment phase and the many treatment options (tactics) available for a brand protection strategy.

Understanding illicit trade risk from a value chain perspective requires insight and experience as to what can go wrong, or what potential loss exposure exists within the system. This is the risk identification step of the assessment. The compilation of risk examples in Table 3.2 provides a head start or reference point for practitioners based on the author's experience and industry research. It breaks the value chain down into a mix of component parts, including value chain areas, business activities, and market channels, and identifies some associated key risk examples for each. In line with the TBS approach, it also lists the business function(s) that is/are typically responsible for each area. These are the stakeholders a practitioner would engage to conduct an assessment, followed by discussions around risk evaluation and treatment options. If a decision is made to implement some form of mitigation or control, then a discussion concerning how to fund, operationalize, and sustain that business process would follow.

Risk analysis for value chain assessment can be done using a risk index scoring model, the same technique applied to product-level risk assessment. A series of questions for each value chain area and/or business activity designed to evaluate likelihood, consequence, and preparedness level, with answers ranked on an ordinal scale, will enable decision makers to prioritize those areas with highest risk and make decisions about treatment options and required resources.

When evaluating consequences in these different areas, it's important to keep in mind that a risk event can have multiple consequences, thereby increasing the severity of outcomes. For example, the stream of events and losses connected with a cargo theft would not only include the initial financial loss from the theft, but also the follow-on sales loss from the likely reintroduction of that diverted product back into the supply chain somewhere, and the potential consumer safety concerns due to product exiting the legitimate supply chain. Unexpected costs for investigation and legal activities could also come into play. This chain of events could also affect multiple business objectives. The consequences can escalate quickly.

Results from a comprehensive value chain assessment can also provide an understanding of the strength and readiness level of the overall system. This understanding can then provide a key input for a business case for brand protection and inform the creation of a strategy and roadmap to address identified gaps and weaknesses, in conjunction with key stakeholders in each area.

Table 3.2   Examples of value chain risk for brand protection

Value Chain Area and/or Business Activity	Key Risk Example(s)	Typical Functional Partner (with Brand Protection)
Intellectual Property Management		
Intellectual Property (IP) Registrations (Trademarks (TMs), Copyrights, Patents, etc.)	• Inability to assert legal rights for IP protection in a given jurisdiction if IP is not legally registered beforehand • Infringers may preemptively register a brand owner's TMs in foreign jurisdictions before the brand owner does	Legal, Commercial
TM Customs Recordals and Training	• Inability to assert legal rights and authorize Customs agents to take IP enforcement actions on your behalf • Infringing product goes undetected due to Customs agents not being well equipped or informed about potential product issues	Legal, Security
New Product Development/Launch		
Product/Market Risk Assessment and Program Determination	• Infringers may target new product launches/ market opportunities and negatively impact market launch objectives • Additional time and expense may be incurred to retrofit product security/brand protection program post-launch	Commercial, Supply Chain, Packaging
Commercial—Go-to-Market Strategy (New and Legacy Products)		
Online Channels	• Infringers leverage easy access/reach and anonymity of online channels to sell counterfeit/illicit products	Commercial, Supply Chain
Offline Channels	• Infringers penetrate legitimate distribution points (retail, wholesale, secondary market) to sell counterfeit/illicit products	Commercial, Supply Chain
Commercial Analytics	• Counterfeit and diversion activity may continue undetected and persist due to lack of proactive monitoring and analytics	Commercial, Sales Analysis, Data & Analytics
Channel Compliance	• Channel partners/retailers engage in incentive abuse and gray-market activity due to lax or non-existent controls	Commercial, Channel Management

Value Chain Area and/or Business Activity	Key Risk Example(s)	Typical Functional Partner (with Brand Protection)
Supply Chain		
PLAN—Value Stream Management	• Consideration must be given to the changing risk profile for brand protection as product attractiveness (to infringers) increases/ decreases over product lifecycle	Value Stream Management, Product Management
SOURCE—Procurement	• Due diligence process (e.g., "Know Your Customer" protocols) must ensure that vendors/suppliers are not known or suspected infringers and are engaged in legitimate trade	Procurement
SOURCE—Quality Control	• Counterfeit or substandard raw materials or components may enter the upstream supply chain and compromise product integrity • Suppliers of raw materials/components may knowingly or unknowingly sell to counterfeit manufacturers	Procurement, Quality
MAKE—Contract Manufacturing Organization (CMO)	• CMOs may produce unauthorized batches or over-runs of genuine product for sale through unauthorized channels • Scrap materials or rejected finished goods may be improperly disposed of or diverted to infringers and then sold as genuine goods	Supply Chain Operations, Security
MAKE—Decommissioning	• Manufacturing assets (e.g., molds, dies, raw materials) for decommissioned products may be improperly sold to infringers who then produce counterfeit versions • Formerly authorized contract manufacturers or licensees may continue to surreptitiously produce genuine goods after termination of contract	Supply Chain Operations, Legal
DELIVER—Distributors	• Rogue or mismanaged distributors may willfully engage in or enable, through poor security practices, the introduction of illicit product into the legitimate supply chain or diversion of genuine product into unauthorized channels (channel compliance)	Supply Chain Operations, Security

Value Chain Area and/or Business Activity	Key Risk Example(s)	Typical Functional Partner (with Brand Protection)
DELIVER—Third-Party Logistics, Contract Packaging Organization (CPO)	• Genuine product in transit or in storage may be stolen and reintroduced into legitimate channels, or diverted into unauthorized channels. Presents health and safety risk if special handing, such as cold storage, is required • CPO operations present opportunities for introduction of counterfeit, diverted, and/or tampered product	Supply Chain Operations, Security
International Commerce	• Infringers employ evasive trans-shipment schemes and exploit lax oversight in free trade zones to facilitate the trafficking of counterfeit goods	Security or Brand Protection in partnership with Customs
Customer Call Centers (Incident Management)	• Indicators of suspect counterfeit/illicit product in customer complaint/service dialogue may be unheeded/not actioned if customer service representatives (CSRs) are not trained to spot them and inquire further	Quality, Commercial
REVERSE—Returns	• Infringers exploit reverse logistics/returned goods policies and process to introduce illicit product for the purpose of refund/credit/ genuine replacement • Returned/expired products may not be properly disposed of and can potentially re-enter the legitimate supply chain	Supply Chain Operations, Security
REVERSE—Destruction	• Returned/expired product marked for destruction may be illegally diverted and re-enter the legitimate supply chain	Supply Chain Operations, Security
Management/Organizational		
Leadership Engagement & Support	• Lack of understanding and awareness of counterfeit/illicit trade risk may lead to uninformed decisions that put business objectives at risk	C-Suite Leaders
Organizational/Employee Communication	• Lack of understanding and awareness of counterfeit/illicit trade risk may lead to gaps in operational controls and inability to identify risk events or emerging issues	Corporate Communications

Value Chain Area and/or Business Activity	Key Risk Example(s)	Typical Functional Partner (with Brand Protection)
Mergers, Acquisitions (M&A) & Divestitures, Discontinued Products	• M&A target may have material (in financial terms) counterfeit/illicit trade problem that is not factored into negotiations/plans • Potential business disruption due to divested assets/brands may increase risk of counterfeit/illicit trade problem • Manufacturing assets/components (e.g., plates, molds, dies, proprietary formulas, etc.) from discontinued products may be acquired illegally and used to manufacture counterfeit/illicit product	Finance/M&A, Business Development, Legal
Preparedness for Response (Incident Management)	• Inability to quickly and effectively respond to a counterfeit/illicit trade incident can worsen business impact and potential patient/consumer safety risk	Quality, Commercial, Security

Note: This list is representative and should not be considered exhaustive. The author welcomes any contributions from the brand protection community.

ORGANIZATIONAL ENGAGEMENT—FORCE MULTIPLIER

The risk assessment process, whether at the product level or the value chain level, gives brand protection practitioners an excellent opportunity to engage their counterparts in a critical brand protection activity. It can serve as a catalyst and first step toward creating awareness and getting buy-in and support for brand protection. If all goes according to plan, it can also lead to eventually establishing operational-level ownership of a required mitigation action or control process. This integration of brand protection risk management into the day-to-day operations of the business is the central organizing principle for a TBS approach, and one of the key principles of ISO 31000.

However, even for best-in-class brand protection programs there is work to be done on the engagement front. While the TBS research tallied a surprising 35 organizational functions that *could* be involved with brand protection (Wilson and Grammich, 2020), it also pointed out that most brand protection programs do not have the desired level of engagement and collaboration across the organization. In fact, many continue to operate in a mostly siloed fashion, with Legal not knowing what Commercial is doing to address the problem, for example. "Many brand-protection programs … are weak and piecemeal" (Wilson and Grammich, 2020, p. 366).

Getting the right level of engagement can be an uphill battle. Perhaps not Sisyphean, but one practitioner described it as much more "push than pull" early in his brand protection team's journey to eventually becoming an "in demand" group (Kaeser, 2019). They did so by consistently engaging and delivering value.

Returning to our earlier examples of risk sources in the value chain, a brand protection professional working with the relevant stakeholder in his organization could identify and anticipate these risks and implement controls to mitigate them before a loss event occurred:

1. Risk of buying from an unauthorized distributor—Anti-counterfeiting clauses and policies included in distributor agreements; education and training to make partners aware of risks and penalties.
2. Risk of suppliers not protecting intellectual property (IP)/designs— Anti-counterfeiting clauses and policies included in supplier agreements; education and training to make partners aware of risks and penalties.
3. Risk of contract manufacturer going rogue—Anti-counterfeiting clauses and policies included in manufacturer agreements; design and implementation of controls for CMO sites; regular auditing of controls at CMO sites.

Using risk assessment as a lever to initiate this type of collaboration is a great strategy. And getting to the ultimate point of operational ownership and integration can create a strong force-multiplier effect for normally under-resourced brand protection teams.

CONCLUSION

Compared to many business disciplines, brand protection is still in the early stages of its evolution. Many of the gold standard programs, such as Pfizer's or Johnson & Johnson's, only came into being in the last 10 to 15 years. While the necessity of keeping up the with the rapidly growing counterfeit trade and protecting patients and consumers continues to spur growth and maturity in the industry, the standard operating model remains mostly reactive and enforcement driven. But that is beginning to change thanks to a strong community of practice, and fruitful partnerships between business, academia, trade organizations, and government agencies. The saying "You can't enforce your way to brand protection" is starting to become gospel in the industry.

One of the challenges has been that there are no widely accepted standards or best practices, or a commonly understood strategic framework and approach for brand protection. Collaborative research projects like the one this book grew out of, and this book itself, help address that challenge by sharing industry knowledge and laying the foundations for those standards and best practices.

The tenets of the TBS coupled with a risk management framework like ISO 31000:2018 give practitioners an excellent platform and toolkit from which to build a more strategic, proactive, and preventive brand protection program, one that is more effective and impactful over time. The all-important risk assessment aspects of that program can be leveraged to open doors and engage all the key stakeholders across the organization who can help you realize and operationalize your vision for a total business solution for brand protection. Risk assessment can also help decision makers better understand the value brand protection brings to the business, which, in turn, can help secure the resources needed to implement recommended actions. Ultimately, brand protection is about protecting and creating value for the business, its patients/ consumers, and society as a whole. And that's something everyone in the organization can buy into.

NOTES

1. ISO also provides resources to support implementation of the standard.
2. This information is based on the author's experience and industry knowledge and is not claimed or intended to be exhaustive in terms of potential risk sources, analysis methods, or treatment approaches. At best, it represents a starting point and foundation to build on and adapt to suit the needs of individuals tasked with brand protection and their organizations.
3. This applies only to the "deceptive" category of counterfeits, where the counterfeiter is attempting to dupe the consumer, and not the "non-deceptive" variety where a consumer is knowingly purchasing a counterfeit (e.g., luxury handbags).

REFERENCES

ASIS International. (2019, September 6). ASIS releases new Enterprise Security Risk Management (ESRM) guideline. https://www.asisonline.org/publications--resources/news/press-releases/asis-releases-new-enterprise-security-risk-management-esrm-guideline.

Chaudhry, P. E. (2017). *Handbook of Research on Counterfeiting and Illicit Trade.* Cheltenham, UK and Northampton, MA, USA: Edward Elgar Publishing.

Frontier Economics Ltd. (2017). *The Economic Impacts of Counterfeiting and Piracy.* Brussels: Frontier Economics Ltd.

Hubbard, D. W. (2014). *How to Measure Anything: Finding the Value of Intangibles in Business.* Hoboken, NJ: John Wiley & Sons.

International Organization for Standardization (ISO). (2018). *ISO 31000 Risk Management—Guidelines.* Geneva.

Investopedia. (2020). Value chain vs. supply chain: what's the difference? https://www.investopedia.com/ask/answers/043015/what-difference-between-value-chain-and-supply-chain.asp#:~:text=While%20a%20supply%20chain%20involves,to%20create%20a%20competitive%20advantage.

Kaeser, R. (2019, June 15). Vice President of Global Brand Protection, Johnson & Johnson (S. O'Hearen, Interviewer).

Kennedy, J. P., and Wilson, J. M. (2017). Towards a more proactive approach to brand protection: development of the Organisational Risk Assessment for Product Counterfeiting (ORAPC). *Global Crime, 18*(4), 329–352.

Kennedy, L. W., and McGarrell, E. F. (2011). *Crime and Terrorism Risk*. New York: Routledge.

Trent, C. A. (2013, November). Assessing the risks of counterfeiting and illicit diversion for health care products. A-CAPP Paper Series. Michigan State University, Center for Anti-Counterfeiting and Product Protection.

Wilson, J. M., and Grammich, C. A. (2020). Brand protection across the enterprise: toward a total business solution. *Business Horizons, 63*(3), 363–376.

Wilson, J. M., Grammich, C. A., and Chan, F. (2016). Organizing for brand protection and responding to product counterfeit risk: an analysis of global firms. *Journal of Brand Management, 23*(3), 345–361.

4. Combatting illicit trade: understanding consumer motivations

Peggy E. Chaudhry and John Reiners

1. INTRODUCTION: THE CHALLENGES OF COMBATTING ILLICIT TRADE

Illicit trade is a persistent and growing threat, as technology, the global economy, and e-commerce continue to open new opportunities for illicit products to infiltrate supply chains and provide consumers with fake products (Chaudhry and Cesareo, 2017; Wilson and Grammich, 2020b). The problem of illicit trade is growing, and the Organisation for Economic Co-operation and Development (OECD) Task Force on Countering Illicit Trade estimated that $460 billion of lost revenue was due to the sale of counterfeit goods in the global marketplace (OECD, 2020). The purpose of this chapter is to provide a synopsis of research that was conducted by Oxford Economics with more than 37,000 consumers and 8,121 stakeholders (policymakers, enforcement officials) across 37 European countries to provide a comprehensive picture of consumer attitudes and behaviors regarding illicit trade (Oxford Economics, 2018).

In this chapter, we specifically address what drives consumers to engage in illicit trade activities. Is cost their only motivation, or do other factors come into play? While many studies attempt to size the market and approximate the volume of illegal trade (Chaudhry, 2017b), our research takes a purposely different angle: to understand consumers' *behaviors*—their attitudes and inclinations toward illicit purchases—and how they might be influenced.

2. RESEARCH METHOD

The data presented in this chapter is based on an independent research study conducted by Oxford Economics, titled *Combatting Illicit Trade: Consumer Motivations and Stakeholder Perspectives* (2018). The Oxford Economics study was financed by PMI IMPACT, a global grant initiative by Philip Morris International to support projects dedicated to fighting illegal trade and related crimes. Both authors of this chapter participated in this research study. Dr. Peggy Chaudhry, Associate Professor of International Business at the Villanova School of Business, served as a member of the advisory panel of four independent experts to provide feedback at key stages of the research. Other members of the advisory panel were Liz Allen, former Divisional Head of Excise for Her Majesty's Revenue and Customs (HMRC of the United Kingdom); Allen Buford, former Deputy Director of the World Customs Organization (WCO); and Stefano Betti, Senior Criminal Justice Expert and Deputy Director of Transnational Alliance to Combat Illicit Trade (TRACIT). The other co-author of this chapter, John Reiners, is the Managing Editor of Thought Leadership EMEA at Oxford Economics. Thus, the data highlighted in this chapter stem from the aforementioned Oxford Economics study, which is referred to as the "study" throughout the chapter.

Two key research questions addressed in this study were:

- What drives consumers to buy illicit goods, and how are these motivations different by product and country?
- How aware are policymakers, law enforcement officers, and business executives of these motivations?

To answer these research questions, the co-authors of this chapter worked with a panel of experts and analysts at Oxford Economics to conduct a year-long study spanning 37 European countries and five product categories: cigarettes and tobacco; alcoholic beverages; films, music, and games; clothing and accessories; and medicines and pharmaceutical products. These five product categories were vetted by the advisory panel overseeing the study and the analysts at Oxford Economics due to the prevalence of illicit goods in each product group. Note that throughout this chapter we shorten the descriptions of these categories.

The consumer survey asked 1,000 purchasers in each country for their motivations for buying illicit goods and how their behaviors are influenced by different interventions to combat illicit trade for a total sample size of 37,000 consumers. The demographics of consumers based on age were 18–24 (10%); 25–34 (21%); 35–44 (23%); 45–54 (21%); 55–64 (17%); 65–74 (7%); and 75+ (1%). The work status of respondents were employed full-time (51%), retired (15%), part-time (14%); unemployed (9%); full-time student (7%); and full-time parent or caregiver (4%). The occupations were technical, admin-istrative, or clerical (35%); manager or professional (26%); skilled worker (14%); other (11%); small business owner (8%); routine occupation (5%); and armed forces (1%). The majority of respondents had either a secondary school, vocational, or technical qualifications (43%) or a university degree (42%). A smaller percentage had a graduate degree (9%) or had not completed secondary school (6%). The respondents reported annual household income of under €10,000 (11%); €10,000–€24,999 (26%); €25,000–€49,999 (26%); and €50,000–€74,999 (11%). Only 13% of the respondents earned greater than €75,000 while 13% of respondents did not disclose their personal income in the survey (Oxford Economics, 2018, pp. 48–49).

The stakeholder survey involved interviews with 150 business executives and approximately 75 public sector officials (comprising policy officials and law enforcement officers) working to combat illicit trade in each of the 37 European countries for a total sample size of 8,121 respondents. The primary roles of stakeholders included law enforcement officers (e.g., police officers, defense officers, and customs officials); policy officials (e.g., trade, finance, and tax/revenue advisors); and business executives (e.g., manufacturing, retail, transport, and media) (Oxford Economics, 2018, p. 50).

Both surveys were administered to consumers and stakeholders from November 2017 to February 2018 (Oxford Economics, 2018).

3.   DISPELLING MYTHS OF ILLICIT TRADE

The Oxford Economics survey of stakeholders in Europe (policymakers, law enforcement, and business executives) estimated that roughly 13% of purchases across the five product segments under study are illicit, with similar levels across all products. Furthermore, illicit trade is an issue for all countries across Europe (see Table 4.1), with no obvious distinction between the regions studied. In fact, stakeholders report fast growth in the overall level of illicit trade over the last three years in several countries considered to have deployed sophisticated approaches to resist it, such as Spain (4.8%), Germany (5.2%), and the UK (4.7%) (Oxford Economics, 2018, p. 8).

Yet when consumers were asked to forecast their future illicit purchases, they estimated a decline over the next three years of 5% (Oxford Economics, 2018, p. 8). Illicit purchases were estimated to decline for all products, from 2.7% for cigarettes to 6.7% for medicines and 6.8% for films. Declines were forecast in all countries, with the largest in Estonia (9.5%), Portugal (7.6%), Turkey (7.3%), Hungary (7.1%), Azerbaijan (7.0%), Romania (6.8%), and Italy (6.5%) (Oxford Economics, 2018, pp. 8–9).

The rapid evolution of technology, globalization, and the development of e-commerce and frictionless supply chains have shifted the traditional patterns of illicit trade on both the demand and supply sides (Chaudhry, 2017a). Perhaps consumers may be underestimating the amount of illicit goods they will buy as supply chains are increasingly compromised (Chaudhry and Zimmerman, 2013; Wilson and Grammich, 2020a, 2020b). Alternatively, it is possible that brand owners of legitimate products are unaware that consumers are concerned about authentication and have developed greater awareness

Table 4.1   Estimated illicit trade by country

Rank	Country	Estimated illicit trade (%)	Growth (prev. 3 years (%))	Rank	Country	Estimated illicit trade (%)	Growth (prev. 3 years (%))
1	Ukraine	16.20	7.20	20	Portugal	13.00	2.50
2	Turkey	15.20	8.40	21	Sweden	12.80	1.00
3	Belarus	15.00	2.10	22	Slovakia	12.80	2.50
4	Russia	14.90	−0.20	23	Austria	12.70	2.90
5	Azerbaijan	14.60	8.80	24	Cyprus	12.70	2.80
6	Hungary	14.20	8.80	25	France	12.50	1.80
7	Lithuania	13.60	0.40	26	Switzerland	12.50	2.90
8	Germany	13.50	5.20	27	Finland	12.50	1.60
9	Italy	13.50	5.00	28	Norway	12.50	2.40
10	Czech Republic	13.50	−0.50	29	United Kingdom	12.40	4.70
11	Serbia	13.50	4.60	30	Latvia	12.20	2.20
12	Denmark	13.30	1.50	31	Romania	12.20	2.70
13	Spain	13.30	4.80	32	Belgium	11.90	2.50
14	Slovenia	13.20	2.40	33	Luxembourg	11.40	−3.50
15	Netherlands	13.10	1.40	34	Malta	11.40	−2.80
16	Croatia	13.10	4.80	35	Bulgaria	11.30	−0.60
17	Poland	13.10	4.10	36	Estonia	11.20	−2.20
18	Kazakhstan	13.10	2.70	37	Ireland	10.90	−5.10
19	Greece	13.00	3.30				

Note: N = 8,121 stakeholders.
Source: Oxford Economics (2018, p. 8).

of the risks and costs of illicit trade (Chaudhry and Stumpf, 2010; Stumpf, Chaudhry, and Perretta, 2011).

But how have these developments affected the attitudes and purchasing decisions of consumers? Based on the prior research that established a disjunction between consumers' and business executives' perceptions of illicit trade, we employed the data from the Oxford Economics survey to shed light on four widely held managerial perceptions about consumers' illicit trading behavior, spanning *what* they understand to be illicit goods, *where* they buy them, *who* engages in it, and most important of all, *why* they buy illicit goods (Chaudhry and Stumpf, 2010; Stumpf, Chaudhry, and Perretta, 2011).

The development of these "myths" regarding the demographic profile and motivations of consumers to knowingly engage in the trade of fakes is based on over a decade of research devoted to providing evidence of generalized concepts of illicit trade. Most of our prior research either investigated managerial perceptions of illicit trade (Chaudhry and Stumpf, 2011; Chaudhry et al., 2009a, 2009b) or developed models to determine the key factors that motivate consumer complicity with counterfeit products (Chaudhry and Stumpf, 2009a, 2009b; Chaudhry, Cesareo, and Stumpf, 2014). Previous research examined a multitude of questions, such as whether consumers authenticate goods purchased by using primarily price cues, or whether they find it increasingly difficult to discern if the product is legitimate (Chaudhry and Stumpf, 2011; Stumpf, Chaudhry, and Perretta, 2011; Chaudhry and Cesareo, 2017). This research stream examined whether demographic variables (e.g., age, income, occupation, and education) predicted a complicit consumer, a person who *knowingly* obtains counterfeit goods, with mixed results (Chaudhry and Stumpf, 2011; Chaudhry, Cesareo, and Stumpf, 2014). A comparative study that examined the disparity between managerial (US and Brazilian executives) and consumer (US and Brazilian) perceptions of illicit trade developed an array of myths to descriptively summarize the results of survey work. For example, one myth asserted that price was the most important information consumers used to determine the legitimacy of a product, but the results suggested otherwise—that consumers in the United States and Brazil used perceived quality of the product more than price to authenticate between real versus fake goods (Stumpf, Chaudhry, and Perretta, 2011). The main purpose of the myths developed for the Oxford Economics study was to deliver a novel narrative for practitioners to better understand the key findings of this multi-country study.

3.1 Myth 1: Consumers Know that They Are Buying Illicit Goods

Myth 1: Most illicit goods are usually clearly signaled by their price, whether it is a free film or a designer handbag at a fraction of the price. Consumers know when they are buying illicit goods.

Reality: Consumers increasingly find it difficult to confirm their purchases are genuine even when they buy through trusted sources.

In a rapidly globalizing economy where more goods are available over the internet—from official online stores to online marketplaces and auction sites, then delivered through extended, low-cost supply chains—it is getting harder for consumers to tell whether a product is genuine (Wilson and Grammich, 2020b). In the Oxford Economics study, consumers ranked the likelihood that products purchased were illicit across the five product categories. These European consumers estimated that 11% of purchases were illicit, but a far greater proportion, 27%, had a degree of uncertainty—what the study defined as "possibly illicit" purchases (see Figure 4.1). For some countries and products this uncertainty is even more widespread. For example, in Slovakia, 61% of films and 54% of total purchases across the five products studied were reported as possibly illicit (Oxford Economics, 2018, p. 10).

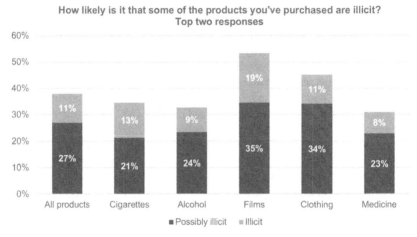

Note: Cigarettes n = 12,998; alcohol n = 18,966; films n = 8,611; clothing n = 22,194; medicines n = 22,448.
Source: Oxford Economics (2018, p. 11).

Figure 4.1   Consumer estimates of illicit trade by product

Undoubtedly some purchases are clearly illicit—such as a video streamed online at an unofficial site (Chaudhry, Cesareo, and Stumpf, 2014). Some consumers deliberately seek out illicit goods, for example buying fake medicines to avoid visiting a doctor (Chaudhry, 2019; Chaudhry and Stumpf, 2013). For some, returning home with fake branded shirts or a designer handbag has become part of the holiday experience (Chaudhry and Zimmerman, 2013). Previous work on customer complicity suggests that some consumers buy illicit goods simply for the hedonic experience, the thrill and adventure of buying from illicit channels (Chaudhry and Cesareo, 2017; Chaudhry, Cesareo, and Stumpf, 2014; Chaudhry and Stumpf, 2011).

But many illicit purchases are not deliberate (Chaudhry and Zimmerman, 2009). Consumers may buy cheaper goods online or from an independent retailer and not realize they could be illicit. There are also many gray areas between legitimate and illicit trade—such as crossing the border to load up a van of goods for personal consumption, receiving a link to a film, buying a locally produced alcoholic drink, or buying a "gray" import of a branded fashion product (Chaudhry, 2014, 2016; Chaudhry, Cesareo, and Stumpf, 2014).

Counterfeiting is often invisible to consumers, as it occurs further down the supply chain, in business-to-business transactions (Chaudhry, 2017a). For many products today, extended and complex supply chains mean that security is in the hands of various intermediaries—such as wholesalers, internet service providers (ISPs), freight forwarders, distribution and postal depots, and payment providers (Chaudhry and Zimmerman, 2013; Wilson and Grammich, 2020b). Ironically, these intermediaries, making decisions on behalf of consumers, also have incentives to sell fake products (Chaudhry and Zimmerman, 2009, 2013).

3.2   Myth 2: Illicit Goods Are Mainly Bought through Illicit Channels

Myth 2: Illicit goods are mostly bought through unofficial retail outlets— such as flea markets or through unofficial websites.

Reality: Illicit trade passes through many retail channels and undermines consumer confidence in legitimate goods. Official online channels, with high volumes and easy access to illicit goods, may post a bigger long-term risk than criminal sites on the dark web.

Based on the purchasing profiles developed for each consumer and product category in the Oxford Economics study, it was not surprising that confidence levels regarding the legitimacy of the product(s) were understandably low for "unofficial sources" of goods, both offline and online, such as buying from a market, a friend or stranger, or an unofficial website. But unofficial sources make up a small share of total purchases from consumers in the study. Of greater concern, the data revealed low levels of consumer confidence regarding the authenticity of the products sold through official outlets—both physical stores and online retailers—such as retailers' websites, apps, auction sites, and popular online marketplaces (Oxford Economics, 2018).

The results of this study clearly present the need for managers to empower consumers with the ability to authenticate the legitimacy of products. We found a startling 56% of consumers have complete confidence that purchases made from official physical stores are genuine, with 36% expressing uncertainty and 8% actively distrusting purchases (Oxford Economics, 2018, p. 12). Confidence is even worse on the internet, with 63% of consumers agreeing it is difficult to tell if a product bought online is legitimate. Forty-four percent of consumers overall say illicit goods are easy to source online, compared with 25% in a physical store. And only 30% of consumers have complete confidence in purchases from official online stores or apps. For online market-places, only 14% of purchasers are fully confident all their purchases are legit-imate products. Unofficial websites (including file-sharing sites and the "dark web") appear mostly to be for illicit purchases, though transaction volumes are much smaller than other channels (Oxford Economics, 2018, p. 13). These data metrics clearly support the need for firms to start using technology that is readily available, such as scanning a QR code with a smartphone, to build trust with consumers regarding the authenticity of the branded product. For example, the apparel industry uses brand protection tactics, such as education and awareness, to help both consumers and law enforcement authenticate goods (Wilson and Grammich, 2020b, p. 12).

Figure 4.2 illustrates a continuing shift toward buying through online retail channels. Fortunately, these consumers report an expected decline in purchas-ing from unofficial outlets, particularly online, a positive trend of reducing their illicit behavior over the next three years.

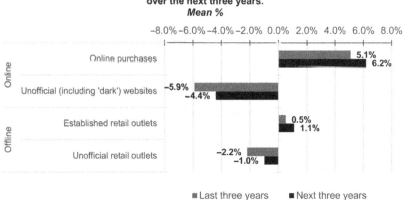

Please tell us how your shopping attitudes and behaviors have changed over the last three years, and how you expect them to change over the next three years.
Mean %

Note: n = 37,370.
Source: Oxford Economics (2018, p. 13).

Figure 4.2   *Consumer estimates of past and future purchasing behavior*

There are several possible reasons to explain why consumers are moving away from unofficial outlets:

- Many businesses are improving their product offerings, introducing new business models like online subscription services and in-app purchases. Retailers are developing more sophisticated "omnichannel" strategies, combining the best of offline and online channels to deliver improved availability, greater convenience, and a better customer experience. All these initiatives could push consumers back to official outlets (Wilson and Grammich, 2020a, 2020b).
- Businesses, often working with public officials, are adapting to the threat, and introducing ways to authenticate products, verify official websites, introduce Codes of Practice with digital retailers, and close unofficial websites. These initiatives may be starting to influence consumers' shopping habits (Chaudhry, 2017b; Wilson and Grammich, 2020a, 2020b).
- Quality assurance is reported in the Oxford Economics study as being the most important reason for buying from official sources. Consumers are generally becoming more demanding of products' authenticity and the traceability of ingredients. The main deterrents experienced to purchasing illicit goods were inferior quality (38%), lack of warranty or after-sales service (32%), dangerous or unhealthy product (15%), and an infected computer (11%). A small fraction of the consumers (3%) reported any type of penalty for engaging in illicit trade (see Figure 4.3).

3.3   Myth 3: Illicit Goods Are Primarily Purchased by Consumers with Low Incomes

Myth 3: Most illicit trade is carried out by low-income consumers, who cannot afford to pay for legitimate goods and have easier access to illicit sources in their communities.

Reality: Illicit trade occurs across all levels of income in society. As illicit trade expands to more products and is increasingly online, it becomes easily accessible to a wider population. There are many reasons why people buy illicit products that are not related to income level.

While this myth is supported by the proclivity to obtain illicit goods among consumers in the lowest-income bands, the study also revealed a high level of complicity in obtaining these illegitimate goods in higher-income bands (see Figure 4.4). Even respondents with annual incomes greater than €150,000,

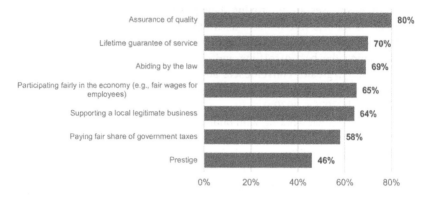

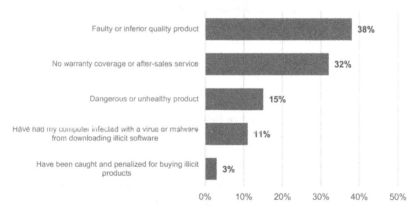

Note: n = 32,023.
Source: Oxford Economics (2018, p. 14).

*Figure 4.3   Consumers' reasons for buying legitimate goods/consumers'
            experiences with illicit goods*

those with a university degree, and those working in managerial and professional roles were complicit in obtaining illicit goods.

    The data show a closer correlation to age than any other factor (see Figure
4.5). Younger people are more likely to be consumers of films, music, and
games, where high levels of illicit trade are almost accepted norms. Older
people are more likely to be concerned about the impact of illicit trade on

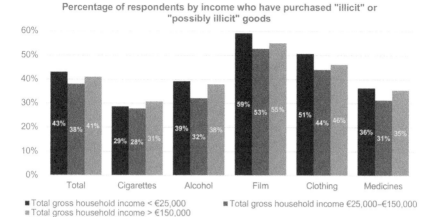

Percentage of respondents by income who have purchased "illicit" or "possibly illicit" goods

- Total gross household income < €25,000
- Total gross household income €25,000–€150,000
- Total gross household income > €150,000

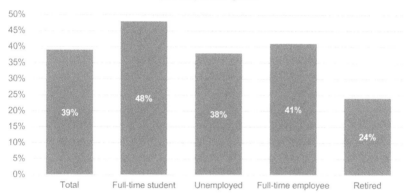

Percentage of respondents by role who have purchased "illicit" or "possibly illicit" goods

Note: Cigarettes n = 12,998; alcohol n = 18,966; films n = 8,611; clothing n = 22,194; medicines n = 22,448.
Source: Oxford Economics (2018, p. 15).

Figure 4.4   Illicit trade by income level and work status

wider society. For example, those over 55 years old agree that illicit trade is harmful to businesses (80% vs. 66% in the youngest group) and that it funds criminals and terrorists (60% vs. 42%).

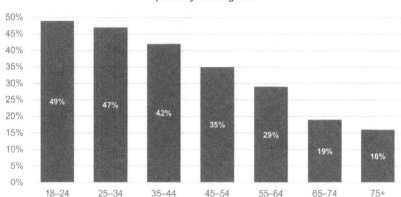

Note: n = 37,370.
Source: Oxford Economics (2018, p. 16).

Figure 4.5   Illicit trade by age group

3.4   Myth 4: Consumers Buy Illicit Goods Since They Are Cheaper, and It Is a Victimless Crime

> *Myth 4: Consumers see illicit trade as essentially victimless—they are buying a cheaper product and no one gets hurt, unlike more serious crimes like drug- or people-trafficking.*
>
> **Reality:** Consumers buy illicit goods for many reasons. Though price is clearly a key factor, there are several other strong influences relating to both the product offering and negative perceptions of illicit trade.

We asked consumers to rate the importance of eight different motivations that spurred their desire to obtain illicit products. Four of these reasons center on the *attractiveness of the product*—price, quality, availability, and convenience. The other four incentives relate to *social factors*—that there is nothing wrong with doing it, others do it, there is little chance of sanction, or that they prefer to buy from unofficial channels. Though the aggregate responses show that most consumers prioritize price, other factors, such as access to the product, are close behind (see Figure 4.6).

In general, stakeholders (policy officials, law enforcement, and business executives) tend to underestimate consumers' awareness of the implications

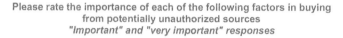

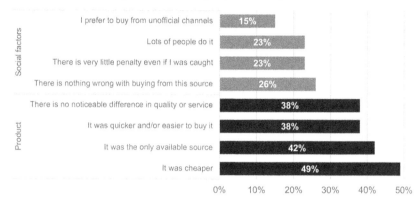

Note: n = 32,023.
Source: Oxford Economics (2018, p. 17).

Figure 4.6   Reasons for buying illicit goods

of illicit trade (Chaudhry and Stumpf, 2010; Stumpf, Chaudhry, and Perretta, 2011). However, the data collected for the Oxford Economics study show that consumers are quite aware of the implications of illicit trade and that this impacts their buying decisions. For example, the respondents of this study agreed that buying illicit goods funds criminals and terrorists (50%), creates health risks (e.g., counterfeit medicines) (56%), and hurts businesses and other stakeholders (66%). However, the results revealed a lack of awareness of the penalties associated with buying counterfeit products (39%) (Oxford Economics, 2018, p. 18).

4.   A NEW WAY OF LOOKING AT CONSUMER MOTIVATION

Effective strategies to reduce illicit consumption need to be based on a solid understanding of why people are buying illicit goods and the factors that would be most effective at influencing them. The results of the study were employed to create an illicit trade matrix that identifies consumers' potentially illicit purchases and then segment them based on two dimensions: (1) their level of complicity (either possible or likely illicit purchases) and (2) the motivations for the illicit purchase (either mostly product related or socially motivated). The remaining illicit purchases are classified as socially motivated, as they score equal or higher on social factors. The matrix creates four separate groups that share distinct characteristics (see Figure 4.7).

The matrix helps to identify the distribution of consumers across the four quadrants, capturing the percentage spread across all potentially illicit European purchases, with "Opportunists" representing the largest group, at 40%. However, the matrix for each country varies significantly by product category—providing insight to those seeking to combat illicit trade into which groups are most important to prioritize.

This study mapped effective strategies for all five products for each country, highlighting how strategies to tackle illicit trade should be customized based on the consumer profiles. The matrix allows the analysis to highlight strategies that most effectively steer consumers away from illicit trade for each product. For each quadrant, the study identified the top three strategies in deterring illicit purchases for each product. The percentage scores reflect the likely effectiveness of the strategy as reported by consumers who fit that quadrant, that is, Critics, Activists, Opportunists, or Bargain Hunters.

For example, Figure 4.8 shows the matrix for alcoholic beverages at the European level (i.e., using all consumer data derived from 37 countries in the matrix), highlighting the most effective strategies for each consumer quadrant. The spread of illicit purchases of alcoholic drinks has more "Critics" and "Opportunists" than other products. Strategies directed at these groups should deter them from progressing to more deliberate illicit purchasing. Authentication initiatives to clarify goods are legitimate could deter the 46% of Critics and Activists. The alcohol industry is introducing QR codes on bottles so that consumers can verify authenticity by using an app on their smartphones. Managers in this sector are also aiming to improve supply-chain security through introducing seals and tamper-proof caps and using track-and-trace technologies (Emler, 2015).

The high level of variation in the study results by product and country makes a strong case for managers seeking to tackle illicit trade to improve their understanding of consumer behavior by collecting detailed data on consumer motivation and analyzing it in a structured way. Oxford Economics gives access to the data from this study at https://www.oxfordeconomics.com/thought-leadership/combatting-illicit-trade. Thus, each unique country matrix can be generated at this website using one (or all) product category for each of the 37 countries.

5.   CONCLUDING REMARKS

Illicit trade is a persistent and growing threat, as technology, the global economy, and e-commerce open new opportunities for counterfeit products to infiltrate supply chains thus providing consumers with illicit products. Our

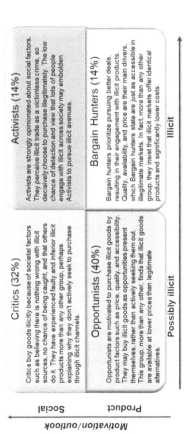

Critics (32%)

Critics buy goods illicitly because of societal factors such as believing there is nothing wrong with illicit sources, no chance of being caught, and that others do it. They have experienced faulty and inferior illicit products more than any other group, perhaps explaining why they don't actively seek to purchase through illicit channels.

Activists (14%)

Activists are strongly opinionated about social factors. They perceive illicit trade as a victimless crime, so decisively choose to purchase illegitimately. The low chance of detection and view that lots of people engage with illicit across society may embolden Activists to pursue illicit avenues.

Opportunists (40%)

Opportunists are motivated to purchase illicit goods by product factors such as price, quality, and accessibility. They may buy illicit goods as opportunities present themselves, rather than actively seeking them out. This group, more than any other, finds that illicit goods are available at lower prices than legitimate alternatives.

Bargain Hunters (14%)

Bargain hunters prioritize pursuing better deals, resulting in their engagement with illicit products. Quality, availability, and price are their main drivers, which Bargain hunters state are just as accessible in illegitimate markets. In fact, more than any other group, they insist that illicit markets offer identical products and significantly lower costs.

Social — Product — Motivation/outlook

Possibly illicit — Complicity to buy illicit — Illicit

What will most influence consumers to change their behavior

Strategies to modify behavior	Description
Assure quality	Providing quality assurance, warranty, reward schemes, and after-sales service for legitimate goods
Reduce cost	Reducing the cost of the legitimate good (e.g., reducing the tax)
Increase availability	Increasing the availability of legitimate products (e.g., quicker, better distribution)
Clarify goods are legit	Clarifying that goods are legitimate (e.g., supplier, website, and product certification)
Track illicit goods	Knowing that retailers and law enforcement can track and identify illicit products
Raise fines and penalties	Raising fines and penalties for buying illicit products
Communicate wider implications	Understanding consequences of buying illicit goods (e.g., health risks, funding organized crime/terrorism)
Increase penalties	Increasing the likelihood of being punished for buying illicit goods
Publish names involved in illicit	Publishing the names of those caught distributing and purchasing illicit goods in local media
Remind illicit harms legit firms	Making clear how buying illicit goods hurts law-abiding companies and their workers

Source: Oxford Economics (2018, p. 20).

Figure 4.7   *Illicit trade consumer matrix, European total averages*

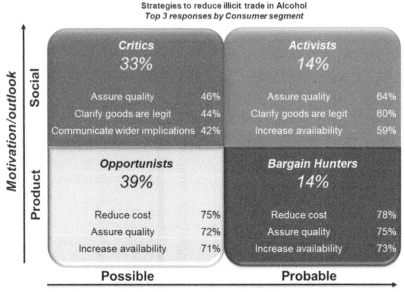

Strategies to reduce illicit trade in Alcohol
Top 3 responses by Consumer segment

Source: Oxford Economics (2018, p. 21).

Figure 4.8   Illicit trade consumer matrix—alcohol

analysis of 37,000 consumers fielded across 37 European countries provides a comprehensive picture of consumer attitudes and behaviors regarding illicit trade. It is important that brand owners and others working to contain illicit trade update their approaches to recognize these realities: the high level of "possibly illicit" purchases, the lack of consumer confidence in the reliability of official online channels, the pervasiveness of illicit trade across all income levels and occupations of society, and above all, the highly nuanced reasons consumers have for buying illicit goods (Wilson and Grammich, 2020a). Though many seek to get a better deal, it is not just about the price—quality, reliability, and availability are also important factors. This study asserts that many consumers are aware and concerned about the implications of illicit trade, for themselves and broader society. Recognition of these realities will help in seeking out effective remedies, such as restoring trust in products through securing supply chains and product authentication (Chaudhry, 2017a; Chaudhry and Zimmerman, 2013; Wilson and Grammich, 2020a). Raising consumer awareness of the prevalence and consequences of illicit trade continues to be at the forefront of decreasing demand for illicit goods (Chaudhry and Cesareo, 2017; Chaudhry and Zimmerman, 2013). However, an important finding is that consumers' motivations are highly nuanced and will vary according to multiple factors, so strategies need to be tailored to different consumer groups. Our illicit trade consumer matrix indicates that the effectiveness of initiatives to combat illicit trade will vary significantly by product and country.

REFERENCES

Chaudhry, P. (2014), 'Confronting the gray market problem', *Business Economics*, **49**, 263–270.

Chaudhry, P. (2016), 'Can consumers be scared into not buying counterfeit goods?', *Marketing Daily*, December 12, accessed 16 February 2021 at http://www.mediapost .com/publications/article/290753/can-consumers-be-scared-into-not-buying-count erfei.html?edition=98785.

Chaudhry, P. (2017a), *Handbook of Research on Counterfeiting and Illicit Trade*, Cheltenham, UK and Northampton, MA, USA: Edward Elgar Publishing.

Chaudhry, P. (2017b), 'The looming shadow of illicit trade on the internet', *Business Horizons*, **60**(1), 77–89.

Chaudhry, P. (2019), 'Confronting a virtual sea of fake medicines on the web: The battle continues', *Global Journal of Enterprise Information System*, **11**(4), 49–59.

Chaudhry, P., and L. Cesareo (2017), 'Fake and pirated: Do consumers care?', *Journal of Business Strategy*, **38**(6), 11–19.

Chaudhry, P., L. Cesareo, and S. Stumpf (2014), 'What influences rampant movie piracy?', *Journal of Management Systems*, **24**(4), 73–96.

Chaudhry, P., and S. Stumpf (2009a), 'The CMO's role in curtailing black-market counterfeits: How you can act as a change agent', *Advertising Age*, 21 December.

Chaudhry, P., and S. Stumpf (2009b), 'Getting real about fakes', *The Wall Street Journal*, 17 August, pp. R4, R8.

Chaudhry, P., and S. Stumpf (2010), 'Country matters: Executives weigh-in on the causes and counter measures of counterfeit trade', *Business Horizons*, **53**(3), 305–314.

Chaudhry, P., and S. Stumpf (2011), 'Consumer complicity with counterfeit products', *Journal of Consumer Marketing*, **28**(2), 139–151.

Chaudhry, P., and S. Stumpf (2013), 'The challenge of curbing counterfeit prescription drug growth: Preventing the perfect storm', *Business Horizons*, **56**(2), 189–197.

Chaudhry, P., and A. Zimmerman (2009), *The Economics of Counterfeit Trade: Governments, Consumers, Pirates and Intellectual Property Rights*, Berlin: Springer-Verlag.

Chaudhry, P., and A. Zimmerman (2013), *Protecting Your Intellectual Property Rights: Understanding the Role of Management, Governments, Consumers and Pirates*, Berlin: Springer-Verlag.

Chaudhry, P., A. Zimmerman, J. Peters, and V. Cordell (2009a), 'Evidence of managerial response to the level of consumer complicity, pirate activity, and host country enforcement of counterfeit goods: An exploratory study', *Multinational Business Review*, **17**(4), 21–44.

Chaudhry, P., A. Zimmerman, J. Peters, and V. Cordell (2009b), 'Preserving intellectual property rights: Managerial insight into the escalating counterfeit market quandary', *Business Horizons*, **52**(1), 57–66.

Emler, R. (2015), 'Technology used to fight back against fakes', accessed 5 June 2020 at https://www.thedrinksbusiness.com/2015/10/technology-used-to-fight-back -against-fakes/.

Organisation for Economic Co-operation and Development (OECD) (2020), *Illicit Trade Estimated International Revenue by Sector*, accessed 14 December 2020 at http://www.oecd.org/governance/risk/oecdtaskforceoncounteringillicittrade.htm.

Oxford Economics (2018), *Combatting Illicit Trade: Consumer Motivations and Stakeholder Perspectives*, accessed 5 June 2019 at https://www.oxfordeconomics .com/thought-leadership/combatting-illicit-trade.

Stumpf, S., P. Chaudhry, and L. Perretta (2011), 'Fake: Can business stanch the flow of counterfeit products?', *Journal of Business Strategy*, **32**(2), 4–12.

Wilson, J., and C. Grammich (2020a), 'Brand protection across the enterprise: Toward a total-business solution', *Business Horizons*, **63**(3), 363–376.

Wilson, J., and C. Grammich (2020b), 'Protecting brands from counterfeiting risks: Tactics of a total business solution', *Journal of Risk Research*, https://doi.org/10 .1080/13669877.2020.1806908.

PART III

Mitigating the risk of counterfeit products

5. Brand protection and organizational silos: integrating tactics and firm functions in the fight against counterfeits

Jeremy M. Wilson and Clifford A. Grammich

In part because of the limited knowledge they have of product counterfeiting, most firms addressing the problem do so only after discovering they have been victimized. As a result, firms typically pursue reactive tactics in their fight against product counterfeiting. These may include seeking monetary damages and injunctions against counterfeiters (Yang et al. 2004; Sonmez and Yang 2005; Firth 2006; Trott and Hoecht 2007; Chaudhry and Zimmerman 2009; Hoecht and Trott 2014). Such tactics may also include organizing evidence for law enforcement officials to investigate and, if warranted, seek prosecution of violations (Foucart 2016). Crackdown operations involving undercover informants, raids, and seizures can have significant deterrent effects (Green and Smith 2002; Reynolds 2011; Hoecht and Trott 2014), but such tactics still result only from reaction to a prior incident.

Firms wanting a more proactive approach may seek to minimize supply chain vulnerabilities or rely on contractual agreements, including penalties for nonconformance, and periodic field audits, such as ones covering how suppliers receive, use, dispose of, and account for materials (Yang et al. 2004; Liu et al. 2005; Chaudhry and Zimmerman 2009; Waring 2013; Hoecht and Trott 2014; Stevenson and Busby 2015). Alternatively, organizations may use anti-counterfeiting labeling and packaging and track-and-trace technology to follow a product through its life cycle (Stumpf et al. 2011). Vertically integrating supply chains, for example where one firm is responsible for products from procurement of raw materials to sale at retailers, can provide the most direct control over a supply chain and minimize risks to counterfeiting (Stevenson and Busby 2015), but can also be costly or even impractical given the proliferation of third-party virtual marketplaces.

Other proactive responses to product counterfeiting may involve raising awareness among consumers, collaborating with competitors to identify sources of counterfeit trade, and facilitating internal education and awareness

(Hoecht and Trott 2014; Wilson and Kinghorn 2014). Such efforts may include aligning brand protection values with daily operations through strategic plans, operating practices, performance appraisal, training, and other mechanisms (Post and Post 2007). Firms may hire a risk officer or specialist to address counterfeiting issues or seek to quantify risks as best they can (Wilson 2017). Firms may also find that diverse approaches have varying levels of effectiveness in dissimilar markets (Stumpf and Chaudhry 2010).

Altogether, previous research notes several strategies that firms may use to address product counterfeiting but offer few systematic approaches. Many current approaches are "siloed," with little interaction across functions (Wilcock and Boys 2014), that is, sets of activities or processes within or across structural units for accomplishing a brand protection goal. In this chapter, we seek to provide insight on the integration of functions and tactics as part of a coordinated effort to facilitate brand protection in a total business approach (Wilson and Grammich 2020a).

THE ROLE OF BRAND PROTECTION TEAMS

Brand protection teams may occupy similar positions across organizations. An analysis of brand protection teams in ten leading firms found half were positioned within a single function, typically legal, but others were positioned across multiple functions (Wilson et al. 2016). For example, one firm reported having a brand protection function within a single corporate stand-alone unit, which also overlapped security and legal resources, and integrating its work into businesses across the firm.

Most successful teams reported having "active" rather than "reactive" programs or being "aggressive" rather than "passive" in their efforts; one "very successful" team reported being both "active" and "aggressive" while one "unsuccessful" team reported being "reactive" and "passive" (Wilson et al. 2016). Firms claiming to be "successful" cited management support, funding, and understanding of the problems as reasons for their success.

There are many practices that teams can implement to facilitate brand protection, including seizures of counterfeit products, legal action against infringers, training customs agents, analyzing supply chain risks, securing excess labels, and embedding track-and-trace technologies in products. Such practices have been categorized in different ways, including by their relation to consumer demand (Stöttinger et al. 2017); their effect on deceptive and nondeceptive counterfeits (Grossman and Shapiro 1988a and 1988b); their proactive versus reactive nature (Clements 2016; Ting and Tsang 2014; Staake and Fleisch 2008; Berman 2004); their substantive focus, for example consumers, distribution channels, international organizations (Wilson and Grammich 2020b; Chaudhry et al. 2009); their internal or external implementation

(Wilson et al. 2016); their perspective of intervention, for example whether they are launched internally within the firm or with global partners (Raman and Pramad 2017); and their relation to elements of total quality management (Wilcock and Boys 2014). These classifications show that firms can and do rely on multiple, diverse tactics to protect their brands. This suggests a multi-faceted or layered approach to combating product counterfeits that appears to integrate multiple stakeholders.

The total business solution for brand protection emphasizes promoting a holistic approach that integrates and coordinates all parts of the firm for brand protection. Brand protection is achieved through an interdisciplinary understanding of and response to brand risks. Yet typical brand protection programs, like individual strategies, are siloed, often emphasizing a singular function such as security, legal, or supply chain. A total business solution requires firms to acknowledge the critical role that virtually all functions of the organization play in brand protection and to integrate these functions in a com-prehensive and meaningful way to protect the brand (Wilson and Grammich 2020a).

This raises two questions for firms. First, which functions should pursue which tactics? Second, which tactics should be integrated across multiple functions? In this chapter, we seek to answer these questions through analysis of brand protection tactics and associated functions suggested by brand protec-tion practitioners and other leading experts.

ASSESSING BRAND PROTECTION FUNCTIONS AND THEIR TACTICS

Definitions

We define a function as a set of activities or processes within or across struc-tural units for accomplishing a brand protection goal. We chose to analyze organizational functions in brand protection given prior research showing that firms locate brand protection responsibilities in a variety of departments and divisions, including in multiple units within a matrix structure, and that a wide array of tactics can help protect brands (Staake and Fleisch 2008; Chaudhry et al. 2009; Wilcock and Boys 2014; Wilson et al. 2016). Likewise, as open systems that interact with their environments, firms structure themselves dif-ferently and do not maintain the same organizational components (Burns and Stalker 1961; Katz and Kahn 1966; Lawrence and Lorsch 1967; Thompson 1967; Meyer and Rowan 1977; Donaldson 1987).

Functions are meant to focus on the substantive nature of the work carried out by the firm as the basis of organization and could be located structurally in different parts of the firm or have different names. The focus on functions helps us to concentrate on substantive work without regard to where it occurs.

Drawing from Experts

To identify the critical functions and tactics that firms might employ in brand protection, we sought to gather information about critical functions directly from brand protection practitioners and experts, creating a purposive sample of expert respondents. We created the sample to primarily reflect large multinational brands in a wide range of industries with recognizable depth and experience in brand protection. To provide some diversity in perspective, we also included some service providers, industry associations, and scholars. To facilitate recruitment, we drew upon many experts with whom we have had previous interaction.

Altogether, 42 respondents provided us information. This included 33 experts, representing 25 global and widely recognizable brand-owning firms, who come from a wide variety of ranks (e.g., managers, directors, vice presidents) and have a broad range of perspectives (e.g., legal, security/enforcement, strategy, licensing, compliance, risk management, enterprise administration). These experts represented a broad range of industries, including agriculture, apparel, auto, construction/farm equipment/machinery, consumer products, electronics, luxury products, pharmaceuticals and medical devices, higher education, and food. The firms where respondents worked varied in size as well; in Fiscal Year 2017, according to MarketLine company profiles or the corporate websites of firms, the firms ranged in revenue from $450 million to more than $165 billion, and in number of employees from 2,000 to more than 230,000. To round out the sample, we included representatives of four brand protection service providers, three academics, and representatives of two brand protection industry associations. (For further information on our methods, see Wilson and Grammich 2020a and 2020b.)

Expert Responses

We asked our respondents to provide us information on the functions and tactics that ideally would be employed in a brand protection program. For practitioners, these could be both tactics they employ and additional others that, ideally, they would employ. We compiled all the resources into a dataset, allowing us to examine all the functions identified along with the tactics respondents associated with them.

Our respondents identified 1,347 individual tactics. Among these we identified 757 unique tactics associated with 35 functions such as legal, supply chain, sales, and marketing. Table 5.1 lists the 20 functions for which at least

Table 5.1   Numbers of unique and total brand protection tactics reported for each function

Function	Number of Respondents (N = 42) Suggesting Tactics Within Function	Unique Tactics Reported Within Function	Total Tactics Reported Within Function
Legal	36	72	122
Supply Chain	35	63	71
Sales	34	73	84
Marketing	33	54	65
Media and Public Relations	33	28	47
Security	32	134	190
Packaging	32	41	57
Customer Relations and Service	30	42	45
Procurement	27	45	57
C-Suite Executive Team	27	29	47
Government Affairs	27	11	42
Brand Protection	26	112	178
Human Resources	26	31	41
Quality Assurance	24	45	50
Finance/Audit	23	29	39
Research and Development	23	27	28
Warehousing and Distribution	21	43	44
Manufacturing	21	40	41
Engineering	16	20	23
Operations	12	22	22

ten respondents suggested brand protection tactics. It shows, for each function, the number of respondents who suggested brand protection tactics within that function, the number of "unique" tactics suggested for that function, and the number of "total" brand protection tactics suggested for that function. Functions are listed by the number of respondents suggesting brand protection tactics within each of them.

The following example illustrates how we counted "unique" and "total" tactics. Seven respondents cited "consider brand protection in packaging design" as a tactic to be applied within the packaging function of a firm. Because seven individuals cited the same tactic for this function, we counted it as only one "unique" tactic within packaging. At the same time, because seven different individuals suggested this as a tactic, we counted these seven different individual suggestions as seven different "total" tactics within packaging. One individual also suggested "consider brand protection in packaging design" as a tactic that could be applied within the engineering function of a firm. Hence, we also counted this as one of the 20 unique brand protection tactics suggested by respondents for the engineering function, and one of the 23 total tactics suggested for that function. (For more on our classification of "unique" and "total" brand protection tactics by firm function, see Wilson and Grammich 2020a and 2020b.)

We are interested in the number of "unique" and "total" tactics that can be identified because of what they say about how widely and how frequently a function might be involved in brand protection. A function for which respondents suggested a wide variety of unique tactics might perform a wide variety of activities in brand protection. Hence, we consider the number of unique tactics cited to be an indicator of the "breadth" of tactics that a function might perform. A function for which respondents suggested a high number of tactics might perform brand protection tactics frequently. Hence, we consider the number of total tactics suggested to be an indicator of the "depth" of tactics that a function might perform.

Perhaps not surprisingly, security and brand protection were the functions that our respondents advised should have both the deepest and widest roles. For each of these two functions, our respondents suggested more than 100 unique tactics and nearly 200 total tactics.

Respondents appear to view a few functions as having different levels of depth or breadth. The most striking example of differing depth and breadth is for tactics suggested within the government affairs function. Respondents suggested 11 unique tactics for government affairs but 42 total tactics. This may indicate the need that brand owners see to increase public awareness of counterfeiting. Furthermore, as noted above, respondents often saw a need to adopt a single tactic across multiple functions. For example, nearly a dozen respondents cited a single tactic, "network with law enforcement," across five functions, including government affairs, brand protection, and security. This may indicate a growing awareness of the need to involve all levels of law enforcement early on and consistently in supporting brand protection (Foucart 2016).

While respondents did note greater breadth or depth for some functions than others, they typically noted the need to involve multiple functions. As Table 5.1 indicates, at least 30 respondents suggested tactics for each of eight functions, and at least 20 respondents suggested tactics for each of 18 functions. While these suggestions by function did not always overlap, they indicate the breadth of functions and tactics that respondents suggest for brand protection. From this, we surmise that brand protection practitioners across ranks and industries understand the value of a total business solution and seek to advance it. (For more on brand protection functions and tactics, see Wilson and Grammich 2020a.)

CATEGORIZING BRAND PROTECTION TACTICS

A further way to identify all dimensions of an enterprise-wide approach to brand protection is to categorize all tactics associated with it. To do so, we employed a grounded-theory approach (Glaser and Strauss 1967) and a multistage content analysis (Aksulu and Wade 2010) to identify categories of tactics independent of organizational function. (For more discussion of how we organized categories of tactics, see Wilson and Grammich 2020b.) As we did for functions, we assessed the depth and breadth of each category in brand protection, with depth being indicated by the total number of tactics cited in a category and breadth being indicated by the number of unique tactics cited in a category.

We ultimately classified our tactics into 12 categories: analysis, communications and coordination, education and awareness, enforcement, firm policy and process, legal, physical security, product protection, public policy, resources, strategy, and supplier compliance. Table 5.2 lists the categories of tactics we derived, the number of respondents who suggested tactics falling into our categories, and the number of unique and total tactics that we identified for each category. This table suggests the categories of tactics that firms may wish to apply to brand protection regardless of their own functional structure.

Table 5.2   *Numbers of unique and total brand protection tactics reported by category of tactic*

Tactic Category	Number of Respondents (N = 42) Suggesting Tactics Within Category	Unique Tactics Reported Within Category	Total Tactics Reported Within Category
Analysis	36	121	182
Communications and Coordination	36	92	166
Education and Awareness	35	66	173
Enforcement	32	53	123
Firm Policy and Process	31	86	100
Legal	31	52	101
Physical Security	16	30	37
Product Protection	39	121	196
Public Policy	25	6	57
Resources	30	42	74
Strategy	24	32	45
Supplier Compliance	29	55	93

Perhaps not surprisingly, product protection tactics were suggested as having the greatest depth and, with analysis, the greatest breadth of all categories. This includes subcategories of tactics such as disposing of excess or reject product, product identification and authentication, packaging, and track and trace. Nearly every respondent suggested tactics that fell into this category.

As noted, analysis had, with product protection, the greatest breadth and the second-greatest depth. This category includes analysis of risks, customer feedback, and market monitoring. Analysis may occur anywhere from product design to market distribution. As one respondent told us, firms should conduct "comprehensive risk assessments for new products in the pipeline to ensure that proper protections are in place prior to launch. [It is b]est to get upstream as far as possible in the planning and package design process[es]." Another noted the need for manufacturing, marketing, sales, and product return personnel to work together to monitor product distribution and returns and to dispose of excess product as needed. Altogether, 36 respondents suggested tactics that fell into this category.

Education and awareness had the third-greatest depth, that is, the third-highest number of total tactics suggested for it, but only the fifth-greatest breadth, that is, the fifth-greatest number of unique tactics. In other words, our respondents indicated that it is highly important for brand protection, but the relative breadth of such tactics is not as great as one might expect. This appears to be a result of the relatively small number of different education and training tactics respondents noted for groups such as consumers and law enforcement. Respondents noted the importance of training law enforcement but had little detail to add beyond the need to do so. By contrast, respondents reported a breadth and depth of tactics for areas such as raising internal and external awareness. This suggests respondents, and firms more generally, have better-developed ways to educate internal and external stakeholders on awareness of counterfeits, but may still be developing lessons for law enforcement.

The communication and coordination category had the fourth-highest number of total tactics and the third-highest number of unique tactics. This indicates a category both relatively broad and deep, that is, a category of tactics that respondents are likely to suggest using and a variety of tactics as well. These tactics include internal and external communication, crisis communication, and networking with others. Such tactics seek to provide more general support for brand protection than education and awareness tactics do. As one respondent said, "protecting the brand should be something embedded in the culture of each company." Among purposes that respondents suggested for networking with peers are "sharing best practices, benchmarking, and innovating brand protection solutions."

INTEGRATING TACTICS AND FUNCTIONS

In devising a total business solution to brand protection, how should firms integrate tactics and functions? What tactics are likely to be used across multiple functions? What functions are most likely to use multiple tactics? Where might functions find synergy in pursuing a common tactic in ways that yield benefits across the enterprise? How do functions differ in the breadth and depth of their uses of different categories of tactics? To address these and related issues, we consider the links between functions and categories, including functions that use multiple categories of tactics and tactics of categories that are used by multiple functions.

Depth of Tactics

Table 5.3 shows the total number of tactics in each category, listed alphabetically across the top, by each function, listed alphabetically along the left-hand side. Overlaying functions by total number of tactics in each category, we see respondents suggested anywhere from 1 to 54 total tactics in each combination of firm function and tactic category. For example, respondents suggested only one enforcement tactic for the customer relations and service function. At the other extreme, they suggested 54 total enforcement tactics for the security function. Table 5.3 highlights function and category tactics with 27 or more total tactics, that is, with at least half the maximum number of tactics suggested for any function and category combination. Although this is a somewhat arbitrary distinction, we chose this threshold to identify cells that have higher numbers of total tactics in a classification scheme we later discuss for prioritizing approaches to brand protection.

As noted earlier, the brand protection function ideally would incorporate many tactics, including analysis, communications and coordination, education and awareness, enforcement, and strategy categories. In some of these, it should perhaps lead enterprise-wide efforts, but in many it should also work with other functions. Indeed, while enforcement tactics are the most common in brand protection, they are more common in the security function, and nearly as common in the legal function.

Similarly, the security function should also incorporate many tactics from different categories. Some of these are predictable, including enforcement tactics. Others are perhaps a bit more surprising or at least less common. For example, our respondents recommended public policy tactics for the security function more than for any other function outside government affairs. Public policy tactics recommended for the security function include networking with law enforcement, networking with other government agencies, and suggesting

Table 5.3   Total tactics by category and function

	Analysis	Communications and Coordination	Education and Awareness	Enforcement	Firm Policy and Process	Legal	Physical Security	Product Protection	Public Policy	Resources	Strategy	Supplier Compliance
"All"					1							
Administration	1											
Brand Management		2	2			1				1		
Brand Protection	27	23	28	31	10	10		11	3	11	22	2
Communications (Internal)			2									
Compliance					1							
C-Suite Executive Team	2	15	13		3	2			2	9	1	
Customer Relations and Service	24	6	12	1	1			1				
Data Analytics	5										1	
Dealers, Franchisees, Licensees	1	1			2							
E-commerce	1	1	1	1	1							
Engineering	2	2			1		2	15			1	

	Analysis	Communications and Coordination	Education and Awareness	Enforcement	Firm Policy and Process	Legal	Physical Security	Product Protection	Public Policy	Resources	Strategy	Supplier Compliance
External Partner Provider	2			1								
Finance/Audit	12	3	1	1	4	1		1		4		12
Government Affairs	2	5	2		1				*31*	1	1	
Human Resources		2	14		9					15		
Information Technology	3							5				
Legal	7	4	6	27	4	*54*	3	4	3	9	4	1
Logistics	1	1					3	2	1			10
Manufacturing		3			5		5	16		1	1	10
Marketing	3	15	21	1	7	11		4			2	1
Media and Public Relations	5	22	17			2				1		
Operations		2	3		5		1	4		2		5
Packaging	2	1				1		52		1		
Procurement	2	2	3	2	9	9		5		1		24
Quality Assurance	11	11	2	2	3	1		12	1	1		6
Research and Development	1	1			4	2		19			1	

	Analysis	Communications and Coordination	Education and Awareness	Enforcement	Firm Policy and Process	Legal	Physical Security	Product Protection	Public Policy	Resources	Strategy	Supplier Compliance
Retail Operations	1		1									
Risk Management	1				1							
Sales	*29*	11	21	2	7	2	1	5			5	1
Security	24	20	23	*54*	9		10	10	16	16	5	3
Service		2										
Styling/Design								1				
Supply Chain	8	6			7	4	7	19			1	19
Warehousing and Distribution	3	5	1		6	1	8	10		1		9

Note: Function and category combinations with 27 or more total tactics are shown in *italicized* font.

enhancements and other improvements to current public policies regarding counterfeiting. Respondents also recommended resources tactics for security and human resources functions more than any other. Many of these tactics involved hiring investigators, suggesting security should help human resources identify and select candidates who can best support brand protection.

Most of the tactics that respondents suggested for the legal function were, not surprisingly, from the legal and enforcement categories. Respondents also suggested nearly a dozen legal tactics for the marketing function, many of which would best be executed in coordination with the legal function. Legal tactics that respondents for the marketing function may coordinate with the legal function include ensuring proper use and identification of registered trademarks, working on rebranding efforts, and working to develop agreements with brand protection features in marketing.

Most tactics that respondents suggested for the government affairs function were, also not surprisingly, from the public policy category. Respondents also recommended public policy tactics for six other functions. Most of these are tactics in which a government affairs function could lead or enhance efforts across functions. Many, for example, involve networking with government agencies, networking with law enforcement, and monitoring and lobbying for improved protections of intellectual property. The government affairs function might find in other functions specific insights on needed policy improvements, while other functions might find in government affairs insights on the best way to pursue such improvements.

Several other functions had a relatively large number of tactics concentrated within certain categories. For example, the C-suite executive team had more than ten total tactics in communication and coordination as well as in education and awareness. C-suite communication and coordination tactics suggested by our respondents focused on the unique roles of corporate leaders and included holding briefings on brand protection, sponsoring the brand protection function, and developing a culture of brand protection such as by "foster[ing] an understanding that the [b]rand's intellectual property is the companies most valued asset." C-suite education and awareness tactics suggested by our respondents focused on increasing internal awareness, including the costs of counterfeiting to the firm and the risks that counterfeiting posed to firm revenues. Customer relations and service had more than ten total tactics in education and awareness and, perhaps more surprisingly, analysis. Marketing had more than ten total tactics suggested for communication and coordination, education and awareness, and, perhaps most surprisingly, legal. Legal tactics that respondents suggested for the marketing function included working with the legal function to ensure proper use and identification of registered trademarks, trademark registration, and rebranding efforts, all suggesting work needed across functions to ensure brand protection.

Similarly, for the human resources function respondents suggested more than ten tactics in the categories of education and awareness and resources. These included not just training incoming staff on brand protection issues but also reminding all staff continually of such issues, assessing brand protection strengths and weaknesses among staff, and developing a brand protection professional career path. Clearly such tactics require cross-functional approaches.

Breadth of Tactics

Table 5.4 shows the total number of unique tactics in each category and for each function. Respondents suggested anywhere from 1 to 37 unique tactics for each combination. For example, while respondents suggested, in total, 27 analysis tactics for the brand protection function, we found only 21 of these were unique. All function and category combinations with only one total tactic suggested would, of course, have only one unique tactic. Table 5.4 highlights function and category combinations with 19 or more unique tactics, that is, with at least half the maximum number of unique tactics suggested for any function and category combination. Again, our decision to highlight cells with 19 or more unique tactics is somewhat arbitrary, but it also helps in our later discussion of where firms should focus their first efforts. For now, by focusing on unique tactics, we can identify the breadth of each category of tactics in brand protection and more of the leadership roles that each function might perform.

Respondents suggested analysis tactics be used for brand protection by 27 different functions. For several functions—brand protection, customer relations and service, finance/audit, sales, and security—respondents suggested both considerable breadth and depth of analysis tactics. The functions suggested for analysis tactics also indicate the breadth of activities that brand protection should consider. Respondents suggested the brand protection, finance, and security functions analyze risks and monitor marketplaces. They also suggested the customer relations function could monitor customer feedback on products, while the sales function monitors sales and trends.

Respondents suggested communications and coordination tactics be used by 25 different functions. Our respondents noted that communications and coordination tactics can differ somewhat by function as well as by phase of response to counterfeiting incidents, though they may overlap as well. Sales personnel, for example, can communicate internal information on discovered incidents. Security can provide communication both on incidents and on how best to network with other private organizations to investigate incidents. Marketing can communicate the dangers of counterfeit products and develop other messaging for brand protection in efforts to prevent brand protection incidents. Media and public relations can prepare communications plans for

Table 5.4   *Unique tactics by category and function*

	Analysis	Communications and Coordination	Education and Awareness	Enforcement	Firm Policy and Process	Legal	Physical Security	Product Protection	Public Policy	Resources	Strategy	Supplier Compliance
"All"					1							
Administration	1											
Brand Management		2	2			1				1		
Brand Protection	*21*	*19*	*13*	*15*	*8*	*6*		*10*	*1*	*7*	*11*	*2*
Communications (Internal)			2									
Compliance					1							
C-Suite Executive Team	2	8	10		3	2			2	1	1	
Customer Relations and Service	23	6	10	1	1			1				
Data Analytics	5										1	
Dealers, Franchisees, Licensees	1	1			2							
E-commerce	1	1	1									
Engineering	2	2		1	1		2	13			1	
External Partner Provider	2			1								
Finance/Audit	11	3	1	1	4	1		1		2		
Government Affairs	2	2	2	1	1				3	1		5

	Analysis	Communications and Coordination	Education and Awareness	Enforcement	Firm Policy and Process	Legal	Physical Security	Product Protection	Public Policy	Resources	Strategy	Supplier Compliance
Human Resources	2	2	6		8					14	1	
Information Technology	2							5				
Legal	7	4	4	10	3	25		4	3	8	4	1
Logistics	1	1					2	2	1			
Manufacturing	3	3			5		5	16		1	1	9
Marketing	5	14	11	1	7	11		4			2	1
Media and Public Relations		10	12			2				1		
Operations	2	2	3		5		1	4		2		5
Packaging	2	1			8	1		36		1		
Procurement	2	2	3	2	3	8		5		1		14
Quality Assurance	9	11	2	2	4	1		9	1	1		6
Research and Development	1	1	1			2		18			1	
Retail Operations	1											
Risk Management					1							
Sales	25	11	14	2	7	2	1	5			5	1
Security	19	14	14	37	9		8	9	5	11	5	3
Service	2	2										
Styling/Design								1				

	Analysis	Communications and Coordination	Education and Awareness	Enforcement	Firm Policy and Process	Legal	Physical Security	Product Protection	Public Policy	Resources	Strategy	Supplier Compliance
Supply Chain	7	6			7	4	5	16			1	17
Warehousing and Distribution	3	5	1		6	1	7	10		1		9

Note: Function and category combinations with 19 or more unique tactics are shown in *italicized* font.

counterfeiting incidents and communicate successes that have been made in the fight against product counterfeiting. Respondents suggested a wide variety of internal and external communications and coordination tactics for the brand protection function, but personnel in this function can also, as shown, enlist the support of many other functions in executing these tactics.

Education and awareness tactics, respondents suggested, could be executed in 19 different functions. Many of these are the same functions that respondents suggested for communications and coordination tactics, but there is some variation in the breadth and depth here. For example, in the C-suite, customer relations and service, media and public relations, and sales functions respondents suggested more unique education and awareness tactics than communication and coordination tactics. Such tactics focus on general education, communications, and awareness of counterfeit products, and might benefit from insights that multiple functions can bring from working with multiple audiences.

Product protection tactics were also suggested for 19 different functions. Respondents viewed product protection tactics as having the greatest breadth in the packaging function, but they noted breadth and depth for many other functions as well. Types of tactics that the packaging function could execute for brand protection include use of tamper-proof packaging, preventing re-use of packaging, and deploying track-and-trace or other packaging technology. Product protection tactics suggested for other functions, including engineering, manufacturing, quality assurance, research and development, supply chain, and warehousing and distribution, include every stage of a product life cycle. Specifically, these tactics range from considering brand protection in product design, ensuring excess production is properly disposed of, and addressing brand protection in product obsolescence.

Respondents also noted the depth of other tactics categories across multiple functions. For example, respondents suggested at least five unique firm policy and process tactics in ten different functions. These include processes for brand protection, personnel background checks for human resources, securing high-risk parts for manufacturing, devising branding schemes for marketing, implementing work rules for brand protection in operations, prioritizing performance elements for suppliers in procurement, managing customers in legitimate and illegitimate markets in sales, and distribution only in authorized channels for warehousing and distribution.

Respondents also suggested at least five strategy tactics in three different functions. Most of these were in the brand protection function, but others were in the sales and security functions. For the sales function, respondents suggested implementing pricing strategies to combat counterfeits and working with sales partners. For the security function, respondents suggested such tactics as benchmarking and developing a strategy for takedowns.

CHOOSING TACTICS FOR INITIATING AND EXPANDING A BRAND PROTECTION PROGRAM

There are myriad brand protection tactics that, our respondents suggest, could be applied across multiple functions. There may also be others that could be applied to functions where they currently are not.

Figure 5.1 provides some directions for future consideration. As noted above, we classified cells by whether they had at least half the maximum of total or unique tactics for any cell. This allowed us to classify the cells in four ways, specifically:

• Deep depth (at least 27 total tactics) and narrow breadth (fewer than 19 unique tactics), shown in solid black.
• Deep depth and wide breadth (at least 19 unique tactics), shown in cross-hatch.
• Shallow depth (fewer than 27 total tactics) and wide breadth, shown in horizontal stripes.
• Shallow depth and narrow breadth, shown in light gray.

Cells with no tactics in them are unshaded.

This figure has several implications for those looking to create or expand their brand protection programs.

The first area to notice are the black cells. These are where our respondents suggested many total tactics but few unique ones. From this, we can conclude that these areas have tactics that are highly important in brand protection and, perhaps just as important, tactics that our respondents are certain should be performed. The best example here may be public policy tactics in the government affairs function. Respondents mentioned 31 total tactics here which were variations of three unique ones: lobbying for anti-counterfeiting laws, networking with law enforcement, and networking with government agencies outside law enforcement. Within the brand protection function, we surmise education and awareness tactics as well as enforcement tactics are good places for brand protection programs to start. Common tactics here include educating staff, law enforcement, and the public on the dangers and identification of counterfeits, and proactively monitoring marketplaces, both physical and online, where counterfeits may be sold. Similarly, enforcement tactics that respondents suggested for the legal function focused on monitoring potential offenses and litigation against violators. In short, the first actions of a brand protection program should involve a mix of basic reactive (e.g., enforcement) and proactive (e.g., education) tactics.

The next areas to address are those indicated by the cross-hatched cells. These are areas that respondents indicated have high importance but where

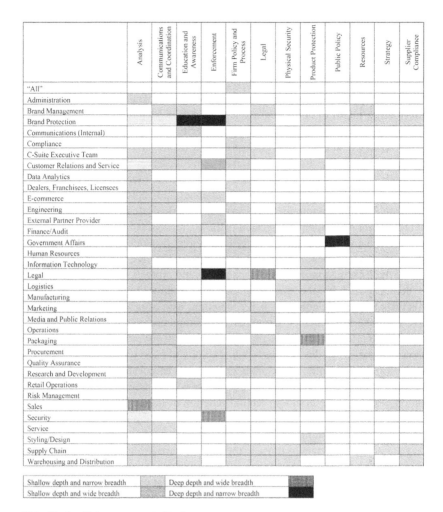

Shallow depth and narrow breadth
Shallow depth and wide breadth
Deep depth and wide breadth
Deep depth and narrow breadth

Note: Blank cells have no reported tactics.

Figure 5.1   *Identifying firm functions and tactic categories for initiating and expanding a brand protection program*

any given action is less certain. Perhaps the best example here is that of enforcement tactics in the security function. Respondents identified 54 tactics for this overlap, of which 37 were unique, indicating an area that is highly important but requires diffuse approaches. Among tactics that respondents suggested here were conducting test buys, developing cases, gathering intelligence, investigating infringements and those participating in them, monitoring marketplaces, performing raids, and working with law enforcement. Legal tactics that respondents suggested for the legal function include trademark registrations and their defense, including and enforcing brand protection clauses in contracts, and overseeing competitive intelligence efforts. Product protection tactics that respondents suggested for the packaging function include considering brand protection in packaging design, deploying track-and-trace packaging and technology, sourcing counterfeit-detection technology, using anti-counterfeit labels, using packaging that deters or inhibits copying, and working with other functions in packaging design. Analysis tactics that respondents suggested for the sales function include monitoring markets and market data, monitoring sales data by channel and region, monitoring sales trends to determine anomalies, and providing market intelligence. The number of tactics that respondents suggested in these four areas highlights their importance, but the variety of tactics suggests different products may require different approaches (depending, for example, on how they are packaged and sold).

The need for customizing approaches as brand protection programs advance is demonstrated by the tactics in the cells indicated by horizontal lines. Analysis tactics are common here, including assessing markets, conducting risk analyses, and developing metrics in the brand protection function; analyzing product returns and claims, providing reporting hotlines for customers, and assessing complaint data for customer relations and service; and gathering and analyzing data on complaints, analyzing suspect counterfeits, and monitoring markets for security. Respondents also suggested communication and coordination tactics for the brand protection function of networking with academia, external providers, and industry, as well as coordinating information sharing. The relatively low numbers of total tactics in these individual cells suggest they are not as important as those in the two previous groupings, but the variety of unique tactics proposed suggests different means for customizing brand protection programs. In particular, we find it striking that while there is deep depth and wide breadth to analysis tactics and to communications and coordination tactics (as seen in Table 5.2), these are concentrated in relatively few functions (as seen in Tables 5.3 and 5.4 as well as Figure 5.1). Some tactics in these categories may be used in multiple functions. For example, respondents suggested conducting some variation of risk analysis in six different functions, and some variation of market monitoring in six functions. Respondents also suggested the communications and coordination tactic of endorsing the message of brand protection throughout a company in 18 different functions. Future research or practices may identify more functions in which analysis tactics or communication and coordination tactics might be more widely applied.

Finally, for a large number of areas, indicated by gray cells, respondents suggested fewer than 27 total tactics and fewer than 19 unique tactics. There is variation here. While there is only one tactic in most of these areas, respondents suggested 22 total tactics and 11 unique tactics for the overlap between strategy tactics and the brand protection function. These include tactics such as aligning strategy with other units, developing and benchmarking programs, and developing strategy across the corporation, the importance of which may vary by the size and diversity of a firm.

IMPLICATIONS FOR PRACTICE AND THE TOTAL BUSINESS SOLUTION

Various forms of enforcement and legal action (e.g., arrests, seizures, cease and desist letters, website takedowns) are commonly thought of as primary ways to protect the brand. However, as this research helps illustrate, there are many more options at a firm's disposal. So many, in fact, that they can be differentiated by substantive type, from analysis and education/awareness to product protection and supplier compliance. Likewise, they can be categorized specifically into the place in the firm that has responsibility for implementation, and this research illustrates the many functions that could have brand protection responsibilities—from legal and supply chain to sales and procurement. This suggests firms have many available approaches to consider in their brand protection strategy.

Our findings indicate all the areas that firms should coordinate in a total business solution to brand protection, and what each function can do to help. At its core, this work provides important information about the need for brand protection programs and the strategy and practices that such programs can use to initiate a conversation with key stakeholders throughout the firm. The diverse options available to firms suggests an opportunity, if not a need, to think creatively and comprehensively about the process, structure, and administration of brand protection and brand protection teams.

Our findings suggest that some functions should implement more forms of tactics and play a more prominent role in brand protection than others. The relative breadth and depth of tactics associated with each function helps to illustrate where firms may first seek to build capacity for new brand protection programs. This insight is also critical for firms with existing programs as it enables them to benchmark their approach against an "ideal" program with virtually every option, thereby suggesting alternatives for expanding both actions and partnerships across the enterprise.

Our analysis of the breadth and depth of tactics that each function should implement provides insight on allocating resources as well. While our analysis, not surprisingly, illustrates the importance of the brand protection function, it also demonstrates the importance of focusing on education and awareness tactics as well as enforcement tactics within it, or providing a mix of reactive and proactive tactics from the launch of brand protection programs. In expand-ing brand protection programs beyond their initial launch, brand owners should prioritize tactics by their importance, as indicated by high numbers of total tactics, and their certainty of implementation, as indicated by low numbers of unique tactics. In other words, we suggest those who are expanding brand protection programs look to see what experts most frequently suggest are key.

Our findings show the importance of the total business solution in multi-ple ways. They illustrate the many parts of the enterprise that play a role in brand protection. Indeed, we find nearly a dozen different functions should help craft brand protection strategy, as indicated in Figure 5.1. Our results also demonstrate that many of the most important actions that firms can take are proactive. These include communicating and coordinating with key stakeholders and educating the public and law enforcement. Actions should also be data-driven, with risk analyses informing decision making. As one respondent suggested, brands should "assess product/market risk and deploy brand protection program/product protection technology, as appropriate" in a "closed-loop system." Similarly, another respondent suggested coordinating "IP/technology risk reviews for companies looking at moving a manufacturing line out of a country or into a particular country." This, the respondent added, may specifically require coordination between research and development, business leaders, legal staff, security, and manufacturers "to assess risk for a particular country and develop risk mitigation strategies." Here, risk analysis would inform decisions to locate or move manufacturing sites.

Finally, in addition to illustrating elements of the total business solution, our analysis suggests firms should implement such a solution. All our respondents noted the role of multiple functions in implementing various brand protection tactics.

FUTURE RESEARCH

While our analysis illustrates the importance of a total business solution for brand protection, along with setting out the components of such a solution and outlining how firms—even if lacking any brand protection program—may begin to implement one, there are several areas that future research should explore.

First, future research might include other experts, such as those in other functions, to assess if there are any key tactics for each function that are missing. For most of the cells in Figure 5.1, for example, our respondents offered no tactics. Future research may wish to consider whether there are any tactics that others use that could fill these gaps, or if there are additional func-tions and categories of tactics to engage in brand protection. Future research might also better distinguish the breadth and depth of tactics. Finally, while this research focused primarily on suggestions from practitioners at large firms on tactics that might ideally be suggested, future research might examine variation in implementation by firm size and industry.

Second, future research might assess the relative cost and effectiveness of each tactic used in brand protection. Perhaps one tactic suffices for many of the areas we explored. Alternatively, perhaps having multiple tactics in these areas can offer customization, a layered strategy with a combination of tactics offering the most effectiveness, or cost-efficiency options. Showing effectiveness empirically would be preferable to simply using the number of total tactics suggested as a proxy for importance.

Third, future research might examine environmental, organizational, and individual characteristics that facilitate or impede the formulation and adoption of a total business solution that is comprehensive, strategic, proactive, and data-driven. It may also evaluate the impact of implementing a total business solution on achieving brand protection goals and an acceptable return on investment. Such research might consider whether some tactic categories, firm functions, or total business solution elements are easier to incorporate than others. This may have implications for how a firm develops and implements a total business solution to meet its own needs.

REFERENCES

Aksulu, A. and Wade, M. (2010), 'A comprehensive review and synthesis of open source research', *Journal of the Association for Information Systems*, **11** (11), 576–656.

Berman, B. (2004), 'Strategies to combat the sale of gray market goods', *Business Horizons*, **47** (4), 51–60.

Burns, T. and Stalker, G. M. (1961), *The Management of Innovation*, London: Tavistock.

Chaudhry, P. and Zimmerman, A. (2009), *The Economics of Counterfeit Trade: Governments, Pirates and Intellectual Property Rights*, Heidelberg, Germany: Springer-Verlag.

Chaudhry, P. E., Zimmerman, A., Peters, J. R., and Cordell, V. V. (2009), 'Preserving intellectual property rights: managerial insight into the escalating counterfeit market quandary', *Business Horizons*, **52** (1), 57–66.

Clements, W. N. (2016), 'Examining and evaluating the effect of brand protection strategies on product counterfeiting', PhD dissertation, Northcentral University, Prescott Valley, AZ.

Donaldson, L. (1987), 'Strategy and structural adjustment to regain fit and performance: in defence of contingency theory', *Journal of Management Studies*, **24** (1), 1–24.

Firth, G. (2006), 'IP protection best practice tips', *The China Business Review*, **33** (1), 18–25.

Foucart, B. (2016, September), 'How to be a good victim', *The Brand Protection Professional*, **1** (1), 18–19, accessed 11 June 2020 at http://joom.ag/k9MQ/p18.

Glaser, B. G. and Strauss, A. L. (1967), *The Discovery of Grounded Theory: Strategies for Qualitative Research*, New Brunswick, NJ: AldineTransaction.

Green, R. T. and Smith, T. (2002), 'Executive insights: countering brand counterfeiters', *Journal of International Marketing*, **10** (4), 89–106.
Grossman, G. M. and Shapiro, C. (1988a), 'Counterfeit-product trade', *American Economic Review*, **78** (1), 59–75.
Grossman, G. M. and Shapiro, C. (1988b), 'Foreign counterfeiting of status goods', *Quarterly Journal of Economics*, **103** (1), 79–100.
Hoecht, A. and Trott, P. (2014), 'How should firms deal with counterfeiting? A review of the success conditions of anti-counterfeiting strategies', *International Journal of Emerging Markets*, **9** (1), 98–119.
Katz, D. and Kahn, R. L. (1966), *The Social Psychology of Organizations*, New York: Wiley.
Lawrence, P. R. and Lorsch, J. W. (1967), *Organization and Environment*, Boston, MA: Harvard Business School.
Liu, K., Li, J. A., Wu, Y., and Lai, K. K. (2005), 'Analysis of monitoring and limiting of commercial cheating: a newsvendor model', *Journal of the Operational Research Society*, **56** (7), 844–854.
Meyer, J. W. and Rowan, B. (1977), 'Institutionalized organizations: formal structure as myth and ceremony', *American Journal of Sociology*, **83** (2), 340–363.
Post, R. S. and Post, P. N. (2007), *Global Brand Integrity Management*, New York: McGraw-Hill Professional.
Raman, R. and Pramod, D. (2017), 'A strategic approach using governance, risk and compliance model to deal with online counterfeit market', *Journal of Theoretical and Applied Electronic Commerce Research*, **12** (3), 13–26.
Reynolds, D. (2011), 'Manipulating perceived risk to deter and disrupt counterfeiters', *Journal of Economic Crime*, **18** (1), 105–118.
Sonmez, M. and Yang, D. (2005), 'Manchester United versus China: a counterfeiting and trademark match', *Managing Leisure*, **10** (1), 1–18.
Staake, T. and Fleisch, E. (2008), *Countering Counterfeit Trade: Illicit Market Insights, Best-Practice Strategies, and Management Toolbox*, Berlin: Springer.
Stevenson, M. and Busby, J. (2015), 'An exploratory analysis of counterfeiting strategies: towards counterfeit-resilient supply chains', *International Journal of Operations and Production Management*, **55** (1), 110–144.
Stöttinger, B., Penz, E., and Cesareo, L. (2017), 'Analysis of anti-counterfeiting tactics to diffuse consumer demand', in P. E. Chaudhry (ed.), *Handbook of Research on Counterfeiting and Illicit Trade*, Cheltenham, UK and Northampton, MA, USA: Edward Elgar Publishing, pp. 387–403.
Stumpf, S. A. and Chaudhry, P. (2010), 'Country matters: executives weigh in on the causes and counter measures of counterfeit trade', *Business Horizons*, **53** (3), 305–314.
Stumpf, S. A., Chaudhry, P. E., and Perretta, L. (2011), 'Fake: can business stanch the flow of counterfeit products?', *Journal of Business Strategy*, **32** (2), 4–12.
Thompson, J. D. (1967), *Organizations in Action*, New York: McGraw-Hill.
Ting, S. L. and Tsang, A. H. C. (2014), 'Using social network analysis to combat counterfeiting', *International Journal of Production Research*, **52** (15), 4456–4468.
Trott, P. and Hoecht, A. (2007), 'Product counterfeiting, non-consensual acquisition of technology and new product development: an innovation perspective', *Journal of Innovation Management*, **10** (1), 126–143.
Waring, A. (2013), *Corporate Risk and Governance: An End to Mismanagement, Tunnel Vision and Quackery*, Burlington, VT: Gower.

Wilcock, A. E. and Boys, K. A. (2014), 'Reduce product counterfeiting: an integrated approach', *Business Horizons*, **57** (2), 279–288.

Wilson, J. M. (2017), 'The future of brand protection: responding to the global risk', *Journal of Brand Management*, **24** (3), 271–283.

Wilson, J. M. and Grammich, C. A. (2020a), 'Brand protection across the enterprise: toward a total-business solution', *Business Horizons*, **63** (3), 363–376.

Wilson, J. M. and Grammich, C. A. (2020b), 'Protecting brands from counterfeiting risks: tactics of a total business solution', *Journal of Risk Research*, online before print.

Wilson, J. M., Grammich, C., and Chan, F. (2016), 'Organizing for brand protection and responding to product counterfeit risk: an analysis of global firms', *Journal of Brand Management*, **23** (3), 345–361.

Wilson, J. M. and Kinghorn, R. (2014), *Brand Protection as a Total Business Solution*, East Lansing, MI: Michigan State University Center for Anti-Counterfeiting and Product Protection, accessed 11 June 2020 at http://a-capp.msu.edu/?p=22008.

Yang, D., Sonmez, M., and Bosworth, D. (2004), 'Intellectual property abuses: how should multinationals respond?', *Long Range Planning*, **37** (5), 459–475.

6. Options for mitigating the risk of product counterfeits: lessons from research and practice

Jeremy M. Wilson and Clifford A. Grammich

Though brand protection and product counterfeiting are increasing in prevalence, academic research on them remains disjointed and sporadic. Much of the research that does exist focuses on estimating its prevalence, addressing risk and opportunity structures for product counterfeiting, and identifying and preventing counterfeits in select industries (Sullivan et al. 2017). Of these areas, that on identifying and preventing counterfeits is least developed, and this insight is critical for the development of a total business solution for brand protection. There are many reasons for this. Academic research is costly, and there is limited funding for research on product counterfeiting. Additionally, brand protection is interdisciplinary, so it does not have a natural "home" in academia. This creates disincentives for scholarly research. Firms, in turn, may not be fully aware of counterfeiting of their own products. Firms that are aware of the problem may closely guard what they know and be unlikely to share data on it. Academic research is time-consuming and complicated, and peer review, while ensuring quality, does not always facilitate timeliness. Much academic research is jargon-laden and written for other academics, published in venues that, to practitioners, are esoteric.

Nevertheless, academic research on product counterfeiting, when available, may provide new insights for practitioners. Academic research is likely to be more independent and comprehensive than what practitioners can undertake for themselves. Peer review may not facilitate timeliness, but it does improve rigor and the likelihood that research findings are applicable in many settings. Academic research considers evidence from multiple perspectives, and scholars can be impartial judges of different aspects of counterfeiting. Finally, academic research can place findings in context, helping readers determine their applicability to their own situation.

In this chapter, we review academic research on anti-counterfeiting tactics that businesses may employ. Specifically, we reviewed 362 peer-reviewed articles from multiple disciplines that mentioned product counterfeiting in some way. From these, we identified more than 1,600 tactics that firms might use for brand protection. We coded these in the same way that we coded tactics suggested to us by brand protection professionals (see Chapter 5), placing each in one of twelve categories as well as subcategories within categories.

In the next section, we describe how we identified articles to review and the brand protection or anti-counterfeiting tactics within them. Using the same categories of tactics we used in our practitioner interviews (see Chapter 5), we then compare the distribution of tactics that practitioners shared with us and the distribution of tactics that we identified in academic research on them. After reviewing these distributions, we explore for each category of tactics differences in distribution by subcategory, what tactics practitioners suggest that researchers suggest as well, and what additions or refinements researchers may suggest. We conclude with a discussion of the implications of our findings for the practice of brand protection.

IDENTIFYING TACTICS IN PREVIOUS RESEARCH

To identify brand protection tactics in previous research, we conducted a systematic literature review of journals, focusing on product counterfeiting issues specifically. To obtain these articles, we searched the Business Source Complete and Criminal Justice Abstracts literature databases for references using the broad search terms "product AND counterfeit." We limited our search to English-language peer-reviewed research articles. Applying these search criteria, we identified 362 journal articles.

We began by conducting an initial review of the title and abstract to determine if the article appeared to offer any insight on combating counterfeiting. To be as comprehensive as possible, we interpreted combating counterfeiting broadly to relate to any lesson, tactic, strategy, or the like that pertained to prevention, detection, investigation, or response to counterfeiting from any perspective. If the title or abstract failed to exhibit insight on combating counterfeiting, we reviewed the source document to determine if its introduction, data, discussion, or conclusion sections offered insight on combating counterfeiting. Of these 362 reviewed results, 228 appeared to offer insight on combating counterfeiting, but 8 of these were inaccessible. Ultimately, this process yielded 220 relevant journal articles for analysis.

We then reviewed these articles for tactics that practitioners themselves might use in brand protection. We excluded tactics that others, such as government agencies or online market operators, would use exclusively on behalf of intellectual property rights owners. For example, one of the articles we examined (Lord et al. 2017) noted the need for public bodies "to identify and disrupt the networks of criminal enterprise involved in the trafficking of fake goods." While this surely is an important means to reduce counterfeiting and its harms, this is something that must be reserved to public law enforcement, and hence excluded from our list of tactics. At the same time, this article noted among other tactics the importance of "[e]ducating potential victims around the risks of counterfeit alcohol and increasing awareness about the indicators of potential counterfeiting, such as suspiciously low prices," which is something firms can undertake.

CATEGORIZING TACTICS IN PREVIOUS RESEARCH

Once we identified the tactics, we categorized them as we did in Chapter 5 as well as in previous research (Wilson and Grammich 2020). We employed a grounded-theory approach (Glaser and Strauss 1967) to organize the data. We adopted a multistage content analysis process that allowed the categories to emerge from the data (Aksulu and Wade 2010). This entailed a systematic process of coding, interpreting, and recoding the data to identify all the categories and subcategories into which the tactics could be classified. (Readers wanting further details of this process may wish to consult Chapter 5 of this volume and, especially, Wilson and Grammich 2020.)

We ultimately classified our tactics into 12 categories: analysis, communications and coordination, education and awareness, enforcement, firm policy and process, legal, physical security, product protection, public policy, resources, strategy, and supplier compliance. Within several of these categories, we identified subcategories of tactics. For example, within the communications and coordination category, we identified six different types of communication (external general, internal general, internal incidents, internal managers, internal partners, and crisis communications) as well as tactics involved in fostering a good internal culture (e.g., treating counterfeiters as competitors, integrating anti-counterfeiting initiatives into quality plans) and networking with industry and professional groups as well as with other (quasi-)private organizations (e.g., International AntiCounterfeiting Coalition).

In Table 6.1 we compare all the tactics that brand protection practitioners previously shared with us in interviews (Wilson and Grammich 2020) with those that we identified from our literature review of previously published research. Though the total number of tactics from each of the two sources are roughly equivalent—1,347 for practitioners and 1,622 for previous research—the distribution of tactics identified by practitioners and those identified by previous researchers by category differs somewhat.[1]

Product protection was the top category for brand protection practitioners and the second category for tactics published in previous research. Education and awareness was the top category of tactics previously published, and the third category for practitioners. Analysis was the second category for practitioners but only the fourth category in previous research. That is, practitioners

Table 6.1   *Total brand protection tactics identified by practitioners and in previous research by categories and subcategories*

Category Subcategory	Practitioner Tactics	Literature Tactics
Analysis	182	161
Analysis—Other	38	13
Analysis—Risks	71	112
Customer Feedback	33	16
Marketplace Surveying and Assessment	23	18
Monitor Product Returns	17	2
Communications and Coordination	166	156
Communications—External General	21	45
Communications—Internal General	26	10
Communications—Internal Incidents	44	3
Communications—Internal Management	20	3
Communications—Internal Partners	7	5
Crisis Communications	10	6
Internal Culture	9	8
Network with Other (Quasi-)Private	12	48
Network with Industry and Professional Groups	17	28
Education and Awareness	173	321
Awareness—External	37	120
Awareness—Internal	32	2
Consumer Education	25	153
Train Law Enforcement	19	10
Train Partners	8	18
Train Staff	52	18
Enforcement	123	160
Enforcement—Legal Authorities	17	66
Enforcement—Litigation	18	25
Enforcement—Other	8	29
Internet Monitoring and Website Seizure	31	19
Investigations—Incidents and Follow-Up	20	13
Investigations—Intelligence or Other	15	2
Test Buys	14	6

Category Subcategory	Practitioner Tactics	Literature Tactics
Firm Policy and Process	100	130
Internal Policy and Rules	51	25
Process	49	105
Legal	101	45
Contracts	29	13
Legal Not Elsewhere Classified	13	4
Trademarks	59	28
Physical Security	37	3
Product Protection	196	307
Disposing of Excess or Reject Product	20	8
Identification and Authentication	23	28
Packaging	63	81
Product Design	38	76
Technology	28	52
Track and Trace	24	62
Public Policy	57	64
Legislative	22	18
Network with Government Agencies (Non-LE)	22	27
Network with Law Enforcement	13	19
Resources	74	81
Budget	20	8
Staffing	54	73
Strategy	45	81
Supplier Compliance	93	113
Audit Supply Chain and Partners	41	12
Supplier Management	52	101

focused more on need for analysis tactics than researchers did. Education and awareness have frequently been recognized at professional conferences as among the most important needs in brand protection, while the importance of analysis has also been increasingly recognized (Wilson 2017). Among less frequently cited tactics, legal was the sixth category for practitioners but the eleventh category of tactics previously published. While physical security was the least frequently cited category for both practitioners and previous research, it was cited 12 times as frequently by practitioners as by researchers.

Comparing the categories individually further illustrates the different lessons that practitioners and researchers offer for brand protection. Generally, practitioner tactics tend to focus on internal operations while tactics published in previous research focus externally. This may be because practitioners are focused on day-to-day operations and areas they can better control, while researchers do not have as much internal knowledge and access and therefore focus on external aspects they can observe and study.

While previous research points to more externally focused tactics than practitioners suggest, it also matches practitioner tactics in some ways. This leads to two further questions. Specifically, what tactics suggested by practitioners are suggested by researchers as well? And what further details may researcher-suggested tactics offer for practice or implementation?

Below we offer some comparisons by tactic category of practitioner-suggested tactics and researcher-suggested tactics. For each of our categories of tactics, we discuss how the distribution of practitioner-suggested tactics and researcher-suggested tactics differs by subcategory. We also discuss what practitioner-suggested tactics appear to be endorsed by researchers. Finally, we explore what refinements or additions researchers may offer to each category of brand protection tactics.

ANALYSIS TACTICS

Among analysis tactics, both researchers and practitioners report more tactics for analysis of risks than any other subcategory. There is some difference in the emphasis each group places on analysis: 70 percent of the researcher tactics suggested for analysis are for analysis of risks, compared to 39 percent of the practitioner-suggested analysis tactics. Practitioners report more tactics regarding customer feedback, marketplace surveying and assessment, and monitoring product returns than researchers do.

Common tactics suggested by practitioners for analysis of risks include "conduct risk analysis," "conduct risk analysis for supply chain," "develop metrics on counterfeiting impact," "monitor market data," and "monitor sales trends." Researchers suggested similar tactics, while adding some details. For example, one article notes the need for "marketers [to] uncover the distribution of social motives in their target population, identify psychographic segments that vary in such motives, and create segment-appropriate communications that trigger counterfeit-inhibiting goals" (Wilcox et al. 2009). In other words, brands, in their marketing, might determine what advertisements can both appeal to the image that buyers want to have of themselves through the purchase of legitimate product and to the desire of buyers to avoid a diminished social standing resulting from consumption of counterfeits. This can, however, vary by nation and the perceptions that consumers have of counterfeit products (see, for example, Stumpf and Chaudhry 2010).

Many of the additional analysis of risk tactics that researchers suggest similarly focus on assessing consumer behavior. One article, for example, advises marketers "to recognize that not all consumers are equally receptive to counterfeits" (Peng et al. 2012). Such receptivity, these authors note, may vary by personality characteristics, which firms should explore in their anti-counterfeiting efforts.

Researchers also suggest assessing counterfeiters' errors. One article notes that counterfeiters often make errors in packaging because "they do not have time to follow the changes operated by the fabricants or to understand the logistics behind the manufacturing of the packaging" (Dégardin et al. 2015). Identifying such errors and teaching staff members how to identify them can enable decentralized identification of counterfeits.

In analyzing customer feedback, practitioners commonly reported maintaining hotlines for customers, maintaining a hub for consumer correspondence, monitoring customer reviews, reporting customer complaints of counterfeits to other functions, and finding other ways to engage customers in anti-counterfeit efforts. Researcher-suggested tactics match many of these, particularly in enabling customer engagement. One article, for example, suggests having cashiers register the mobile phone number of purchasing customers, who would then receive a product reference code to check product information and register the product on a company portal at their convenience (Ting and Tsang 2013).

Both practitioner- and researcher-suggested tactics for marketplace surveying and assessment emphasize physical and virtual monitoring of marketplaces. The researcher-suggested tactics provide more specific details here. Practitioners suggested tactics such as "eyes-on-the-ground surveillance of markets," "increase market vigilance," and "market surveys." One researcher provides more detail here, suggesting "[c]onstant monitoring of the product environment ... conducted by either internally specified personnel or externally through private investigators ... Private investigators can be used to continuously sample product offerings at the retail level" (Harvey 1988). Here, practitioners may understandably not want to reveal their tactics so as to not alert counterfeiters, while researchers can be more open—and perhaps more helpful for those starting new programs.

Practitioners suggest a wider variety of tactics for monitoring product returns. These include analyzing the material of returned products, monitoring for inconsistencies among returns, and properly segregating return products. Two research articles suggest monitoring warranty claims and collecting data on them, but none suggest the variety of tactics that practitioners do.

Practitioners also suggest a wide variety of other analysis tactics. These include analyzing data on global distribution, conducting forensic analysis of infringing products, and developing metrics. Researcher-suggested tactics match some of these but provide more detail or add others. One article suggests using "a Customer Relationship Management System ... to record the anti-counterfeit enquiries to understand the customer purchase behavior," including which products are most frequently checked by customers (Ting and Ip 2013). Another suggests using chemometric analysis to differentiate components of legitimate and illicit products (Gomes et al. 2016).

The analysis tactics suggested by practitioners and those suggested by published research highlight different principles of the total business solution. Practitioner tactics such as monitoring market data, surveillance of physical and virtual marketplaces, and monitoring product returns can all help identify and monitor the counterfeiter as an unseen competitor. Researcher-suggested tactics such as assessing counterfeiter errors and gathering and assessing data on counterfeit products point toward using metrics and analysis to assess counterfeiter risk. Given the differences we noted in the perspectives of researchers and practitioners, with practitioners having more insight on what firms can do internally, this is not surprising. But it does point to where those building brand protection programs may wish to look as they develop or expand tactics for their work.

COMMUNICATION AND COORDINATION TACTICS

Suggested communication and coordination tactics show the contrast in focus between researchers and practitioners. Of the 166 practitioner-suggested tactics, 116 are on internal communications and culture; of the 156 researcher-suggested tactics, 121 are on external communications or networking.

Tactics suggested by practitioners regarding internal general communication tactics as well as culture focus on endorsing the message of brand protection throughout the company. Regarding incidents, they focus on ensuring hotlines are available both within the company for employees to use, particularly for sensitive products (e.g., medicines), and to organizations (e.g., customs, law enforcement) with whom firms should work in fighting counterfeits. Regarding internal management, they focus on providing briefings and regular communications to functions (e.g., C-suite, finance, sales) that should be continuously updated on brand protection. Regarding crisis communications, they focus on developing a communications plan for incidents.

Researcher-supported tactics support many of these and provide additional detail on some. One article, for example, suggests developing a culture of brand protection by "demonstrat[ing] a respect for [intellectual property] in business practices and policies, explicitly forbidding employees to engage in piracy and counterfeiting[, t]rain[ing] employees to identify counterfeit products[,] reward ongoing vigilance[, and d]evelop whistleblower mechanisms and protections" (Wilcock and Boys 2014). For incidents and crises, researchers suggest developing a management plan to forward complaints to a designated specialist, to track the progress of complaint resolution, and to address complaints as well as media and related issues (Wilcock and Boys 2014).

Regarding external communications, practitioner-suggested tactics focus on communicating brand protection objectives with customers and, especially, communicating successes in thwarting counterfeiting. Researcher-suggested tactics focus on advertising that the company pursues counterfeiters, communicating the dangers of counterfeiting, and focusing on consumer self-image in advertising. Some advertising on the company's pursuit of counterfeiters may also note success in doing so. Firms that perceive demand for counterfeits as being buyer-driven may, for example, seek to inform consumers of the illegal nature of the act and make consumers aware of legal actions against counterfeiting (Stumpf and Chaudhry 2010). Regarding self-image in advertising, researchers suggest seeking to increase consumer accountability, that is, increasing their anticipation of a need to explain their purchase to others, to deter the purchase of counterfeit products (Kim et al. 2012).

Practitioner-suggested tactics for networking include working with other industry leaders, participating in industry and intellectual property organizations, monitoring the market with trade partners, networking with news media, and sharing information. Researcher-suggested tactics include these and others. One additional tactic that several research articles raise is collaborating with online service providers to achieve effective trademark protection, though researchers noting this also identify difficulties in doing so (Saunders and Berger-Walliser 2011). Research also discusses how industry sources can use media to inform consumers and shape public perception of counterfeiting (Sullivan and Chermak 2013). Researchers explain that small businesses in particular can help extend guardianship of their products by developing relationships with supply chain partners, peer firms, customs agencies, law enforcement, and other relevant stakeholders (Kennedy 2016).

Communication and coordination tactics suggested by practitioners and researchers highlight different elements of the total business solution. Practitioner tactics of gathering additional information from customers and providing briefings and regular communications to functions, as well as tactics for networking, illustrate ways in which brands can identify procedures that will allow them to continuously improve. Researcher-suggested tactics such as demonstrating a respect for intellectual property and developing plans for handling complaints illustrate ways to continuously improve and to be proactive in brand protection.

EDUCATION AND AWARENESS

Education and awareness tactics also show a split between practitioners focusing on internal tactics and researchers focusing on external ones. Of the 173 education and awareness tactics that practitioners suggested, 111 are on internal awareness or training. Of the 321 tactics suggested by researchers, 273 are on external awareness or consumer education.

Internal awareness tactics suggested by practitioners focused on communicating the dangers of counterfeits, the importance of brand protection, and the need to educate leadership. Researchers suggested only two internal awareness tactics, but both confirmed the need to increase knowledge and raise awareness.

Practitioners suggest training law enforcement, partners, and staff to increase awareness and understanding of counterfeit issues. They note that training of partners can include a template identifying specific counterfeit issues. They also note that training of staff should begin with onboarding sessions for employees. Researcher-suggested tactics confirm these and provide more details. One article, for example, suggests training customs personnel to differentiate fake and legitimate products and providing them with easily read dossiers and training cards to increase the likelihood of detecting fake products (Cooper and Eckstein 2008). Another suggests working directly with suppliers to integrate counterfeit identification into employee training and ensure contact information for those responsible for anti-counterfeiting programs is readily available (Wilcock and Boys 2014).

To increase external awareness of counterfeits, practitioners recommend such tactics as communicating the dangers of counterfeits, including through public service announcements and other marketing materials on specific products, promoting brand protection in advertising, and providing a web page with information on counterfeits. Researchers suggested many of these tactics as well but provided more details and suggested still others. For example, one article suggested differentiating between economic and individual motivations in awareness campaigns (Viot et al. 2014). Another article noted that stressing linkages to organized crime, particularly how counterfeiting can fund terrorism and human trafficking, was at least somewhat effective in raising consumer awareness in several nations (Chaudhry and Cesareo 2017). Marketing campaigns might seek "not only [to] communicate a positive brand meaning … but, equally important, project negative" images of counterfeit products (Bian and Moutinho 2011). Brands may also seek to foster communities of those loyal to them where customers may share experience of, and information on, genuine product (Castaño and Perez 2014).

Consumer education tactics suggested by practitioners focus on general customer education, education on the dangers of counterfeits and how to identify counterfeit products, and providing online education, including on how to identify authorized retailers. Researchers suggest many of these tactics, providing additional detail, and others. To deter counterfeit purchases, one article suggests consumer education emphasizing socially centered values supporting genuine goods and the negative economic outcomes of counterfeit goods (Marcketti and Shelley 2009). Another suggests educating consumers on the means to differentiate genuine from counterfeit products (e.g., by incorrect consistency, size, or color) and providing them an online means to verify genuine products (Hollis and Wilson 2014). One additional means that researchers suggest for educating customers is social media, which brands may use to educate customers on means to combat counterfeiting and how to determine if a product is authentic (Raman and Pramod 2017). Another is using nongovernmental organizations to educate the public about counterfeiting and the need to combat it (Ahmed 2016).

The differing focus of education and awareness tactics suggested by practitioners and researchers means that they support different areas of the total business solution. Practitioner tactics in this category, being internally focused, can support firms as they seek to create a culture of continuous improvement and learning. Researcher tactics, being externally focused, can support firms as they seek to emphasize prevention and proactivity. Here, as elsewhere, the lesson is not necessarily that practitioners and researchers are demonstrating different levels of interest in the total business solution, but that the tactics they suggest will be of differing uses for those seeking to build or expand a brand protection program.

ENFORCEMENT

For enforcement, practitioners are more likely to recommend investigation and monitoring tactics that rely more on a firm's own resources and initiative. Of the 123 enforcement tactics that practitioners recommended, 80 were related to Internet monitoring and website seizures, investigations, and test buys. Researcher tactics relied more on outside authorities. Of the 160 enforcement tactics that researchers recommended, 120 were related to enforcement by legal authorities, through litigation, or by other means.

Practitioner-suggested tactics for Internet monitoring and website seizure are typically general, though some practitioners suggest some specific tactics such as monitoring social media platforms, deterring bulk buyers and resellers, and using web-crawling technology and optical character recognition software to detect counterfeit sites. Researchers concur with these while adding other detailed or proactive tactics. One article suggests using "trust seals and other mechanisms to improve consumer confidence in the marketplace" (Wimmer and Yoon 2017). Another suggests identifying and prioritizing efforts to deal with cybersquatters (Raman and Pramod 2017).

Practitioner-suggested tactics for investigations are similarly general, though some suggest investigating specific topics, such as sources of illicit product and suppliers suspected of violating the terms of purchase orders, and developing an approach to prioritize investigation of incidents by their assessed risks. Researchers make similar and fewer suggestions but add some novel ones. One is to collaborate with competitors to identify sources of counterfeits under the assumption that counterfeiters are likely to target competing brands and not just one (Wilson et al. 2016). Another is to keep internal records on violations for leads and context on future cases (Cooper and Eckstein 2008).

Practitioners suggest several test-buy tactics, including documentation of such purchases and hiring third-party shoppers. Researcher tactics generally match these. One article suggests organizing a product purchase program to identify counterfeits (Wilson and Sullivan 2016). Another suggests using test buyers to purchase goods from unauthorized resellers (Berman 2004).

In addition to seeking legal enforcement against counterfeiters, practitioners suggest maintaining lists of contacts to support investigations and managing cases for presentation to law enforcement. Litigation enforcement tactics suggested by practitioners include filing lawsuits, assisting in case preparation, and sending cease-and-desist letters. Other enforcement strategies suggested by practitioners include supporting raids and developing a reputation for aggressively pursuing infringers and counterfeiters.

Researchers suggest all these tactics and others, some in detail. Regarding enforcement, one author notes the importance for multinationals to use local litigators who are familiar with local courts, as well as the possibility of using civil enforcement, even if riskier than criminal enforcement, to publicize the case and create a deterrent effect (Chow 2001). Another article notes that developing relationships with responsible regulators can help increase guardianship over legitimate products (Lord et al. 2017). Regarding litigation, one article suggests litigating against manufacturers, distributors, and sellers of counterfeit goods, both to demonstrate commitment to combating counterfeiting and "to move up the ladder" to identify others responsible for counterfeiting (Cooper and Eckstein 2008). Still other enforcement suggestions include understanding consumption of counterfeiting in different geographical contexts to identify the most effective ways to enforce anti-counterfeiting policies (Gistri et al. 2009).

Enforcement tactics suggested by practitioners and researchers may help support the prevention and control elements of a total business solution for brand protection. Both practitioners and researchers note the need for monitoring and deterring counterfeiters in their potential marketplaces. They both also suggest conducting and documenting test buys and other internal means for monitoring the problem, though researchers also suggest external means for controlling the problem, such as litigating against external parties responsible for counterfeit goods.

FIRM POLICY AND PROCESS

Regarding firm policy and process, practitioners suggested tactics that were nearly evenly divided between internal policy and rules and process, while researchers suggested more than four times as many tactics for process than for internal policy and rules.

Practitioners recommended a variety of internal policies and rules for brand protection. The most common involved implementing a corporate social responsibility program for avoiding nefarious conditions, such as poor labor practices, associated with counterfeiting. Others included controlling trademark design files, developing a brand protection policy, developing branding schemes, aligning compensation programs with brand protection goals, requiring bonds from suppliers, and restricting access to proprietary information. Researchers suggest similar but additional tactics. Among researcher-suggested tactics are ways to develop employees as guardians of a firm's intellectual property (Hollis and Wilson 2014).

Practitioners also recommend a variety of process tactics for brand protection. These include auditing brand protection controls, conducting background checks for personnel, monitoring access to facilities and equipment, placing all purchase orders through a system visible to the brand protection function, and regular review of protection measures. Researchers suggest many of these and others that are less conventional. One study suggests that firms should disperse their research and development across locations to minimize threats to intellectual property at any one location (Stevenson and Busby 2015). One of the less conventional suggestions is for firms to consider converting counterfeiters who produce a quality product into a legitimate franchisee (Harvey 1988). Another researcher suggests "shifting the 'certification' process from the upstream state, i.e., the trademark holder, to the downstream state, i.e., the exclusive distributor or retailer," while adding this "is more likely to be effective when expertise adds significant value in the downstream stage" (Globerman 1988).

Many of these tactics can help brands highlight the value of internal and external controls and mechanisms for detecting and responding to infringements. Practitioners, from their perspective within firms, recommend internal tactics such as implementing corporate programs to minimize the opportunities for counterfeiting. Researchers suggest more external controls such as developing ways for a brand to have external guardians of its intellectual property and even shifting certification of authentic product elsewhere.

LEGAL

Researchers suggest fewer legal tactics than practitioners do. This may be because the legal tactics that are suggested (e.g., those involving brand protection clauses in contracts and registration of trademarks) are those that firms themselves would execute internally in their daily work.

Contract tactics that practitioners recommend include developing master sourcing agreements and inserting brand protection clauses, including clauses specific to particular parties (e.g., distributors, licensees, printers). Researcher-suggested tactics are fewer but generally match these, occasionally offering more specificity. For example, one article suggests inserting a clause requiring that goods be shipped in original manufacturer cartons or cases and that the manufacturer seal remain intact throughout the shipping process (Cooper and Eckstein 2008).

Trademark tactics suggested by practitioners focus on registrations, including those with specific entities in market countries, manufacturing countries, and counterfeiting countries, as well as with multiple organizations, such as both trademark and customs offices. They also include considering defensive trademark registrations. Researchers suggest similar but fewer tactics, sometimes with more specificity. For example, one author suggests using copyright registration to protect advertising, promotional material, creative work, and product designs (Harvey 1988).

Other legal tactics that practitioners suggest include having legal staff review communications and legal documents for brand protection implications. We found only four other legal tactics suggested by researchers, one of which is ensuring penalties are associated with counterfeit use (Yoo and Lee 2012).

The legal tactics that practitioners and researchers suggest may support internal controls and proactivity elements of the total business solution. Contract tactics can support internal controls while tactics such as defensive trademark registrations may represent proactivity to thwart potential infringements of intellectual property.

PHYSICAL SECURITY

Both practitioners and researchers were least likely to suggest physical security tactics. Nevertheless, practitioners suggested more than a dozen times as many physical security tactics than researchers did. We surmise this is because practitioners are more immediately concerned with, and have more direct oversight on, these issues.

Physical security tactics suggested by researchers included camouflaging products during testing and development, securing facilities where products are made, and securing transportation routes, all tactics that firms would largely conduct internally. All three researcher-suggested tactics here involved securing transportation of products. One article suggested increasing transparency and diligence in transportation of goods at the point of collection and delivery to ensure transport companies are transporting what is stated (Lord et al. 2017).

Physical security tactics suggested by practitioners and researchers help highlight the value of controls and mechanisms for thwarting counterfeit products. Controlling access to plants and transportation of product may lead to fewer vulnerabilities that counterfeiters may exploit.

PRODUCT PROTECTION

For product protection, both researcher-suggested and practitioner-suggested tactics focus more on packaging, product design, technology, and track and trace, tactics that are more externally focused or "customer-facing." Researcher-suggested tactics focus less than practitioner-suggested ones on disposing of excess or reject product and product identification and authentication.

Practitioners recommend developing procedures to dispose of damaged, excess, obsolete, rejected, and scrap product so that it is beyond use and cannot be resold. They also note the need to monitor scrap processes and, in some cases, to purchase excess product. Among the works published by researchers, one article notes the need to reacquire obsolete products so that they do not become counterfeit and to use reverse logistics to recover products as necessary (Stevenson and Busby 2015).

Practitioners also note the need to develop and use means for identifying product, including establishing procedures to compare suspicious products to authenticated ones. Another article published by researchers suggests developing a web platform for authenticating products and updating such a platform as needed (Ting and Ip 2013). Others suggest chemical analysis to identify authentic products such as alcoholic beverages (Arslan et al. 2015).

Packaging tactics are the most common ones that both practitioners and researchers recommend in product protection. Packaging tactics that practitioners suggest for brand protection include considering brand protection in packaging design, designing packaging to prevent reuse, including brand protection features (e.g., holograms) on packaging and labels, monitoring packaging and label suppliers, and using packaging that is counterfeit-resistant.

Researchers suggest many of these same tactics, emphasizing the use of anti-counterfeit labels. One article suggests "incorporating special inks and dyes into product labels for product authentication, or serialisation and bar codes that allow a package to be tracked across the globe" (Kennedy et al. 2017). Another article suggests using "microscopic particles, tiny planchettes or threads with microtext, labels with special print, holograms with microtext, and materials with spectroscopic properties" (Wang and Alocilja 2012).

Product design tactics that practitioners suggest for brand protection include considering brand protection in conceptualizing and designing new products, embedding anti-counterfeiting features in new products, and placing trademarks directly on product. Researchers suggest many of these as well, but also suggest product improvements to stay ahead of counterfeiters. One article, for example, suggests product innovation, improved product features and reliability, and after-sale services can all help maximize corporate competence against counterfeiters, just as they can against other competitors (Sonmez et al. 2013).

Many practitioner-suggested tactics for technology are general, for example "source appropriate anti-counterfeit technology for overt and/or covert detection," though a few are more specific. Among the more specific practitioner-suggested tactics for technology are establishing a formal innovation program to evaluate emerging product protection technologies and using hang tags and price tickets to track authentic product. Researcher-suggested tactics for technology are similar but more numerous and detailed, with some focused on enabling customers to check authentication of their products. One author notes a need for low-power portable devices that do not require much user training that can be used by pharmacists and patients to check chemical composition and authenticate legitimate medicines (Strickland 2017). Another article suggests using radio-frequency identification (RFID) technology and antenna technology to validate pallets, cases, and products throughout their journey from distribution centers to consumers, providing data security features to prevent cloning of tags with electronic information (Wong et al. 2006).

Practitioner-suggested tactics for track and trace are general, such as implementing "serialization and tracking capability," using "batch code and serial number confirmation," and "scan[ning] at every transition." Researchers suggest similar tactics, often for specific industries and in more detail. One article, for example, suggests "pharmaceutical shipments could be fitted with RFID tags that allow patients to access information about where the drug was manufactured and how it traveled through the supply chain, record when medication is dispensed to patients and taken by patients, and automate the inventorying of products at health care facilities" (Kennedy et al. 2018). Another suggests embedding RFID technology as a chip on each item a manufacturer produces to uniquely identify manufacturers and their products and to trace products in the supply chain, with information transmitted to the Internet and received by manufacturers, distributors, retailers, and third-party logistics providers (Bose and Pal 2005).

The various practitioner- and researcher-suggested tactics for product protection can support several elements of the total business solution. Indeed, the variety of elements they support demonstrate how they promote a holistic approach that integrates all parts of the firm for brand protection. This includes developing means for identifying genuine and counterfeit product, such as packaging and product designs that can help verify products, and means for monitoring products throughout their life cycle.

PUBLIC POLICY

There is little difference in the distribution of public policy tactics as suggested by practitioners and by researchers. We surmise this is because both these tactics overall and their subcategories must focus externally, and hence are not differentiated by an internal or external focus.

All the practitioner-suggested legislative tactics are to lobby for or monitor anti-counterfeiting laws. This includes involving local, state, and federal representatives of the places where the firms are located, working with a firm's government affairs function, and supporting government actions against countries that do not adequately prevent the manufacture of counterfeit products. Nearly all researcher-suggested legislative tactics also involve lobbying for anti-counterfeiting laws, which one article describes as efforts to address the supply of counterfeits (Stumpf and Chaudhry 2010).

Practitioner-suggested tactics for networking with law enforcement include designating a liaison to work with law enforcement agencies and establishing relationships with different arms of law enforcement such as prosecutors and customs officials. Researcher-suggested tactics are similar, with some calling attention to the different roles of different law enforcement agencies in other nations (Chow 2001).

Practitioner-suggested tactics for networking with other government agencies focus on developing relationships with government agencies such as the Consumer Product Safety Commission, the Department of State, or the National Intellectual Property Rights Coordination Center in the United States, and similar government agencies for other countries. Researcher-suggested tactics here are similar, with a few offering more details. One article suggests coordinating with government agencies to develop and maintain a database on intellectual property cases and issues (Wilcock and Boys 2014). Another suggests establishing relationships on intellectual property issues with multiple agencies so as to amplify a firm's voice (Cooper and Eckstein 2008).

Public policy tactics as suggested by practitioners and researchers focus on broad elements of preventing counterfeit product. Working with public authorities to define and identify counterfeit product as well as to remove it from the marketplace can help reduce the opportunities that counterfeiters have and help eliminate more quickly the ones that still develop.

RESOURCES

Regarding resources, both researchers and practitioners suggest focusing most on staffing, but practitioners do suggest more budgetary tactics, which are focused internally, than researchers do.

Many of the budgeting tactics suggested by practitioners are simply to budget support for brand protection programs. Some more specific practitioner tactics include budgeting resources for a product throughout its life cycle and seeking budgetary support and endorsements from the highest levels of management one can reach. Researcher-suggested tactics are also general, with a few specific recommendations. One specific researcher-suggested tactic is to build a model that can budget brand protection needs for a product throughout its life cycle in a clean product environment, a contaminated market, and a repaired environment (Harvey 1988).

Suggested tactics for staffing are more specific. Practitioners noted the need to add security personnel at warehouse locations, designate experts for consultation, develop a brand protection career path, hire investigators both externally and internally, hire legal staff, and include brand protection duties in quality inspection positions. Researcher-suggested tactics were similar, with a focus on organization and specific skills needed for brand protection. One author suggested using "a team with members from the sales, finance, legal, and manufacturing departments … finance personnel can be on the lookout for increased potential global [counterfeit] sales resulting from currency valuation shifts, the legal department can explore the firm's legal options to deter transshipping, and production personnel can evaluate alternative measures to trace diversion" (Berman 2004). Another noted that "[h]aving qualified field representatives almost assures that no counterfeit good can go undetected once it has been found in a retail setting. Counterfeit investigators who know their business can spot a counterfeit product on the street and immediately begin actions necessary to lay the foundation for prosecuting the impostor" (Harvey 1988).

Resources tactics suggested by practitioners and researchers may support brands as they seek to develop a holistic approach that integrates all parts of the firm for brand protection. Providing resources for protecting a product throughout its life cycle as well as addressing the needs of products in different environments requires uniting all parts of the firm in the fight for brand protection. No one element of the firm can provide continuous support; rather, each has something to contribute. As research notes, brand protection teams with members from across a firm will be able to draw from different areas of expertise as needed when different issues of brand protection arise.

STRATEGY

Researchers suggest nearly twice as many strategy tactics than practitioners do. Practitioner-suggested tactics for strategy focus on aligning brand protection strategy across units, benchmarking programs, developing country-specific metrics, having the brand protection function lead strategy, using data to plan strategy, and working with sales partners.

Researcher-suggested tactics for strategy match many of these, but also emphasize minimizing price differentials between genuine goods and counterfeiters. Such an emphasis, of course, may not be possible for all products, and may also contradict other tactics relying on product innovation to thwart counterfeiters. Other researcher-suggested tactics may be more applicable. A supply-side strategy tactic recommended by researchers is to eliminate shortage of legitimate products in high demand (Harvey 1988). A demand-side strategic tactic recommended by researchers is to address consumer character-istics, cultural aspects, product characteristics, and institutional characteristics that may influence the purchase of counterfeit products (Raman and Pramod 2017). A supply chain strategy against counterfeit products would focus on preparation and shipment of goods at their place of manufacture, transport of goods, freight forwarding, and operation of handling and storage facilities and terminals (McGreevy and Harrop 2015).

Strategy tactics suggested by researchers and practitioners clearly support any emphasis that brands may place on strategy in their efforts to implement a total business solution to brand protection. Researchers, perhaps because of their position outside a firm and resulting ability to share tips, offered tactics that can help control both the supply of and the demand for counterfeits.

SUPPLIER COMPLIANCE

Both researchers and practitioners focus most on supplier management tactics. Practitioners cite more tactics regarding the audit of the supply chain and part-ners than researchers do. So here, too, practitioners focus more on internally initiated tactics than researchers do.

In auditing the supply chain and partners, practitioners suggest focusing on ensuring no leakage of products or components. They also suggest monitoring all tiers of the supply chain. Practitioners also recommend auditing partners to detect return fraud, auditing parts deliveries to manufacturers, and auditing supplies of raw material and product outputs. Researchers suggest similar tactics. One article proposes tracing recalls and product returns to ensure that expired product, defective product, and sold product combined equal the amount distributed (Hollis and Wilson 2014). Manufacturers outsourcing production may also wish "to have their own staff independently test goods during pre-production, production, and post-production stages; use independent, third-party auditors; and employ parallel testing by separate laboratories to confirm results" (Berman and Swani 2010).

Practitioners recommended several general supplier management tactics as well. These included having a supplier database and scorecard, regular quality inspections and monitoring of the supply chain, conducting due diligence on new suppliers, validating third-party logistics security, and visiting supplier factories to ensure performance with brand protection standards. Researchers suggested similar tactics, while calling attention to special initiatives or products. One article, for example, notes the need to monitor programs that streamline the process of acquiring parts from suppliers because they can increase vulnerability to counterfeiting and are at risk for misuse (Sullivan and Wilson 2017). Another notes the possibility of analyzing pollen on a plant-based product to determine its origins and whether it is authentic (Donaldson and Stephens 2010).

Both practitioner- and researcher-suggested tactics for supplier management can support controls in a total business solution. Practitioners, having a perspective within a brand, offered a balance of tactics for auditing partners and managing suppliers. Researchers, with a perspective outside of brands, offered relatively few tactics for auditing the supply chain but dozens of tactics for managing suppliers. Again, the difference is likely one of perspective rather than of desired emphasis. But the difference does point to ways in which those developing or expanding their brand protection programs may wish to pick and use tactics in implementing a total business solution.

CONCLUSION

Those seeking to launch or improve brand protection programs would do well to start with what other practitioners recommend. Practitioners can offer the most insight on what is currently being done, the breadth of activities that should be undertaken, and at what depth such activities should be undertaken.

Researchers, however, have many insights to contribute as well. While practitioners must be guarded in some circumstances, researchers can be more open and provide more details. Researchers may not have the day-to-day insight that practitioners do, but they do have a broad perspective that can place findings in context and offer more information for those seeking to apply their recommendations.

Researchers may also have insight on new tactics as well. They can raise tactics, such as collaborating with online providers, and note the cautions that need to be followed, while practitioners may be more guarded. Researchers may also offer more insight on why some tactics may or may not work in some situations, while practitioners may have valid reasons not to provide such additional detail.

One possible limitation in the application of researcher-suggested tactics is the focus of many on certain industries. There is a good deal of research, for example, on counterfeits in the luxury goods industry, much of which may not be applicable to other industries. Nevertheless, some of its general principles may be applicable, and those seeking to develop or improve brand protection programs can likely judge the context of differing research and its application to their own context. Future research may wish to explore the applicability of different tactics to different markets and industries, and their relative ease of implementation, cost, and effectiveness. An encyclopedia of tactics, both those recommended by practitioners and those suggested in research, can also help guide practitioners and researchers in exploring new ways to thwart counterfeiting, particularly as counterfeiting threats evolve. Future research may also explore matching tactics to particular risks and associate tactics to varying frameworks for mitigating risk.

In sum, practitioner-suggested tactics may give the best insight on current tactics used, as well as insights on issues other practitioners likely need to address. Researcher-suggested tactics, however, can provide additional context and detail that practitioners may not always have the time or even motivation to share. Firms seeking to implement a total business solution to maximize protection of the brand would be well-advised to consider insight from both practitioner and academic perspectives. Together, they can help firms identify ways to be more strategic, proactive, evidence-based, and comprehensive in their approach.

NOTE

1.   Note that in this chapter we consider only total tactics—that is, the total number of tactics that respondents reported to us or that we identified in previous research—and not, as we did in Chapter 5, unique tactics as well. One reason for this, as we later discuss, is that the tactics described in previous research are typically provided in much greater detail. This means that it would be easier to classify researcher-suggested tactics than practitioner-suggested tactics as unique. For example, while several practitioners simply told us to "monitor sales trends to determine anomalies," one of the tactics suggested in research for detecting anomalies is use of a counterfeit network analyzer that integrates automatic data captured from a variety of sources (Kwok et al. 2010). Practitioners, of course, may have valid reasons for not providing such detail, with available time to respond to our questions and need to protect trade information among them. But this means that any effort to identify "unique" tactics among practitioner tactics will systematically differ from that to identify unique tactics published in

research. Hence, in this chapter comparing practitioner and research tactics, we focus on total tactics, and not on unique tactics mentioned across the sources.

REFERENCES

Ahmed, T. (2016), 'Countering counterfeit branding: implications for public-sector marketing', *Journal of Nonprofit and Public Sector Marketing*, **28** (3), 273–286.

Aksulu, A. and Wade, M. (2010), 'A comprehensive review and synthesis of open source research', *Journal of the Association for Information Systems*, **11** (11), 576–656.

Arslan, M. M., Zeren, C., Aydin, Z., Akcan, R., Dokuyucu, R., Keten, A., and Cekin, N. (2015), 'Analysis of methanol and its derivatives in illegally produced alcoholic beverages', *Journal of Forensic and Legal Medicine*, **33**, 56–60.

Berman, B. (2004), 'Strategies to combat the sale of gray market goods', *Business Horizons*, **47** (4), 51–60.

Berman, B. and Swani, K. (2010), 'Managing product safety of imported Chinese goods', *Business Horizons*, **53** (1), 39–48.

Bian, X. and Moutinho, L. (2011), 'Counterfeits and branded products: effects of counterfeit ownership', *Journal of Product and Brand Management*, **20** (5), 379–393.

Bose, I. and Pal, R. (2005), 'Auto-ID: managing anything, anywhere, anytime in the supply chain', *Communications of the ACM*, **48** (8), 100–106.

Castaño, R. and Perez, M. E. (2014), 'A matter of love: consumers' relationships with original brands and their counterfeits', *Journal of Consumer Marketing*, **31** (6/7), 475–482.

Chaudhry, P. E. and Cesareo, L. (2017), 'Fake and pirated: do consumers care?', *Journal of Business Strategy*, **38** (6), 11–19.

Chow, D. C. K. (2001), 'Counterfeiting in the People's Republic of China', *Washington University Law Review*, **78** (1), 1–57.

Cooper, S. and Eckstein, G. M. (2008), 'Eight ways to minimize the risk of counterfeiting', *Intellectual Property and Technology Law Journal*, **20** (8), 15–17.

Dégardin, K., Roggo, Y., and Margot, P. (2015), 'Forensic intelligence for medicine anti-counterfeiting', *Forensic Science International*, **248**, 15–32.

Donaldson, M. P. and Stephens, W. E. (2010), 'Environmental pollen trapped by tobacco leaf as indicators of the provenance of counterfeit cigarette products: a preliminary investigation and test of concept', *Journal of Forensic Sciences*, **55** (3), 738–741.

Gistri, G., Romani, S., Pace, S., Gabrielli, V., and Grappi, S. (2009), 'Consumption practices of counterfeit luxury goods in the Italian context', *Journal of Brand Management*, **16** (5–6), 364–374.

Glaser, B. G. and Strauss, A. L. (1967), *The Discovery of Grounded Theory: Strategies for Qualitative Research*. New Brunswick, NJ: AldineTransaction.

Globerman, S. (1988), 'Addressing international product piracy', *Journal of International Business Studies*, **19** (3), 497–504.

Gomes, C. L., de Lima, A. C. A., Loiola, A. R., da Silva, A. B. R., Cândido, M. C. L., and Nascimento, R. F. (2016), 'Multivariate classification of original and fake perfumes by ion analysis and ethanol content', *Journal of Forensic Sciences*, **61** (4), 1074–1079.

Harvey, M. (1988), 'A new way to combat product counterfeiting', *Business Horizons*, **31** (4), 19–28.

Hollis, M. E. and Wilson, J. (2014), 'Who are the guardians in product counterfeiting? A theoretical application of routine activities theory', *Crime Prevention and Community Safety*, **16** (3), 169–188.

Kennedy, J. P. (2016), 'Proposed solutions to the brand protection challenges and counterfeiting risks faced by small and medium enterprises (SMEs)', *Journal of Applied Security Research*, **11** (4), 450–468.

Kennedy, J. P., Haberman, C. P., and Wilson, J. M. (2018), 'Occupational pharmaceutical counterfeiting schemes: a crime scripts analysis', *Victims and Offenders*, **13** (2), 196–214.

Kennedy, J. P., Wilson, J., and Labrecque, R. (2017), 'Towards a more proactive approach to brand protection: development of the Organisational Risk Assessment for Product Counterfeiting (ORAPC)', *Global Crime*, **18** (4), 329–352.

Kim, J., Kim, J.-E., and Park, J. (2012), 'Effects of cognitive resource availability on consumer decisions involving counterfeit products: the role of perceived justification', *Marketing Letters*, **23** (3), 869–881.

Kwok, S. K., Ting, S. L., Tsang, A. H. C., and Cheung, C. F. (2010), 'A counterfeit network analyzer based on RFID and EPC', *Industrial Management and Data Systems*, **110** (7), 1018–1037.

Lord, N., Spencer, J., Bellotti, E., and Benson, K. (2017), 'A script analysis of the distribution of counterfeit alcohol across two European jurisdictions', *Trends in Organized Crime*, **20** (3–4), 252–272.

Marcketti, S. B. and Shelley, M. C. (2009), 'Consumer concern, knowledge and attitude towards counterfeit apparel products', *International Journal of Consumer Studies*, **33** (3), 327–337.

McGreevy, C. and Harrop, W. (2015), 'Intentional cargo disruption by nefarious means: examining threats, systemic vulnerabilities and securitization measures in complex global supply chains', *Journal of Business Continuity and Emergency Planning*, **8** (4), 326–345.

Peng, L., Wong, A. H. K., and Wan, L. C.-Y. (2012), 'The effects of image congruence and self-monitoring on product evaluations: a comparison between genuine and counterfeit products', *Journal of Global Marketing*, **25** (1), 17–28.

Raman, R. and Pramod, D. (2017), 'A strategic approach using governance, risk and compliance model to deal with online counterfeit market', *Journal of Theoretical and Applied Electronic Commerce Research*, **12** (3), 13–26.

Saunders, K. M. and Berger-Walliser, G. (2011), 'The liability of online markets for counterfeit goods: a comparative analysis of secondary trademark infringement in the United States and Europe', *Northwestern Journal of International Law and Business*, **32** (1), 37–91.

Sonmez, M., Yang, D., and Fryxell, G. (2013), 'Interactive role of consumer discrimination and branding against counterfeiting: a study of multinational managers' perception of global brands in China', *Journal of Business Ethics*, **115** (1), 195–211.

Stevenson, M. and Busby, J. (2015), 'An exploratory analysis of counterfeiting strategies: towards counterfeit-resilient supply chains', *International Journal of Operations and Production Management*, **35** (1), 110–144.

Strickland, E. (2017), 'Fake malaria meds meet their match in a handheld spectrometer', *IEEE Spectrum*, **54** (8), 9–10.

Stumpf, S. A. and Chaudhry, P. (2010), 'Country matters: executives weigh in on the causes and counter measures of counterfeit trade', *Business Horizons*, **53** (3), 305–314.

Sullivan, B. A., Chan, F., Fenoff, R., and Wilson, J. M. (2017), 'Assessing the developing knowledge-base of product counterfeiting: a content analysis of four decades of research', *Trends in Organized Crime*, **20** (3–4), 338–369.

Sullivan, B. A. and Chermak, S. M. (2013), 'Product counterfeiting and the media: examining news sources used in the construction of product counterfeiting as a social problem', *International Journal of Comparative and Applied Criminal Justice*, **37** (4), 295–316.

Sullivan, B. A. and Wilson, J. M. (2017), 'An empirical examination of product counterfeiting crime impacting the U.S. military', *Trends in Organized Crime*, **20** (3–4), 316–337.

Ting, S. L. and Ip, W. H. (2013), 'Combating the counterfeits with web portal technology', *Enterprise Information Systems*, **9** (7), 661–680.

Ting, S. L. and Tsang, A. H. C. (2013), 'A two-factor authentication system using Radio Frequency Identification and watermarking technology', *Computers in Industry*, **64** (3), 268–279.

Viot, C., Le Roux, A., and Kremer, F. (2014), 'Attitude towards the purchase of counterfeits: antecedents and effect on intention to purchase', *Recherche et Applications en Marketing* (English edition), **29** (2), 3–31.

Wang, Y. and Alocilja, E. C. (2012), 'Sensor technologies for anticounterfeiting', *International Journal of Comparative and Applied Criminal Justice*, **36** (4), 291–304.

Wilcock, A. E. and Boys, K. A. (2014), 'Reduce product counterfeiting: an integrated approach', *Business Horizons*, **57** (2), 279–288.

Wilcox, K., Kim, H. M., and Sen, S. (2009), 'Why do consumers buy counterfeit luxury brands?', *Journal of Marketing Research*, **46** (2), 247–259.

Wilson, J. M. (2017), 'The future of brand protection: responding to the global risk', *Journal of Brand Management*, **24** (3), 271–283.

Wilson, J. M. and Grammich, C. (2020), 'Protecting brands from counterfeiting risks: tactics of a total business solution', *Journal of Risk Research*, DOI:10.1080/13669877.2020.1806908.

Wilson, J. M., Grammich, C., and Chan, F. (2016), 'Organizing for brand protection and responding to product counterfeit risk: an analysis of global firms', *Journal of Brand Management*, **23** (3), 345–361.

Wilson, J. M. and Sullivan, B. A. (2016), 'Brand owner approaches to assessing the risk of product counterfeiting', *Journal of Brand Management*, **23** (3), 327–344.

Wimmer, H. and Yoon, V. Y. (2017), 'Counterfeit product detection: bridging the gap between design science and behavioral science in information systems research', *Decision Support Systems*, **104**, 1–12.

Wong, K. H. M., Hui, P. C. L., and Chan, A. C. K. (2006), 'Cryptography and authentication on RFID passive tags for apparel products', *Computers in Industry*, **57** (4), 342–349.

Yoo, B. and Lee, S.-H. (2012), 'Asymmetrical effects of past experiences with genuine fashion luxury brands and their counterfeits on purchase intention of each', *Journal of Business Research*, **65** (10), 1507–1515.

7. Communicating the value of brand protection through a persuasive internal communications approach

Kami J. Silk, Brandon D.H. Thomas, Ashley Paintsil and Jeremy M. Wilson

A 2018 report from the Organisation for Economic Co-operation and Development (OECD) indicates a 154 percent increase in internationally traded counterfeits from 2005 to 2016, making it a more than $500 billion illicit trade industry (OECD, 2018). The problem only continues to increase, with e-commerce opportunities for counterfeiters fueling its rise. A recent report from the US Department of Homeland Security's (US DHS) Office of Strategy, Policy, and Plans calls for action among private industries to enact best practices for brand protection so they are better able to prevent and detect counterfeit and pirated goods, and monitor the trade landscape (US DHS, 2020). An aggressive, scaled-up brand protection strategy with a strong communications function is necessary for organizations to appropriately address the extensive growth of counterfeiting. Simply put, brand protection needs to be at the forefront of all organizational functions, and this requires a persuasive internal communications strategy that can aid in facilitating organizational change.

Businesses strive to be clear in their communication about brand protection. Yet leaders charged with brand protection may wonder why it is not a priority to other organizational members, and why some of their colleagues seem unaware of policies that are in place and have been communicated repeatedly to them. These brand protection program leaders know that policies exist, are reviewed periodically, are often posted internally on the firm's website, and perhaps are even emailed to employees annually. These efforts are not enough. Nor are these efforts likely to be part of an intentional communications strategy designed to ensure consistent and clear communication about brand protection. Communicating internally about the importance and role of brand protection is essential to implementing any plan designed to protect an organization from counterfeiting. Brand protection programs need to have a communication strategy inclusive of all levels of the organization so that every employee within the enterprise understands their role in protecting the brand. In a survey about brand protection efforts, Wilson and Grammich (2020a, 2020b) found that respondents rarely identified internal communications as an important function for brand protection even though they identified the importance of many communication tactics, indicating communication as a brand protection strategy may be underutilized or at least uncoordinated.

Communicating internally (i.e., communications efforts that occur within and across the organization) about what the enterprise must do to protect itself from counterfeits across all organizational functions is one of the greatest challenges for brand protection programs. This chapter makes the case for a strategic internal communications approach within organizations and across their functions, with the goal of communicating the *value* of brand protection, something that is central to the overall brand protection strategy. This chapter discusses the role of communication planning and internal persuasive communication approaches in influencing organizational culture, considers a data set of communication tactics identified by brand protection experts, and then recommends how those tactics might be integrated into an overall internal communications strategy.

ORGANIZATIONAL CULTURE AND LEARNING ORGANIZATIONS

Organizational culture impacts how employees perceive and prevent counterfeiting. If brand protection seems a peripheral concern to most departments and employees in a firm, it has a minimal chance of being prioritized in the activities of those departments, either at the work group level, or by individual employees. Fostering an organizational culture where attitudes, norms, and expectations about brand protection are visible and accepted across all levels of the organization is fundamental to ensuring that brand protection is a consistent priority. Thus, in addition to the policies that organizations create and strive to monitor and enforce, norms also influence the socialization of employees and help to establish organizational culture. Norms can help to not only improve compliance, but also influence the willingness of employees to engage in an organization's brand protection initiatives. Just as consumers are impacted by others in their behavior of purchasing counterfeits (Fejes, 2016), employees' attitudes can be impacted by their colleagues and supervisors. The internal organizational and communication networks of colleagues and supervisors can influence employees' attitudes and perceived norms about prioritizing brand protection to reduce counterfeits. Establishing a brand protection strategy that incorporates internal communications will help in influencing knowledge, attitudes, intentions, norms, and subsequent behavior related to brand protection, which will positively impact organizational culture such that brand protection is the concern of everyone across the enterprise rather than just an individual department, unit, office, or function.

Central leadership is necessary to elevate brand protection across the organization. The real challenge is *how* to make this happen. Thinking about the total enterprise as a "learning organization" provides some guidance for brand protection leaders and reveals the critical implications for internal communications. Senge (1990) defines *learning organizations* as places "where people continually expand their capacity to create the results they truly desire, where new and expansive patterns of thinking are nurtured, where collective aspiration is set free, and where people are continually learning to see the whole together" (p. 3). This definition is certainly aspirational in its vision of organizations and their transformational capacity; however, adopting a learning organization approach can help to provide a roadmap for building a culture where internal communication is fundamental to the overall brand protection strategy. The learning organizations concept provides the context for considering Senge's five flows (shared vision, systems thinking, mental models, personal mastery, and team learning), and how they might apply to the context of making brand protection a salient part of organizational culture.

Shared vision refers to the collective goals that organizational members have for the long term. Organizations should create a clear and shared vision for brand protection that is communicated through strategic planning. This means that organizational leaders need to carefully consider how different functions within the organization (i.e., security, sales, packaging, engineering, operations, etc.) can uniquely and synergistically contribute to brand protection goals. Comprehensive thinking about how the different organizational functions can contribute to brand protection is an example of *systems thinking* in Senge's approach. In other words, all business members need to see beyond their own roles in their respective functions so they are able to see how their own actions, or even inactions, impact the entire brand protection strategy. For example, unreported suspicions of counterfeits in the marketplace have implications across the organization, such as by increasing complaints and warranty costs and reducing sales, which will potentially expand if not monitored or addressed quickly.

Mental models refer to the fundamental assumptions and generalizations a person has at the individual level that inform their understanding and actions within the organization. In the brand protection context, firm members might have mental models that reduce the severity of consequences of counterfeit products for their organization; therefore, influencing those mental models with information and perhaps data to support the real risk that counterfeits pose may help organizational members to accept, implement, and advocate for brand protection strategies within their roles and departments. *Personal mastery* is not simply an accumulation of knowledge or accomplishment of milestones, but rather a process of continual learning. Personal mastery allows for the introduction of brand protection as another layer of knowledge for firm members to consider, understand, and integrate into their ways of implementing their roles. *Team learning* requires dialogue that allows members to think together so that foundational or deep-seated issues can be effectively addressed (Senge, 1990). Team learning also requires systems thinking and shared vision. Thus, if staff members are to creatively and critically consider brand protection, organizational leaders need to foster an organizational culture where team members can take risks and feel safe and confident that suggestions will be considered fully.

This section provided insight on how shared vision, systems thinking, mental models, personal mastery, and team learning can help to shape an organizational culture that is pro-active, aligned, and assertive with regard to brand protection strategy. Moving a culture forward so that it embraces brand protection across the organization is a process and it takes time, planning, commitment, and communication. A wide range of approaches is necessary to influence organizational culture. Recent brand protection research provides a starting point for considering the types of activities that might be effective in attempting to influence all business stakeholders for a total business solution.

A PERSUASIVE ORIENTATION TO BRAND PROTECTION

Organizations seeking to adopt new approaches to better protect against counterfeiting threats likely have goals and specific objectives they would like to achieve with their novel efforts. While these objectives will undoubtedly include financial metrics to indicate level of success, brand protection related goals might also include persuasive goals to influence employees to actively support and enact organizational brand protection policies. For example, employees may have low knowledge or indifferent attitudes about brand protection, and goals with specific objectives to increase knowledge and positive attitudes toward brand protection can be articulated and measured. While different persuasive strategies potentially can be employed to meet goals, identifying specific brand protection tactics currently used in organizations also would help in building communication strategies for a total brand solution.

In a survey of 42 brand protection experts, Wilson and Grammich (2020a) compiled organizational functions and specific tactics that respondents identified as associated with brand protection efforts. Tactics identified by brand protection experts included strategies and actions that they grouped by *organizational function*, defined as "a set of activities or processes within or across structural units for accomplishing a broad organizational goal" (p. 368). Tactics may occur across single or multiple units or departments within an organization, such as security, legal, supply chain, engineering, human resources, and so on. A total of 35 functions were reported and within those functions there was quite a high number of unique tactics (757) indicated by brand protection experts. The number of unique tactics found within functions ranged from 1 to 134 tactics with a median of 22 tactics; for example, within the security function 134 unique tactics were reported, while the number of unique tactics reported in the quality assurance function was 45 and in the engineering function 20. In many functions, such as brand management, service, risk management, and many others, less than ten tactics were reported. Organizational functions, and even categories within them, offer a structure for considering the wide range of tactics that exist for brand protection experts to leverage as part of their brand protection strategy.

Persuasive messages are intended to shape, reinforce, or change the responses of another or others (Miller, 1980; see McGuire (2013) for an excellent review of persuasive strategies). Focusing on persuasion helps to increase the likelihood of positive impact so that the resources invested in brand protection have the greatest potential for success. When brand protection experts identified tactics to reduce counterfeiting and to improve brand protection, the tactics represented different strategies and activities that are persuasive in nature and have varying impacts and levels of effectiveness. Thus, the tactics identified by Wilson and Grammich can be considered through a persuasion lens to evaluate their potential effectiveness for getting organizational members to adopt a brand protection orientation across all levels of the organization.

A closer look at specific tactics reveals they are inclusive of auditing, enforcement strategies, networking and collaborative approaches, education and training, and a wide range of communication activities. If these tactics were framed as attempts at persuasion—and many easily fall into that framework—they could be organized based on the desired brand protection outcome they might achieve if successful. In particular, many of the tactics might also be overtly trying to change a behavior, which means they would be considered compliance gaining strategies (Wheeless, Barraclough, and Stewart, 1983). Unlike persuasive tactics, compliance gaining refers to specific attempts to change a behavior. Compliance gaining has high relevance in the industry context as firms expect specific outcomes based on organizational functions as well as members' job duties and tasks, or the overt behaviors that lead to productivity. When an organizational goal such as increasing the value of brand protection changes, leaders set goals and take actions to influence their colleagues and expect that the organizational change will be adopted and tangible positive outcomes will occur. However, compliance with an organizational goal does not guarantee personal acceptance of it. These strategies to influence behavior, or compliance gaining strategies, can take many forms.

A classic typology from Marwell and Schmitt (1967) identified 16 compliance gaining strategies that included pre-giving, promise, threat, expertise, moral appeal, altercasting, debt, and altruism strategies among others. A comprehensive explanation of each of these strategies is beyond the scope of this chapter, and readers can pursue additional information through the references that are provide at the end. It is more productive and manageable to more broadly discuss the five categories in which the 16 compliance gaining strategies were classified; those five categories included rewarding, punishing, expertise, impersonal commitments, and personal commitments. The categorization does eliminate distinctions of each individual strategy, and it is important to acknowledge that some strategies within these broader categories have the ability not only to influence compliance among employees, but also to influence attitudinal change. Each of these categories of tactics can be more or less effective based on the situation and individual-level variables (Boster and Levine, 1988; Miller et al., 1977), indicating discernment is necessary in selecting which type of strategy should be employed. In the current brand protection context, many of the tactics identified by Wilson and Grammich (2020a) can be organized into one of these five categories.

Reward and punishment as tactics are common in the organizational context, for example, and they are clearly apparent in the tactics identified by brand protection experts in the Wilson and Grammich data set. One respondent noted a reward strategy where organizations could "establish Brand Protection Hero Awards, or the like, across departments so brand protection becomes everyone's job." Many respondents recommended enforcement or punishing strategies, particularly within the security function. These included statements about partnering directly with enforcement agencies (e.g., "establish strong relationship with Customs and Law Enforcement"), presumably to better identify and punish counterfeiters, and about auditing comprehensively across the organization as a protective strategy (e.g., "audit suppliers, at all tiers, to ensure no leakage of products" and "conduct audits on supply chain to prevent counterfeiting").

Tactics also included using expertise as a compliance gaining strategy for brand protection efforts. For example, respondents noted that industry should "work with academic centers and trade associations to share and develop best practices" and "establish feedback mechanisms to enable engineers to see first-hand the counterfeit products to help drive improvements." In other words, to influence real change, brand protection experts sought to turn to subject matter experts to help directly reduce counterfeiting.

Activation of personal and impersonal commitments is a bit more difficult to identify in the data. However, tactics such as "establish expectations that suppliers develop brand protection programs for their operations and their suppliers" and "monitor for inconsistencies, anomalies, and suspect activities at all levels of the manufacturing process" can be couched in commitment appeals that remind organizational members that if they are committed to their jobs and their team members, they will take recommended actions to support an overall brand protection strategy.

The reason for discussing tactics and their relationship to persuasion and compliance gaining is to expand thinking and the choices that brand protection leaders and internal communications professionals have at their fingertips to influence an overall strategy. To bring about organizational change requires policies and processes in support of a change, and it also requires social power, defined as "the *potential* for such influence, the ability of the agent or power figure to bring about such change, using resources available to him or her" (Raven, 2008, p. 1). Social power is not simply power based on position within an organizational hierarchy such as C-suite leaders or brand protection experts in the current context; rather, social power is drawn from a range of potential bases, which align somewhat with the compliance gaining categories discussed previously. These potential bases of power include: *informational power* where the agent has persuasive reasons for why a change is necessary; *reward power* where the agent can offer incentives to encourage the change; *coercive power* where the agent has the ability punish or threaten to encourage the change; *legitimate power*, typical in industry, where supervisory or organizational position/status is used to encourage the change; *expert power* where the advanced or unique knowledge of a person encourages the change; and *referent power* where the change is motivated because organizational members identify with, and want to emulate, the change agent (see Raven (2008) for a complete overview of social power). If brand protection program leaders and internal communication professionals want to see their efforts influence organizational change, they need to understand where their power to influence comes from, because it is a mistake to think that power comes only through position (legitimate power), a typical assumption in organizational hierarchies. The wider the bases of power used, the greater the potential for the persuasive attempt to be effective.

For example, brand protection programs have legitimate power over brand protection efforts, and they may be considered to have expert power. However, if brand protection programs are not located within the highest levels of the organizational hierarchy, their power to influence change may be reduced; thus, people running and using these programs should consider how else they might more broadly tap other sources of power for their efforts. An obvious way is to get C-suite executives on board with the new overall brand protection strategy and ask them to publicly commit to and enforce its implementation (legitimate power, and potentially expert and referent power). As one brand protection expert put it, "remember to reach up high in the corporate hierarchy and secure management endorsement and championship" (Wilson and

Grammich, 2020a). Another source of power is to identify incentives and use reward power, which was noted by brand protection experts when they indicated "Brand Protection Hero Awards" as a compliance gaining tactic. Cooperating with security functions within the organization is another power to leverage because security functions can be perceived as a punishing strategy if threats or coercive strategies are used to influence brand protection outcomes. For example, auditing was repeatedly identified as an important tactic to hold the supply chain accountable for protecting brands (e.g., "audit suppliers, at all tiers, to ensure no leakage of product or components" and "conduct physical audit of supplier spaces to identify diversion; alert brand protection for abnormalities"). Overall, using persuasive and compliance gaining tactics in concert with an understanding of how brand protection programs can exert influence across the organization creates the greatest likelihood for organizational change related to brand protection. While this may be a new frontier for internal communications, accounting for social power within brand protection efforts can give employees the ability to leverage their roles as internal communicators.

LEVERAGE INTERNAL COMMUNICATIONS FOR BRAND PROTECTION

Internal communications have a key function in communicating the value of brand protection. One brand protection expert agreed with this assertion, indicating that organizations should "create internal communications about brand protection issues that fit company culture" (Wilson and Grammich, 2020a). There are plenty of professionals in organizations who are responsible for internal communications and these professionals are very capable communicators. They have been trained to think broadly, precisely, and creatively as they consider the fundamental communication model that includes key decisions about who is initiating and guiding the communication (*message source*; e.g., company president, legal, security), what is the message (*content*; e.g., promoting audits, establishing awards, announcing training), how is the message to be disseminated (*channel decisions*; company email, in person, posters, etc.), who is the message intended for (*receiver/s*; e.g., engineering, marketing, retail partners), and what is the goal (*intended impact*; e.g., to increase awareness, share new knowledge). These internal communications professionals have the knowledge and skills to develop a communications strategy for integrating brand protection into the organizational culture in a defined, systematic, and effective way to achieve the goal of "broadly based brand protection strategies" within organizations (Wilson and Grammich, 2020a, p. 370).

Only two unique tactics related to internal communications function were reported by brand protection experts in Wilson and Grammich's (2020a) research. This is surprising, especially as an examination of individual tactics reveals that many of them could easily be connected to an internal communications function too. It is quite possible that the small sample of brand protection experts surveyed did not directly work in or represent the internal communications function of their organizations, and thus did not fully consider how their respective organizations might actually be engaged in internal communications for brand protection purposes. It is also possible that the low use of internal communications is indeed accurate, and other functions within the organization are engaging in communications separate from the internal communications function. Whatever the reason, the lack of awareness of what internal communications might be doing in support of brand protection and/ or the lack of understanding for how it might be used for brand protection is a problem that should be remedied because the internal communications function is integral to building, maintaining, and changing an organizational culture so it is more broadly focused on brand protection.

Staff whose primary role is internal communications may have less legitimate power over other functions within the organization, but they clearly have informational power and can use informational tactics to increase awareness and educate organizational members. Informational tactics can serve to "share risks of unauthorized sellers/competitors" and other reasons to combat counterfeiting so that organizational members can be persuaded to prioritize brand protection within their own roles. And internal communications can amplify all the other types of power because they have the role of communicating expert knowledge, rewards, and potential punishments that exist in relation to a brand protection strategy from others in high-status organizational positions who have perceived and real legitimate power. As they consider the functions of the entire organization and strategize about *who* needs to *know what* so they can *play* their part in brand protection, internal communications professionals can consider the different tactics associated with brand protection and package them into persuasive communication strategies that lead to compliance, which ultimately can then shift organizational culture around brand protection.

For example, in partnership with the brand protection program, those responsible for internal communications may decide to reach out to procurement, marketing, and sales teams to raise awareness about brand protection and their expected roles in it. After engaging in research about these three audiences and their role in brand protection (see Chapter 5 for organizational functions in brand protection), they might determine that increasing awareness about reporting policies is key for these functions and create "moral appeals" to activate employees' sense of commitment. These types of appeals or messages can highlight the importance of protecting the brand against fraud and theft as moral traits, emphasizing that by not protecting against counterfeiting, employees will be violating moral and ethical beliefs. The incorporation of reward tactics might also be useful for procurement, marketing, and sales functions. Specifically, internal communications can highlight "bottom-line" issues, indicating that wages and salaries are influenced by both failures and successes with brand protection; thus, by protecting the brand against fraud and counterfeiting, the firm will be more apt to increase salaries and incentives for their employees.

Other audiences that internal communications functions might prioritize are quality assurance, security, and legal. These groups are perhaps more captive audiences for brand protection as they are already part of an established system that aims to guarantee authenticity and quality of products as well as to provide safeguards, with legal ready to take action when counterfeiting occurs. However, it is possible and perhaps even likely that those functions are less prepared and knowledgeable about a total brand solution than might be anticipated, which is why it is important to consider all functions of the organization when communicating brand protection strategy. The consideration of all organizational stakeholders is necessary to appropriately enlist and activate their help with brand protection via their roles within their organizational functions. Staff can also strive to communicate brand protection strategies pertinent to their roles and firm functions in a persuasive fashion to help further diffuse brand protection strategies. Different functions will require more or less persuasive and compliance gaining tactics to work toward an organizational culture that seamlessly supports a brand protection strategy.

IDENTIFY WHAT MAKES SENSE FOR YOUR ORGANIZATION

If internal communications functions are tapped as a key resource to help organize and communicate brand protection strategy, there are decisions to be made. Every employee needs to have some minimum amount of information about brand protection, with some functions playing more central roles. First, there is a need to identify and prioritize relevant functions so information can be tailored to their needs and roles in brand protection. Who is well-suited to make the greatest impact on brand protection quickly? What functions do they serve within the organization, and how do those relate to brand protection? What receiver variables, constraints, and facilitators for communication exist? How can brand protection be made relevant to them? What persuasive strategies have the greatest potential to influence? All these questions are part of the situational analysis and formative research necessary to understand the priority audiences. Identifying the goals and objectives specific to brand protection for each audience is necessary. How will those be communicated to different groups and individuals within the organization? How will the effectiveness of communication efforts be assessed to determine if investments in internal communications approaches to brand protection are effective?

Tara L. Smith, an internal communications and public relations expert, who also teaches communication courses and leads a strategic communication graduate program, provides an excellent template of considerations for internal communications functions. Smith has applied this approach to public relations programs and the template adapts easily to brand protection efforts. Smith (2020) recommends that internal communications strategists take systematic steps in approaching a new communication endeavor that include:

- conduct a situational analysis so you can make the case for a brand protection communications strategy;
- engage in research so you can make informed decisions about communication objectives and priority audiences;
- set specific and measurable goals rooted in the organization's mission to protect the brand;
- identify the strategies, key content, persuasive tactics, and collateral materials (brochures, apps, podcast, etc.) necessary to reach different organizational functions and stakeholders;
- set the timeline, with attention to key moments relevant to the organization;
- assess communication efforts via ongoing evaluation strategies to be able to continue to adjust.

Smith also notes that a realistic budget that supports a comprehensive communication effort is necessary for success. Thus, considering the digital media writing and production as well as print costs and image acquisition should be factored into an internal communications budget to fully support the communication plan for promoting an organization's brand protection strategy.

CONCLUSION

Persuasive strategies to improve the value of brand protection are necessary to influence up, down, and across chains of commands as well as to influence audiences external to the organization. This chapter provided guidance on available tactics and how to improve internal communications by adopting a persuasive orientation that maximizes power in selecting different tactics to influence staff. It used data collected from brand protection experts to support a persuasive communication approach from internal communications functions. Firm members need to be "on board" with the brand protection strategy so they play their part in it, and a persuasive orientation is recommended to influence their knowledge, beliefs, attitudes, and actual behaviors related to brand protection. A planned internal communications strategy helps support building an organizational culture where new approaches are adopted, because staff understands that counterfeiting is everyone's challenge and brand protection is everyone's responsibility. In sum, incorporating internal communications into an overall brand protection strategy so it can serve its function of facilitating the brand protection strategy is necessary for organizations to make progress toward a total business solution.

REFERENCES

Boster, F. J., and Levine, T. R. (1988). Individual differences and compliance-gaining message selection: The effects of verbal aggressiveness, argumentativeness, dogmatism, and negativism. *Communication Research Reports*, *5*, 114–119.

Fejes, Z. L. (2016). Investigating consumer demand for counterfeit goods: Examining the ability of social learning and low self-control to explain volitional purchase of non-deceptive counterfeit products in an eastern European college sample. Doctoral dissertation, Michigan State University. ProQuest Dissertations and Theses Global.

Marwell, G., and Schmitt, D. (1967). Dimensions of compliance-gaining behavior: An empirical analysis. *Sociometry*, *30*(4), 350–364.

McGuire, W. J. (2013). McGuire's classic input-output framework for constructing persuasive messages. In R. E. Rice and C. K. Atkin (Eds.), *Public Communication Campaigns* (4th Edn.), pp. 133–145, Thousand Oaks, CA: SAGE.

Miller, G. (1980). On being persuaded: Some basic distinctions. In M. E. Roloff and G. R. Miller (Eds.), *Persuasion: New Directions in Theory and Research*, pp. 11–28, Beverly Hills, CA: SAGE.

Miller, G., Boster, F., Roloff, M., and Seibold, D. (1977). Compliance gaining message strategies: A typology and some findings concerning effects of situational differences. *Communication Monographs*, *44*(1), 37–51.

Organisation for Economic Co-operation and Development (OECD). (2018). *Governance Frameworks to Counter Illicit Trade*, Illicit Trade, Paris: OECD Publishing, https://doi.org/10.1787/9789264291652-en.

Raven, B. H. (2008). The bases of power and the power/interaction model of interpersonal influence. *Analyses of Social Issues and Public Policy*, *8*(1), 1–22.

Senge, P. M. (1990). *The Fifth Discipline: The Art and Practice of the Learning Organization*, London: Random House.

Smith, T. (2020). Public relations campaign template. In *COMM 607: Principles of Strategic Communication: Summer 2020* [Class Handout], Newark: University of Delaware.

US Department of Homeland Security (US DHS). (2020). *Combatting Trafficking in Counterfeit and Pirated Goods*. Retrieved from https://www.dhs.gov/sites/default/files/publications/20_0124_plcy_counterfeit-pirated-goods-report_01.pdf.

Wheeless, L. R., Barraclough, R., and Stewart, R. (1983). Compliance-gaining and power in persuasion. *Annals of the International Communication Association*, *7*(1), 105–145.

Wilson, J. M., and Grammich, C. A. (2020a). Brand protection across the enterprise: Toward a total-business solution. *Business Horizons*, *63*, 363–376.

Wilson, J. M., and Grammich, C. A. (2020b). Protecting brands from counterfeiting risks: Tactics of a total business solution. *Journal of Risk Research*, DOI:10.1080/13669877.2020.1806908.

PART IV

Resource allocation for and measuring the value
of brand protection programs

8. Counterfeiting and anti-counterfeiting costs: an application of cost of quality concepts[1]

B. William Demeré, Karen L. Sedatole and Jeremy M. Wilson

1. INTRODUCTION AND BACKGROUND

Product counterfeiting is a challenge faced by many firms and affects a wide range of industries and products. "Any product for which [intellectual property] adds economic value to rights holders and that creates price differentials becomes a target for counterfeiters" (OECD/EUIPO 2016, 12). Indeed, according to a recent collaborative research report by the Organisation for Economic Co-operation and Development (OECD) and the European Union Intellectual Property Office (EUIPO), customs officials found counterfeit products in 77 of 96 industry sectors (80 percent) (OECD/EUIPO 2016).

Intellectual property (IP) is an umbrella term which refers to the rights related to creative works or inventions, and which may be provided legal protection in the form of patents, trademarks, or copyrights. While the term counterfeiting is often used generally to refer to a broad range of IP infringement and illicit activities, there are technical differences between specific forms of IP infringement. Various definitions of counterfeiting include the production and sale of "tangible goods that infringe trademarks, design rights or patents" (OECD/ EUIPO 2016, 16), "the manufacturing or distribution of goods under someone else's name, and without their permission" (IACC, n.d.), or the "unauthorized use or application of an existing trademark or brand to goods that were not intended to bear the brand" (GIPC 2016, 7). Common across these definitions is the infringement of protected IP rights involving the use of trademarks or patents for a tangible product. Distinctions are also often made between counterfeiting and piracy, where pirated goods refer to either tangible or intangible goods which infringe copyrights (OECD/EUIPO 2016). Consistent with the World Trade Organization's definition of the term "counterfeit," we use the general term "counterfeiting" to refer to all types of IP infringement, including piracy. Additionally, in this chapter we classify and discuss the costs of both counterfeiting and piracy using a common framework.

While the magnitude and scope of the worldwide counterfeit problem is difficult to quantify, the OECD/EUIPO report provides an upper bound for imported counterfeit and pirated goods in international trade of almost half a trillion dollars globally ($461 billion or 2.5 percent of global imports) for 2013 (OECD/EUIPO 2016).[2] When compared to the 2008 estimates of $200 billion (1.9 percent of global imports),[3] this suggests a substantial increase in both the prevalence and magnitude of counterfeiting, a trend exacerbated with the dramatic shift to the virtual marketplace (Wilson 2017).

Counterfeiting can occur in both primary and secondary markets. When counterfeit purchases are made in the primary market—that is, when buyers are unaware that they are purchasing counterfeit goods (e.g., the purchase of UGG boots from an online vendor at a reduced price)—the IP owner immediately incurs losses of revenue from customers who believe they are purchasing genuine products. In addition, the inferior quality of counterfeit products is detrimental to a firm's brand image and can lead to increases in warranty costs. Counterfeiting in secondary markets—that is, when buyers knowingly purchase counterfeit products (e.g., purchasing a Rolex watch on the streets of New York City)—may not appear to affect legitimate sales. However, these secondary markets can expand over time, resulting in long-term consequences for the IP owner. Counterfeiting continues to expand into new industries and products, such as wine, fine art, and cutlery, creating new challenges for brands. A particular concern is when counterfeit products pose health and safety risks to consumers who either intentionally or unintentionally purchase and use counterfeit products. For instance,

> counterfeit automotive parts are often of very poor quality and lead to failure, fake batteries and chargers may explode or catch fire, counterfeit clothes and alcohol contain excessive levels of dangerous chemicals, and fake toys may contain hazardous and prohibited chemicals. In addition, counterfeit medicines may be composed of dangerous or contaminated substances and sometimes do not even contain an active ingredient. (GIPC 2016, 5)

Societal costs to product counterfeiting are also significant. Counterfeiting not only undermines investments in innovation, reduces tax revenues, and results in job losses, it also undermines, aids, and abets organized crime and even poses a risk to national security when it involves the defense supply chain (Heinonen and Wilson 2012; Wilson and Kinghorn 2015). As Warren MacInnis, Director of Global Security & Brand Protection at Underwriters Laboratories, notes, "Make no mistake: the trade in counterfeit products is a clear, persistent, and direct threat to our economies, businesses, and the health and welfare of consumers all around the world" (Wilson 2015, 13).

Given the magnitude of the counterfeiting problem, and the significant individual, organizational, and societal costs, it is the general sentiment among industry experts that more needs to be done (see, for example, comments from industry experts in Wilson (2015)). The problem, however, is in identifying where resources should be expended. While industry associations (e.g., IACC), governmental entities (e.g., OECD, Interpol), and for-profit service organizations (e.g., MarkMonitor, Security Executive Council, Underwriters Laboratories) provide insight and research into technology-based product counterfeiting solutions, individual brand owners are primarily tasked with determining the magnitude of resources to devote to product protection and, perhaps more importantly, deciding how to allocate those resources across various activities to prevent product counterfeiting and pursue legal and financial remedies when counterfeiting is discovered.

Brand protection resource allocation decisions are difficult to make because of challenges associated with measuring their financial and nonfinancial impact. A challenge with traditional return on investment (ROI) calculations is that they often focus on returns in the current period, which tends to understate ROI when investments are expected to yield benefits over multiple periods. Further, the measurement challenges, and the corresponding strategies, are different depending on the type of IP infringement (e.g., product counterfeiting vs. license infringement). Not unlike investments in other intangible assets such as quality, information technology, human capital, and advertising and marketing, an impediment to effective decision-making lies in evaluating the returns to these investments. As these challenges primarily relate to a problem of cost/benefit measurement, we seek to use a cost analysis lens to shed light on the problem. More specifically, we apply concepts from the Cost of Quality (CoQ) literature to counterfeiting and use these concepts to provide insights into the nature of anti-counterfeiting investments and the returns to these investments. We use the CoQ framework to shed light on how firms can best invest in anti-counterfeiting activities and dynamically assess their relative impact. In doing so, we seek to shift the narrative from a focus on whether or not investments in brand protection are "worth it" from an ROI standpoint to a focus on how best to allocate product protection resources across various activities, and how those allocations might vary across settings and through time.

Accordingly, the CoQ framework aligns closely with a total business solution. Specifically, by understanding the types of costs and their relationships, as well as the characteristics of those costs, firms can be better positioned to detect and prevent counterfeiting and IP infringement. This chapter specifically relates to three of the operational principles outlined by Wilson and Grammich (2020). First, the use of the CoQ framework can help brands to emphasize prevention, proactivity, and strategy. With an understanding of the different types of costs and their characteristics, managers can be better equipped to develop and communicate strategies that focus on prevention. Second, the CoQ framework can help managers in using performance metrics and data analysis to assess and mitigate risk. While there are many measurement challenges associated with counterfeiting, understanding how different costs behave and how they influence other types of cost can facilitate resource allocation decisions and guide the development of metrics. The CoQ framework further highlights that investments are expected to yield benefits over multiple periods, so focusing only on the current period understates ROI estimates. Third, the dynamic feedback effects in the CoQ framework highlight the importance of continuous improvement and learning. Further, investments in anti-counterfeiting activities can have positive feedback effects in reducing future counterfeiting. Considering the dynamic nature of counterfeiting activities, it is important for managers to recognize how current costs and investments influence future outcomes and related metrics.

2.   MEAUREMENT CHALLENGES ASSOCIATED WITH COUNTERFEITING

In contrast to research examining the measurement of other intangible investments, a review of academic business research reveals very little empirical research that attempts to measure counterfeiting and its related costs. This is likely due in large part to a lack of data. As counterfeiting is a criminal activity, data on the extent and magnitude of counterfeiting are difficult to collect. Most estimates of the magnitude of national and global counterfeiting rely heavily on assumptions and estimation, and estimates can be very sensitive to how data are collected and what assumptions are incorporated into measures (US GAO 2010, 2013; Wilson and Sullivan 2016). Estimates of counterfeiting are further complicated by the evolving nature of counterfeiting activities as counterfeiters continually adapt to avoid detection and apprehension.

Firms likewise cannot accurately assess the magnitude and extent of counterfeiting of their products, and it is even more difficult to assess their potential lost sales, damage to their brand image, and health and safety impacts for their customers. Further, firms face an investment decision with respect to their anti-counterfeiting efforts. Firms have many investment opportunities, and it can be difficult to support the use of funds for anti-counterfeiting efforts when the very nature of the activity makes it difficult to measure its impact. Finally, measurability is a special challenge for many (anti-)counterfeiting costs. Given that it is very difficult to assess the magnitude and costs of counterfeiting, it is even more difficult to determine the returns to anti-counterfeiting efforts. This creates an enormous challenge for firms attempting to formulate and execute an effective anti-counterfeiting strategy. Firms currently struggle with developing appropriate metrics to assess the effectiveness of their anti-counterfeiting efforts, tracing outcomes to investments, and knowing where and how much to spend on a variety of brand protection and anti-counterfeiting activities.

Brand protection and anti-counterfeiting investments pose measurement challenges similar to those for other intangible investments, such as investments in human resource development, intellectual capital, information technology, advertising and marketing, and product quality, to name just a few. Each of these other intangible investments can be measured with relatively high precision (e.g., dollars spent on a marketing campaign) but influences an outcome which can be difficult to measure (e.g., improvement in brand image from an advertisement), and even harder to tie back to the underlying investment. Much of this prior research thus focuses on intangible asset valuation from a relatively narrow ROI view of correlating easily measured investments (e.g., investments in marketing and advertising) to proxies for the hard-to-measure outcomes (e.g., increase in repeat customers as a proxy for brand image benefits). In contrast, our approach mirrors that of the CoQ literature and considers the *relative* costs and benefits of different types of resource allocation decisions and how those may change through time.

3.   THE COST OF QUALITY FRAMEWORK

CoQ models have been used since at least the 1950s (Juran 1951; Feigenbaum 1956). These models were originally created to better understand and assess the costs associated with quality problems in manufacturing products, and how to more effectively manage those costs. CoQ models provide a classification of costs relating to the prevention and appraisal of quality failures, and the costs of quality failures. CoQ models also demonstrate the tradeoffs between different categories of quality costs. Early CoQ models broadly distinguished between conformance costs and nonconformance costs. Conformance costs are incurred to prevent poor quality (because quality problems *can* occur) and can be further classified into prevention costs (incurred to prevent quality problems) and appraisal costs (incurred to identify quality problems). Nonconformance costs are incurred when quality problems *have* occurred and can be further classified into internal failure costs (quality problems have not reached the customer) and external failure costs (quality problems have reached the customer) (Albright and Roth 1992). Prior CoQ research has focused extensively on the opportunity, or "hidden," nonconformance costs related to quality (see Schiffauerova and Thomson 2006 for a review). While these can be very large in magnitude and are critical to determining the appropriate level of investment in conformance costs, they pose significant measurement challenges.

Importantly, there are also tradeoffs between the cost categories. Greater investments in prevention and appraisal should reduce failure costs. At some point, however, there may be diminishing returns to preventing quality problems, as it may not be practical to completely eliminate failure costs due to potentially prohibitive costs in achieving such a goal. The goal instead is to minimize total costs, where some failure costs may be too costly to eliminate, but up to that point additional investments in prevention and appraisal should yield returns in the form of reduced failure costs. That optimal point will vary by industry and firm, however, and depends on factors such as health and safety implications.

Over time, the static CoQ model evolved into a model that incorporated the dynamic nature of quality costs, reflecting how learning and continuous improvement affect quality investment decisions and quality outcomes. Additionally, as companies learn, their relative emphasis on conformance and nonconformance costs changes, as do their relative levels of quality failures. Thus, there is not a static equilibrium, but as companies adapt and change, and build upon previous quality improvements, the tradeoff between conformance and nonconformance costs also changes (Foster and Sjoblorm 1996; Fine 1986; Ittner 1996).[4]

4.   COST OF QUALITY MODELS APPLIED TO COUNTERFEITING

Given the measurement challenges associated with counterfeiting and anti-counterfeiting efforts, developing metrics in this area is particularly challenging. Many brand protection professionals are unable to develop precise metrics due to a lack of data and the inherent issues with measuring counterfeiting. This poses a challenge for brand protection groups in establishing the importance of their work in promoting brand value, limiting the damaging effects from counterfeiting, and providing protection for consumers. When executives require monetary metrics, such as ROI calculations, brand protection groups face additional barriers to obtaining sufficient resources to manage their efforts effectively. While there is not a perfect solution to these challenges, better models can help to highlight important cost–benefit tradeoffs and dynamic effects over time, as well as the limitations of metrics in fully capturing difficult-to-measure costs and returns. We propose that the CoQ model can be a useful tool for examining counterfeiting. In particular, we use concepts from this model to examine the investments that firms make to mitigate counterfeiting, and to assess the impact of counterfeiting. At the broadest level, we distinguish between *anti-counterfeiting* costs and *counterfeiting* costs. Anti-counterfeiting costs are incurred to prevent counterfeiting and to assess the extent of counterfeiting faced by the firm. These costs correspond to the categories of prevention costs and appraisal costs in CoQ models. Prevention costs include costs related to training customs and law enforcement officials, educating customers, and registering trademarks, as well as other costs incurred to prevent counterfeiting. Appraisal costs include costs related to monitoring online sales and conducting physical merchant audits, along with other costs incurred to identify counterfeiting. Investments in prevention and appraisal are made because counterfeiting *can* occur, and we refer to these collectively as *anti-counterfeiting* costs.

On the other hand, counterfeiting costs are incurred when actual counterfeiting has occurred, and correspond to failure costs (both internal and external) in CoQ models. The distinction between internal and external failure costs rests on whether the counterfeits have reached the customer. Internal failure costs are incurred when counterfeits exist but have not yet reached the customer, while external failure costs are incurred when counterfeits have reached the customer. Some failure costs are related to actions taken in response to counterfeiting, such as costs incurred in carrying out raids and seizures and executing website shutdowns as well as legal costs to stop counterfeiters and make recoveries. Other failure costs are not directly controlled by the firm, such as lost sales and lost brand image. Thus, failure costs are incurred because counterfeiting *has* occurred. We refer to both internal and external failure costs as *counterfeiting* costs (in contrast to *anti*-counterfeiting costs).

We provide an illustration of the CoQ model applied to counterfeiting in Figure 8.1, and we provide an overview of our classifications in Table 8.1, including examples of costs in each category. While this list is not comprehensive, we believe the costs listed represent important examples of counterfeiting and anti-counterfeiting costs, and are based on our interviews with firms.

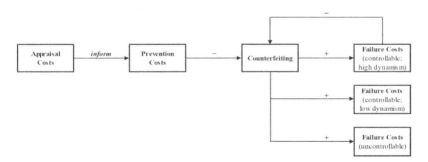

Note: Figure 8.1 provides a diagram of the CoQ categories applied to (anti-)counterfeiting costs. The figure presents the relationships between the cost categories, including the feedback effect of certain failure costs on the likelihood of counterfeiting.

Figure 8.1   *Dynamic counterfeiting and anti-counterfeiting costs*

Table 8.1   *(Anti-)counterfeiting costs classified using the Cost of Quality framework*

Category	Examples	Controllability	Dynamism	Measurability
Prevention	Identification of products at risk	High	High	Low
	Training law enforcement and customs officials	High	High	High
	Customer education	High	High	High
	Legal costs (registering trademarks and patents)	High	High	High
Appraisal	Calculation of the prevalence of counterfeit and pirated goods	High	Low	Low
	Monitoring online websites	High	High	Low
	Purchasing devices for testing potential counterfeits	High	Low	High
	Purchasing goods for testing	High	Low	High
	Physical merchant audits	High	High	High
Internal Failure	Coordination with law enforcement officials (raids, seizures, and counterfeit manufacturer shutdowns)	High	High	High
	Removal and destruction of counterfeit goods	High	Low	High
	Litigation costs (offensive)	High	High	High
External Failure	Coordination with law enforcement officials (raids, seizures, and counterfeit manufacturer shutdowns)	High	High	High
	Removal of counterfeit goods	High	Low	High
	Loss of brand image	Low	Low	Low
	Loss of sales	Low	Low	Low
	Product recalls	High	Low	High
	Customer returns and warranty claims	Low	Low	High
	Litigation costs (offensive)	High	High	High
	Litigation costs (defensive)	High	High	High

Note: Table 8.1 presents an example of (anti-)counterfeiting costs classified using the CoQ framework. For each cost, we identify whether the cost is high or low in terms of controllability, dynamism, and measurability. For controllability, we classify a cost as high if the firm can decide the cost level, independent of the actions of counterfeiters. For dynamism, we classify a cost as high if the cost is likely to have an effect on the likelihood of future counterfeiting (i.e., a feedback effect). For measurability, we classify a cost as high if the cost can be easily measured (even if associated reductions in the likelihood of future counterfeiting are difficult to measure).

Greater investments in preventing counterfeiting (anti-counterfeiting costs) should reduce the costs of counterfeiting. At some point, however, there may be diminishing returns to anti-counterfeiting investments. Just as the goal is often not to completely eliminate quality problems due to potentially prohibitive costs in achieving such a goal, it may not be practical to completely eliminate counterfeiting. The goal instead is to minimize total costs, where some counterfeiting may be too costly to eliminate, but up to that point additional investments in anti-counterfeiting should yield returns in the form of reduced counterfeiting costs.

Finally, while there are many similarities between quality costs and (anti-) counterfeiting costs, we also point out important differences. First, a critical difference between quality costs and counterfeiting costs is the controllability of the problem. With quality, while firms face quality problems if suppliers fail to deliver materials and components of adequate quality, the firm can still exert some control through contract stipulations and quality control procedures. Firms with greater vertical integration also face fewer uncontrollable quality problems and can substantially reduce their uncontrollable quality costs. With counterfeiting, however, because they are engaged in elicit and illegal activities that the firm is unaware of, counterfeiters represent an external, and largely uncontrollable, influence on costs. Thus, even with strong anti-counterfeiting efforts, firms can never completely control counterfeiting costs.

Second, the cost of counterfeiting is determined both by actions that the firm takes (to prevent and address counterfeiting) and by actions taken by counterfeiters. This multi-party setting exacerbates the dynamic nature of counterfeiting as firms attempt to design approaches to mitigate it. Both the firm and counterfeiters continually adapt and learn, often attempting to preempt each otherwhile also being forced to react accordingly. As a result, unlike efforts aimed at ensuring product quality, counterfeiting must be approached in a more strategic way by considering the potential actions and reactions of counterfeiters. What works today as a deterrent to counterfeiting may not work tomorrow once counterfeiters have adapted. Thus, the nature of anti-counterfeiting investments and the returns to these investments are constantly evolving.

Cost Characteristics

In addition to classifying (anti-)counterfeiting costs using a CoQ model, we consider additional cost characteristics which yield important insights into the nature of (anti-)counterfeiting costs. While traditional CoQ models consider the tradeoffs between prevention/appraisal and failure costs, by incorporating additional characteristics we can better understand important linkages between costs in different categories. We look at three specific characteristics in more detail below, and provide an assessment of the examples in Table 8.1 with respect to each of these cost characteristics.

Controllability

We start by incorporating the controllability of costs into our models (Feltham and Xie 1994; Demski 1976). We define controllable (anti-)counterfeiting costs as those costs whose levels are chosen by the firm. As described above, counterfeiters attempt to continually adapt to avoid detection and to continue their operations. As a result, some costs of counterfeiting are not directly controlled by the firm, as these costs arise based on the actions of counterfeiters. As shown in Table 8.1, most prevention and appraisal costs are highly controllable, but some failure costs are not controllable. However, firms can still indirectly affect uncontrollable costs by taking a proactive approach. Specifically, we find that many controllable costs have a dynamic feedback effect on the likelihood and magnitude of future counterfeiting, which we discuss next.

Dynamism

The dynamic nature of counterfeiting results in an evolving nature of (anti-)counterfeiting costs, which has implications for the metrics used to assess the effectiveness of anti-counterfeiting activities. First, investments in anti-counterfeiting reduce the likelihood of both current *and* future counterfeiting. This is important to recognize as metrics for the current year often fail to capture the long-term benefits associated with reductions in future counterfeiting. Comparing metrics across years may also result in the impression that success has decreased (e.g., fewer seizures and fewer counterfeit website shutdowns), but this may actually be due to reductions in counterfeiting. Further, success in mitigating counterfeiting may cause counterfeiters to pursue alternate approaches. Thus, while an improvement in metrics may signal improvement in some areas, it can also be suggestive of the need to continually scan the environment and invest in new areas to stay ahead of the curve and proactively address evolving counterfeiting challenges.

Second, some controllable counterfeiting costs (failure costs) that are incurred in response to actual instances of counterfeiting can also reduce the likelihood of future counterfeiting, creating a feedback effect. This is particularly pronounced for costs which are visible and send credible signals to the market (and counterfeiters) that counterfeiting the firm's products will be less profitable, or subject to higher risk. This occurs due to the dynamic nature of counterfeiting, in which the firm and counterfeiters continually adapt and learn, and the firm's responses affect both the likelihood of counterfeiting and the return to investments in anti-counterfeiting. Further, feedback effects may also contribute to the effectiveness of other investments, resulting in a multiplicative effect. These feedback effects are also illustrated in Figure 8.1.

In much the same way as the "Broken Windows Theory" of law enforcement suggests that addressing petty crimes and disorder (e.g., broken windows) prevents more serious crimes (Wilson and Kelling 1982), firms that litigate even small cases of counterfeiting provide a credible signal of increased risk for counterfeiters. That is, if the firm has the willingness and, perhaps even more importantly, the *resources* to pursue small acts of counterfeiting, they will certainly aggressively pursue more serious acts of counterfeiting.

Measurability

Finally, measurability is a special challenge for many (anti-)counterfeiting costs. The extent of counterfeiting is very difficult to assess, and thus determining the costs associated with counterfeiting is even more challenging. Of the many costs that firms identified during our interviews (described below), external failure costs were the most difficult to measure. Measurability is also closely related to controllability, as more controllable costs are also generally more easily measured.

Unfortunately, the most serious counterfeiting costs (both in terms of frequency and magnitude) are also the most difficult to measure. These are primarily external failure costs, such as lost future sales, reduction in brand image, product recalls, and litigation costs related to customer safety. Since these are not as easily measured, it is difficult to incorporate these costs in ROI calculations. However, failure to consider these potentially severe costs can undermine efforts to mitigate counterfeiting and assess the value of anti-counterfeiting efforts.

Return on Investment for Anti-Counterfeiting Investments

Investing in anti-counterfeiting activities involves resources which could be used for other purposes. While many firms recognize there is value associated with these activities, it can be difficult to establish a quantitative estimate of the ROI. Estimating an ROI metric is inherently difficult, but the additional measurement challenges associated with counterfeiting make ROI estimates even more difficult. While we cannot completely resolve these challenges, by incorporating concepts from CoQ models and the additional cost characteristics described above, we provide an approach to evaluating anti-counterfeiting investments that is more comprehensive, better captures causality, and captures dynamic effects through time.

Another challenge with traditional ROI calculations is that they often focus on returns in the current period. For investments which are expected to yield benefits over multiple periods, focusing only on the current period understates ROI estimates. Further, measuring estimated future returns is inherently difficult, but much more so with respect to counterfeiting. Another challenge is that ROI calculations tend to ignore some costs, particularly those which are difficult to measure (e.g., external failure costs). While many of these hard-to-measure costs are difficult to incorporate into quantitative calculations, by better understanding the relationships between different cost categories, firms can better understand the value of investments. Finally, investments often have a feedback or iterative effect. Thus, costs incurred in one period may not only benefit future periods, but may contribute to the effectiveness of other investments.

In terms of assessing an ROI for anti-counterfeiting efforts, we view anti-counterfeiting costs as investments to reduce counterfeiting costs, as these investments should reduce the likelihood of current and future counterfeiting. As discussed above, certain failure costs (classified as counterfeiting costs) can also have feedback effects which further reduce the likelihood of counterfeiting. Thus, from an ROI perspective, anti-counterfeiting costs (and some controllable counterfeiting costs) represent investments, while reductions in current and future counterfeiting costs and increases in recoveries represent returns.

5.   GATHERING INSIGHT FROM FIRMS

To better understand firms' anti-counterfeiting strategies, measurement challenges, and estimated returns to anti-counterfeiting investments, we conducted interviews with brand protection professionals from a variety of firms. Our initial contacts were identified through our ongoing outreach with industry. Building on these contacts, we identified a potential sample of brand protection professionals from firms across a broad range of industries. Our final sample included ten firms, each of which was a large multi-national company. This small, purposive sample was designed to provide a range of experiences and perspectives from the brand protection professionals we interviewed at each firm.

We designed an interview instrument with a blend of structured and semi-structured questions (Qu and Dumay 2011). The structured questions were designed to categorize the firm and its actions into pre-specified categories (e.g., the firm's industry and size, details about the brand protection group, categories and changes in brand protection spending, perceived success of brand protection efforts). The semi-structured questions were designed to elicit elaborated responses about (1) investments in brand protection, (2) a categorization of investments based on the CoQ framework, (3) the evaluation and reporting of brand protection effectiveness, and (4) metrics related to measuring brand protection performance. We piloted the interview instrument with two brand protection professionals from one firm, who reviewed an initial draft of the interview instrument and provided comments.[5]

In each of the ten interviews, we interviewed one or two brand protection professionals, one of which directed the brand protection group for the firm. We conducted the interviews either in person or by phone, with at least two researchers present for each interview. Each interview lasted between 60 and 120 minutes. We used the interview questions flexibly and asked additional questions to follow up on the brand protection professionals' responses. We took notes during each of the interviews, which we later used to code the structured questions, and to identify themes and insights from the semi-structured questions.

We recognize there are limitations to the data we collected through our interviews. We have a small, nonrandom sample of firms that was developed based on existing partnerships with brand protection professionals. As a result, our data and inferences may not generalize to other firms, particularly much smaller firms. Nevertheless, brand protection professionals working at the firms in our sample have strong experience with brand protection and anti-counterfeiting, and these firms represent a wide range of industries, operating in multiple markets and countries. We also interviewed only one or two brand protection professionals at each firm, and other professionals at the firms may have provided different responses. However, in each case, we interviewed the director of the firm's brand protection group, who was well qualified to respond to our questions.

6.   FIRM EXPERIENCE AND LESSONS

Overview of Participating Firms

To preserve the anonymity of the firms that participated in our interviews, we use broad industry classifications. Specifically, we classify firms into one of three broad groups of industries: (1) apparel, luxury, and consumer products, (2) microelectronics and computer products, or (3) food, agricultural, and pharmaceutical products. Table 8.2 provides descriptive statistics based on these industry classifications. Our final sample has three firms in the apparel, luxury, and consumer products industries, three firms in the microelectronics and computer products industries, and four firms in the food, agricultural, and pharmaceutical products industries.

The number of employees at these firms ranged from 1,500 to 120,000 individuals, and annual sales ranged from $1 billion to $70 billion. An important difference among firms was the number of distinct brands. Some firms only had a single brand, while others had more than 1,000 different brands. For firms with multiple brands, we found that they tended to focus their brand protection efforts on brands with the highest sales, products with the greatest susceptibility to counterfeiting, or products which posed the greatest risks

Table 8.2   Brand protection spending by Cost of Quality category (by industry grouping)

Industry	Number of Sample Firms	Average Number of Brand Protection Employees	Spending by CoQ Category			
			Prevention (%)	Appraisal (%)	Internal Failure (%)	External Failure (%)
Food, Agricultural, and Pharmaceutical Products	4	20	33	43	5	19
Microelectronics and Computer Products	3	29	49	27	17	7
Apparel, Luxury, and Consumer Products	3	8	12	8	38	43

Note: Table 8.2 presents average brand protection spending by CoQ category using broad industry classifications. The number of sample firms and average number of brand protection employees are presented for each industry classification. The average spending by CoQ category is based on the percentage allocations determined by each respondent, averaged within each industry classification (each row sums to 100 percent, with minor differences due to rounding).

to consumers if counterfeited. Most firms had a formal brand protection or IP protection group (9 of 10 respondents, or 90 percent). The smallest brand protection group had two employees, while the largest had fifty.

Respondents indicated there are important differences between different types of IP infringement in terms of measurement, impact, and mitigation approaches. In particular, counterfeiting (of tangible products) differed from piracy (of intangible products, such as licenses), as discussed previously. Among the firms we interviewed, counterfeiting was the primary concern, as most of these firms produced tangible products. For the purposes of our discussion, we consider both of these together, particularly as investments in brand protection for both counterfeiting and piracy are classified in the CoQ framework in the same way.

The Cost of Quality Framework and Resource Allocation

While our interviews covered many topics, for the purposes of this chapter, we focus on responses pertaining to the CoQ framework and how brand protection groups allocate resources across cost categories. In terms of the CoQ framework, respondents sometimes classified costs into different categories depending on the nature of their products. In general, as shown in Table 8.2, we found that failure costs are much higher than prevention and appraisal costs in the apparel, luxury, and consumer products industries. Failure costs are much lower than prevention and appraisal costs in the food, agricultural, and pharmaceutical products industries and the microelectronics and computer products industries. We found that respondents provided more examples of prevention and appraisal costs. Below we describe some of the specific costs incurred by brand protection groups, how these costs were classified, and insights we gleaned from our interviews.

Respondents described a number of costs which they classified as preventative. First, firms often had contractual safeguards in place with suppliers and invested in building supplier relations to maintain supply chain integrity. Second, many respondents discussed the importance of consumer education. They sought to make consumers aware of counterfeit products and promoted the benefits of purchasing legitimate products. Third, many firms provided training to law enforcement and customs officials. This was generally viewed as a relatively low-cost investment which yielded valuable benefits in terms of future seizures and other actions by law enforcement and customs officials. Fourth, many firms incurred legal costs related to registering trademarks and logos, not only in the United States, but in other countries. Finally, many firms built security features into their products to ensure that the products were not counterfeited or otherwise illicitly copied and distributed. These were usually recorded as product costs and were incorporated into the design cost of the product. As a result, these costs were often not included in the budgets of the brand protection groups.

Interestingly, many of our respondents focused on the appraisal of counterfeiting. Monitoring was commonly employed by brand protection groups, and was a major driver in determining the allocation of resources across different anti-counterfeiting activities, based on an assessment of the frequency and severity of identified risks. Monitoring took a variety of forms, including scanning for counterfeit websites, monitoring physical retailers, and monitoring the supply chain. Some firms also conducted market-based surveys and used other intelligence tools. In many ways, appraisal was viewed as the most fundamental aspect of brand protection, and was used to determine the strategies and approaches to follow and how to invest resources.

In terms of internal and external failure costs, the most common cost described by respondents was the use of investigations and litigation, but these were also often viewed as preventative. Many costs that might normally be classified as external failure costs were viewed by the firms as preventative. This is consistent with our earlier discussion of the dynamic nature of investments, as many controllable failure costs have a subsequent preventative effect, and may thus be classified as prevention costs as well. Importantly, the magnitude of failure costs can be much higher than that of prevention and appraisal costs. Some of the less tangible costs, such as lost sales and damage to brand image, were not explicitly mentioned in all our interviews, but were often alluded to as part of the overarching challenge associated with counterfeiting and developing metrics associated with brand protection.

Finally, we also found important differences across firms and industries in whether brand protection is viewed as a cost or profit center. One factor that influenced this classification was whether a brand protection group was able to convert consumers of counterfeit products into consumers of legitimate products. An important point from our interviews is that the emphasis of spending depends on the potential benefit of the investment, not the cost (some very inexpensive actions can be very effective). Thus, subsequent reductions in counterfeiting and other benefits should guide where and how firms invest to maximize the return on their brand protection investments.

7.   CONCLUSION

Brand protection resource allocation decisions are difficult to make because of the challenges associated with measuring their financial and nonfinancial impact. In this chapter, we apply concepts from the Cost of Quality (CoQ) literature to counterfeiting and use these concepts to provide insights into how firms can best invest in anti-counterfeiting activities and dynamically assess their relative impact. We also provide insights from interviews with brand protection professionals at large multi-national firms about how firms in different industries are allocating resources in response to counterfeiting.

We recognize there are substantial limitations and measurement challenges in developing precise metrics regarding the returns to anti-counterfeiting activities. This is especially challenging for brand protection groups in obtaining resources to protect brand value, limit the damaging effects from counterfeiting, and protect consumers. We also recognize that metrics will vary depending on the type of IP infringement, as actions and metrics designed to combat product counterfeiting will differ from those designed to address licensing infringement. While there is not a perfect solution to these challenges, we show how the CoQ model can help to highlight important cost–benefit tradeoffs and dynamic effects over time, as well as the limitations of metrics in fully capturing difficult-to-measure costs and returns.

As the nature of counterfeiting costs is similar to that of quality costs, we find that the CoQ model is a very useful tool for examining counterfeiting. We use these concepts to examine the investments that firms make to address counterfeiting, and to assess the impact of counterfeiting. While we cannot completely resolve existing measurement challenges, by using concepts from the CoQ model and incorporating additional cost characteristics we provide an approach to evaluating anti-counterfeiting investments that is more comprehensive, better captures causality, and captures dynamic effects through time. This model aligns closely with a total business solution, and by understanding the types of costs and their relationships, as well as the characteristics of those costs, firms can be better positioned to detect and prevent counterfeiting and IP infringement.

NOTES

1. We thank the brand protection professionals that graciously participated in our interviews. We thank Cliff Grammich for his assistance in data collection. This research was supported by a gift from Dolby.
2. These estimates were generated using global data on customs seizures of counterfeit and pirated products from 2011 to 2013 (OECD/EUIPO 2016). Note that these estimates do not include counterfeit and pirated goods produced and consumed domestically or online piracy. Including domestic production and digital piracy, the magnitude of counterfeiting and piracy could be as high as $1.13 trillion, potentially rising to $2.81 trillion by 2022 (Frontier Economics 2017).
3. There are some differences in the data and estimation methods between the 2008 and 2013 estimates.
4. As an example, based on the quality costs reported by a sample of 49 manufacturing units in 21 companies, Ittner (1996, 114) finds "ongoing reductions in nonconformance costs while maintaining or reducing reported prevention and appraisal costs. These findings are consistent with recent quality-based learning and continuous improvement models that suggest that, once an effective quality program is established, companies can reduce nonconformance costs over time with little or no subsequent increase in conformance expenditures."
5. These brand protection professionals were part of our final sample, as the professionals subsequently participated in an interview and responded to the final set of questions.

REFERENCES

Albright, T. L., and H. P. Roth. 1992. The measurement of quality costs: An alternative paradigm. *Accounting Horizons* 6(2), 15–27.

Demski, J. S. 1976. Uncertainty and evaluation based on controllable performance. *Journal of Accounting Research* 14(2), 230–245.

Feigenbaum, A. V. 1956. Total quality control. *Harvard Business Review* 34(6), 93–101.

Feltham, G., and J. Xie. 1994. Performance measure congruity and diversity in multi-task principal/agent relations. *The Accounting Review* 69(3), 429–453.

Fine, C. H. 1986. Quality improvement and learning in productive systems. *Management Science* 32(10), 1301–1315.

Foster, G., and L. Sjoblom. 1996. Quality improvement drivers in the electronics industry. *Journal of Management Accounting Research* 8, 55–86.

Frontier Economics. 2017. *The Economic Impacts of Counterfeiting and Piracy: Report Prepared for BASCAP and INTA*. https://www.inta.org/Communications/Documents/2017_Frontier_Report.pdf.

Global Intellectual Property Center (GIPC). 2016. *Measuring the Magnitude of Global Counterfeiting: Creation of a Contemporary Global Measure of Physical Counterfeiting*. US Chamber of Commerce. http://www.theglobalipcenter.com/wp -content/themes/gipc/map-index/assets/pdf/2016/GlobalCounterfeiting_Report.pdf.

Heinonen, J. A., and J. M. Wilson. 2012. Product counterfeiting at the state level: An empirical examination of Michigan-related incidents. *International Journal of Comparative and Applied Criminal Justice* 36(4), 273–290.

International AntiCounterfeiting Coalition (IACC). n.d. What is counterfeiting? http://www.iacc.org/resources/about/what-is-counterfeiting.

Ittner, C. D. 1996. Exploratory evidence on the behavior of quality costs. *Operations Research* 44(1), 114–130.

Juran, J. M. 1951. *Quality Control Handbook*. New York: McGraw-Hill.

Organisation for Economic Co-operation and Development/European Union Intellectual Property Office (OECD/EUIPO). 2016. *Trade in Counterfeit and Pirated Goods: Mapping the Economic Impact*. Paris: OECD Publishing. http://dx.doi.org/10.1787/9789264252653-en.

Qu, S. Q., and J. Dumay. 2011. The qualitative research interview. *Qualitative Research in Accounting and Management* 8(3), 238–264.

Schiffauerova, A., and V. Thomson. 2006. A review of research on cost of quality models and best practices. *International Journal of Quality and Reliability Management* 23(6), 647–669.

US Government Accountability Office (US GAO). 2010. *Intellectual Property: Observations on Efforts to Quantify the Economic Effects of Counterfeit and Pirated Goods*. http://www.gao.gov/new.items/d10423.pdf.

US Government Accountability Office (US GAO). 2013. *Intellectual Property: Insights Gained from Efforts to Quantify the Effects of Counterfeit and Pirated Goods in the U.S. Economy*. http://www.gao.gov/assets/660/655781.pdf.

Wilson, J. M. 2015. Brand protection 2020: Perspectives on the issues shaping the global risk and response to product counterfeiting. Center for Anti-Counterfeiting and Product Protection Paper Series. East Lansing, MI: Michigan State University.

Wilson, J. M. 2017. The future of brand protection: Responding to the global risk. *Journal of Brand Management* 24(3), 271–283.

Wilson, J. M., and C. A. Grammich. 2020. Brand protection across the enterprise: Toward a total-business solution. *Business Horizons* 63, 363–376.

Wilson, J. M., and R. Kinghorn. 2015. The global risk of product counterfeiting: Facilitators of the criminal opportunity. Center for Anti-Counterfeiting and Product Protection Backgrounder Series. East Lansing, MI: Michigan State University.

Wilson, J. M., and B. A. Sullivan. 2016. Brand owner approaches to assessing the risk of product counterfeiting. *Journal of Brand Management* 23(3), 327–344.

Wilson, J. Q., and G. L. Kelling. 1982. Broken windows: The police and neighborhood safety. The Atlantic, March. https://www.theatlantic.com/magazine/archive/1982/03/broken-windows/304465/.

9. Performance measurement for brand protection: a strategic scorecard approach

Sean O'Hearen

"What gets measured gets done." (Accepted wisdom)

"Not everything that can be counted counts, and not everything that counts can be counted." (Albert Einstein)

INTRODUCTION

Leading a "cost center" can be a challenge.[1] Leading a cost center that deals with risk and uncertainty is even more difficult. One must constantly battle for resources, do more with less, and justify one's existence to get the job done. And the cost center manager rarely gets all the budget she requests, which means having to drop some promising initiatives from the plan. Most brand protection practitioners can probably relate to some version of this ongoing resource challenge (who are those lucky few with all the budget they need?). Winning or losing this battle often boils down to a question of how to measure value and return on investment (ROI), which has been a hot topic in brand protection circles in recent years.

Profit center managers, on the other hand, have it relatively easy.[2] They employ well-established metrics, key performance indicators (KPIs), and standard methodologies to report profit and loss, operating efficiencies, customer satisfaction, and other metrics deemed relevant and essential to their strategy. Typically, managers compile the data and report progress to bosses via some version of a balanced scorecard (Kaplan, 1996), which succinctly displays all essential KPIs and targets. As experienced businesspeople, all concerned then readily absorb and understand the meaning and implications of the data shown. Decisions then get made. Resources get allocated. Goals are achieved.

Unfortunately, in the brand protection business it's not that easy. The path from investment to clear representation of value and ROI presents many challenges. The biggest, of course, is uncertainty related to illicit trade. A brand protection practitioner can never answer unequivocally the main business question of "What's the size of the problem?" This naturally leads to a question of what level of resources is required to fix an unknowable problem. Another challenge concerns the fact that significant value is gained from brand protection efforts when nothing happens—that is, no counterfeits have been detected. Thus, unexpected, incremental costs related to responsive actions or field actions are avoided, as is potential damage to reputation and customer trust that can accrue from these events. Also vexing is the question of what it means when counterfeit detections are increasing versus decreasing. Business minds react positively to trend lines showing growth, and a brand practitioner will certainly be pleased to report that, for example, the value recovered from raids and seizures of counterfeit products has been increasing. Perhaps a new high has even been achieved for the last 12-month period. But wait, wouldn't the business prefer the counterfeit trend line and need for raids to be decreasing, evidencing that the problem is being mitigated? Different practitioners may interpret these observations differently. On top of these challenges, and despite a lot of attention having been paid to the topic, there remains no widely adopted, industry standard way for valuing brand protection activities and outcomes (Wilson, Grammich, and Chan, 2016).

One other point that must be highlighted concerns the challenge of educating business leaders/decision makers about how, given the aforementioned difficulties, brand protection programs do actually deliver value to the business and its customers. After all, business leaders are paid to be experts in legitimate trade and business practices. Counterfeiting, grey markets, and the world of dark commerce and criminal opportunists is not, in most cases, their bailiwick. This makes regular stakeholder engagement and "solutions selling" an important factor for success.

Given these valuation and communication challenges inherent in the brand protection discipline, this chapter offers some ideas about how practitioners can shed their "cost center" image and be viewed by business leaders as centers for value creation and protection. Taking a page from our profit center friends, we consider what a balanced scorecard type of approach for brand protection could look like, and how that can be applied in practice to inform and educate decision makers, and effectively make the business case for brand protection.

The balanced scorecard has become a widely accepted framework for performance measurement and management in business. The original notion was that traditional approaches for performance measurement were too narrowly focused on financial measures and did not account for key non-financial drivers of organizational performance. Thus, balance was introduced by adding additional perspectives: customers, internal processes, and innovation and learning. Importantly, measures chosen for inclusion in the scorecard had to be linked to an organization's mission and strategy and be rigorously vetted and prioritized, so that only the essential ones—the key performance indicators (KPIs)—appeared on the scorecard. By applying this approach, businesses could distill a comprehensive set of KPIs that enabled clarity and alignment among managers and employees. In theory, this would lead to improved organizational performance and the achievement of goals and objectives.

As with the traditional business focus on financial measures, research into performance measurement for brand protection suggests that current practices may be too narrowly focused on response and enforcement metrics, including results from raids and seizures, site takedowns, arrests, and other stock-in-trade activities. Results of these actions are important, no doubt, but they don't always translate well for business decision makers who are seeking to understand the bigger picture of how brand protection is delivering value and supporting the organization's strategic goal attainment.

What follows is a proposal for what a comprehensive performance measurement and management system (PMMS) for brand protection—a balanced scorecard—could look like. Consistent with both the balanced scorecard and Total Business Solution approaches, which dovetail nicely, we take a holistic view and identify KPIs on both the preventive and responsive sides of the ledger. The scorecard perspectives for brand protection are necessarily different from those for general business in most respects—we're not transforming raw materials into finished goods after all. What we chiefly borrow from Kaplan, author of *The Balanced Scorecard*, is the idea of having balance and multiple perspectives in the framework. The result is a multi-dimensional management and reporting tool—a basket of measures—that can help drive performance and better communicate the value of brand protection to senior leaders.

While choices about what KPIs to include or exclude are based on practical, real-world experience, this scorecard should be considered a hypothetical example from the healthcare industry. It serves as an explanatory case based on a hypothetical, multi-national healthcare company, with significant and persistent exposure to illicit trade risk and a well-established and sufficiently funded global brand protection program. The goal is to proffer a reasonable framework and starting point that can be modified according to the needs of one's own industry, organization, and brand protection program.

DESIGN OF PERFORMANCE MEASUREMENT AND MANAGEMENT SYSTEM AND SCORECARD FOR BRAND PROTECTION

The objective of any risk management program is the creation and protection of value. In the case of brand protection for a safety-critical industry like healthcare, the valuable assets at risk include brand equity, business reputation, revenue, and market share, and, of course, patient/consumer health, safety, and trust. These are inarguably the crown jewels of any organization. The primary job of the brand protection lead is to advise the business about whether risk related to counterfeiting, grey markets/diversion, or product tampering has the potential to disrupt or jeopardize the attainment of the business's objectives or negatively impact its most valuable assets. Where the line is drawn about what level of risk is acceptable versus what needs to be addressed is subjective, and each business will apply its own calculus. In advising the business, brand protection must make the risk picture as clear as possible based on the best available information, provide options for mitigating and controlling the risk, and then make recommendations tied to results and estimated valuation/ROI. Then, it is up to a business leader to decide what to do and what resources to commit to the effort. Thus, the brand protection scorecard should be designed to support this decision-making process on an ongoing basis. Once a program has been established, the scorecard should communicate the status and effectiveness of the chosen strategy, mitigations, and controls.

Target Audience

Because the main goal is to help business stakeholders make informed and intelligent decisions about illicit trade risk, the scorecard is designed with that audience in mind. Of course, it can and should be used as a performance management tool for the brand protection team, but the primary audience consists of internal stakeholders/decision makers. The metrics chosen are at a high level and all can be fairly easily explained to a general business audience without prior brand protection knowledge or experience. We also deliberately use relatable business terminology for KPIs, such as "Sales Loss Exposure (SLE)," "Total Value Recovery (TVR)," and ROI.[3] Initially, these metrics may require more explanation than others to establish understanding, but in our experience, and with the support of Finance, as mentioned below, they readily gain acceptance.

Link to Strategy

Perhaps the most important aspect of the balanced scorecard approach is how it links to mission and strategy. The scorecard measures selected must be indicators of progress against goals and objectives that have been set forth in the brand protection team's strategy. And that strategy should also cascade from and align with the business's strategy. It's important for the head of brand protection to be able to demonstrate and articulate this linkage between brand protection strategy and business strategy, and how the brand protection team is supporting the attainment of the business's objectives. The worst case would be for brand protection to be perceived by management as operating in a silo, racking up enforcement points, let's say, but having no apparent connection to the overall business strategy and priorities.

Strategies vary across industries and between businesses in the same industry, but strategies for brand protection tend to comprise three or four major themes. To illustrate our case, we will assume our brand protection strategy includes the following four primary objectives:

1. *Disrupting the Illicit Supply Chain*—This involves activities to detect and disrupt the illicit supply chain, including monitoring, intelligence gathering, forensic analysis, and investigation and enforcement.
2. *Strengthening Supply Chain Security*—This involves activities undertaken to improve the security of the end-to-end supply chain, including conducting assessments, deploying product security technologies, conducting audits of control measures, and communicating to stakeholders.
3. *Partnering and Influencing to Protect*—Internal and external collaboration are essential for effective brand protection, including developing and managing relationships with cross-functional partners, suppliers, government agencies, law enforcement, trade associations, and other parties.
4. *Executing and Building Capabilities*—These are activities related to operational excellence for the team, including effective management (of people, budget, resources, initiatives, etc.), continual improvement, and innovating to build future capabilities.

The detailed strategic and operational plans that follow from these four primary objectives—sometimes called strategic pillars—will consist of various programs, projects, and tactics, and their associated goals and measures, all designed to achieve the mission and strategic objectives.

Benefits

Building a performance measurement and management system (PMMS) and scorecard offers many benefits for brand protection teams. In addition to being a tool used to support decision making and create awareness and understanding among stakeholders, the scorecard has other important benefits. It:

1. Provides clarity and alignment across the brand protection team as to how performance will be measured and how those measures link to strategy.
2. Makes results visible across the team and promotes accountability for achieving them.
3. Helps drive performance and improve overall management of the team.

4. Enables managers to make timely adjustments to plans and revise expectations with stakeholders, if necessary, if goals are not being met according to plan, or if a goal has been met ahead of schedule.
5. Provides data to regularly assess what's working and what's not—a strategic feedback loop—and adjust priorities and resources, as needed.

Scorecard Perspectives

Based on our hypothetical brand protection strategy above (for healthcare) and applying a balanced scorecard type of framework and approach, we have constructed a scorecard composed of three perspectives. Each perspective includes a logical grouping of performance measures and/or data points linked to one or more of the strategic objectives. These measures include both outputs and outcomes from various brand protection inputs and activities. The three perspectives, which are explained in further detail in the next section, are as follows:

1. *Total Program Perspective*—These are the highest-level measures that quickly convey the current risk picture and the overall value the program is delivering.
2. *Program Execution Perspective*—These measures include outputs from core tactical programs and activities that support the strategy and drive overall performance. The measures are grouped into offensive actions and defensive actions.
3. *Operating Excellence Perspective*—These measures include those related to brand protection team management, collaboration, and capability building.

Together, these three perspectives and their associated measures give a balanced view of topline results, core program activities that are contributing to those results, and key operational measures. In a reasonably succinct package, the scorecard allows a brand protection manager to tell a coherent and compelling story that covers results/KPIs for value and risk and provides a holistic view of the group's operations. Importantly, the scorecard also supports a Total Business Solution approach to brand protection by linking to strategy and including measures that account for cross-functional collaboration and integration of best practices.

An important perspective that is not represented in this scorecard concerns how brand protection is deployed for specific, at-risk brands. That is, each brand may have a strategy tailored to its unique risk and incident profile, including a select mix of mitigation tactics and control measures, and resources allocated to it depending on the priority assigned to it by the business. Since this is a hypothetical case, we chose to represent only the total programmatic/ capabilities view of the department's activities, inclusive of all the brands it protects. While we didn't drill down to the brand level here, this perspective should be considered as you create your own scorecard. The idea would be to show the prioritized, at-risk brands, along with any tactics and resources deployed for their protection. The KPIs, targets, and results reported would correspond to the tactics used.

Speaking of drilling down, in our proposed scorecard, each measure, such as Value Recovery, or program, such as market monitoring (with multiple measures), may have additional contributing or underlying measures, data points, or important information associated with it—in some cases much more. By all means, managers should build underlying data dashboards or scorecards to show greater detail and track specific measures and/or programs as completely as necessary. These would be part of the overall PMMS and be used by members of the brand protection team to manage accordingly. In the event a stakeholder needed a deeper dive on a particular program or measure, they could be referenced for that purpose too.

Selected Measures

Consistent with a balanced scorecard approach, measures we chose for this scorecard are at the highest level. We methodically selected those measures/ KPIs that we judged to be the best indicators of progress and performance linked to the generic strategy that we outlined, along with factoring in some standard operational measures (e.g., budget, project management office, people, innovation) that could apply to any functional area. Depending on your strategy, the selected measures and design of your own scorecard may look different.

In the next section, we specify and give a brief explanation for each of the measures selected (What is it? and Why is it important?). Practitioners will be familiar with most of them, though a few are likely novel approaches stemming from a Total Business Solution philosophy, such as a measure for "Best Practice Integration," for example. In most cases, how these measures are derived is easily explained. However, two of the most important KPIs, "Value Recovery" and "Sales Loss Exposure," involve multiple factors, assumptions, and relatively complex calculations, which are beyond the scope of this chapter. We do provide a detailed summary to ensure the reader understands their basic meaning and importance to the scorecard, but we do not provide detailed computational instructions.

On that note, concerning the more complex calculations, it is highly recommended that you engage your Finance and/or corporate risk partner as you develop your models and processes for valuation and risk quantification.

These partners possess the mathematical training, business logic, and acumen to support development of these types of models and can help both guide and challenge the necessary assumptions and estimates. They may also have models already in use within the organization that can be leveraged, such as those used to assess risk in other areas of the business. Ultimately, the goal and best practice would be for the Chief Finance Officer or Chief Risk Officer to validate and sign off on the KPIs and how they are calculated. Taking this important step shows the brand protection team's alignment with key business stakeholders and imparts confidence and credibility in the measures.

Targets and Forecasts

The practice of associating a target with each selected measure is fundamental to a PMMS and scorecard. However, as mentioned in the introduction to this chapter, this poses some challenges for brand protection practitioners. The uncertainty inherent in illicit trade and numerous factors outside of one's control are the main culprits in not being able to assign a target in every case. For those measures where a target does make sense, generally speaking, one would be wise to take a conservative approach—for example, setting a range within which the result is likely to fall—and also keep in mind the old forecasting mantra, "under-promise and over-deliver." This, again, owing to factors outside of one's control. Of course, it's easier to set a target and forecast when you have baseline data and some program history to work with. But when you're first launching a brand protection program or a new capability/tactic, you may need to initially forgo setting a target altogether, or seek advice from fellow practitioners, suppliers, or consultants who have had experience with the matter.

Data Management

The approximately 50 data points in our example healthcare brand protection scorecard would be derived from multiple information sources, such as databases, spreadsheets, open-source intelligence/data, and various business applications and corporate data repositories. Ensuring data quality and managing how all that data is ingested, stored, compiled, maintained, and made accessible to the brand protection team for reporting purposes is obviously a complex undertaking and a critical part of the overall process. We leave these endeavors up to the experts in IT/IS and data management and will not be delving into the subject here, but there are some important considerations to keep in mind as you work with your IT support services to define your use cases and set up your data management and reporting system:

1. *One Source of Truth*—Incident data typically comes from multiple sources, including QMS (Quality Management Systems), market monitoring, investigative services, employees, and so on. Compiling all incident data into one database (and data structure) accessible by all those involved in brand protection work is vital to coordination, alignment, and consistent reporting.
2. *Data Assets*—Understanding what data assets are available inside and outside your organization and how those assets may be applicable to your brand protection KPIs and scorecard is important as you develop your system. For example, calculating Sales Loss Exposure and quantifying risk requires access to commercial and supply chain data that may or may not be readily available to you.
3. *Process Automation*—Data collection, cleansing, and analysis can be a tedious and time-consuming task. Excellent software tools are available today to automate data and analytics processes. Whenever possible, leverage these tools for efficiency and to reduce the time it takes to gain actionable insights, make decisions, and deliver value.
4. *Data Visualization*—As with process automation tools, excellent and easy-to-use software tools for data visualization are also becoming standard for presenting business data and intelligence. These tools produce excellent graphical representations of data and enable presenters to drill down into data sets in real time.
5. *Keep It Simple*—This age-old design principle is especially important to keep in mind as you consider what measures to include in your scorecard and how easy or hard it is to obtain and maintain the data needed for your report. Strive for simplicity and efficiency whenever possible.

Stakeholder Engagement

Once designed and built, the scorecard becomes a centerpiece for communications with stakeholders and a vehicle for brand protection performance management. The brand protection leader should have regular engagement with key stakeholders based on the needs of the business and the prevailing risk picture—let's assume quarterly meetings in our case. Armed with a well-designed and strategically aligned scorecard, brand protection will be prepared to consistently tell its story and relay the status of its program, including the current risk situation and the value it is delivering to the business.

As the brand protection team covers each perspective, program area, and/ or measure, it can address key questions, elicit feedback, and build a narrative toward any decisions that need to be made—for example, an ask for additional resources. The team can describe what's working, what's not; set expectations based on current progress toward goals; highlight where more (or less) resources are needed; discuss whether resources are allocated in the best way possible; and overview what adjustments need to be made as the risk picture changes, as it inevitably does. Essentially, the scorecard becomes a tool to drive the conversation, discuss what is actionable, and dive deeper, if necessary, into various program areas to further inform, educate, and/or problem solve.

As a practical matter, time with key stakeholders is usually limited, and the higher up the org chart a person is, the less time you will likely have. By concentrating on what's most important and impactful, the scorecard's design helps manage this challenge by enabling the presenter to deliver a clear and concise message. For example, in a short meeting, the brand protection leader could choose to focus mainly on the Total Program Perspective measures, which are top line indicators, and then touch on one or two other key areas from the Program Execution and/or Operating Excellence perspectives that are noteworthy or in need of attention. Once the base scorecard and KPIs are defined, what gets presented can be tailored to the needs of the audience and/or the brand protection team's agenda. The scorecard becomes the constant messaging tool and focal point that business presentations can revolve around.

Now let's learn what is in our balanced scorecard.

BALANCED SCORECARD COMPONENTS

Total Program Perspective

The first section of the scorecard includes the most important program measures—the "headline measures," you might call them. These measures quickly convey both value and risk at a high level. In a business scorecard, these would be the financial measures (revenue, expense, net margin, profit margin, etc.). These data points answer questions and enable conversation about the following:

1. What value is the program delivering? (Total Program Value Recovery and Patients Protected)
2. What is the size of the problem? (Sales Loss Exposure)
3. Is the problem getting better or worse? (Incident Trends and Sales Loss Exposure)
4. Are we using resources efficiently and effectively to combat the problem? (Program ROI)

Going back to the earlier point about how much time you have with a business leader, if you only have 30 minutes, as an example, this section answers key business questions and provides a good synopsis for how the team is performing. It also frames a discussion for diving deeper into any other areas of concern or opportunity, or, if necessary, sets up an ask for additional resources. Perhaps the risk picture has changed, or resources have been inadequate to execute raids and seizures on known targets, thereby impacting Total Program Value Recovery (TPVR).

Total Program Value Recovery (TPVR)
What is it? TPVR aggregates *all* calculated proceeds or outcomes from brand protection activities, both soft and hard measures. The idea is to have one universal figure you can point to that accounts for the value of all reasonably computable outcomes from the variety of tactics undertaken by brand protection. Total VR for each component of TPVR is also shown in its respective area of the Program Execution Perspective in the next section.

The categories that would comprise TPVR in our hypothetical healthcare industry example are as follows:

1. *Mitigations and Controls*—Includes the estimated value of the reduction in potential illicit trade risk and loss exposure due to implementation of best practice mitigations and controls. For example, a brand protection intervention has reduced the prevalence of counterfeit product in a market by 75 percent. The value of this reduction would be calculated and tallied here. Another example: an intervention in the returned goods process has stopped the flow of counterfeit product and associated fraudulent claims. This would be valued and included here. Again, the assumptions and estimates that go into these calculations are beyond the scope of this chapter, but the idea in each case is to appropriately value the reduction or difference between the pre- and post-intervention situations.

2. *Online Enforcement*—Includes the total value of goods removed from the takedown of illicit listings across various online platforms, marketplaces, web sites, social media, and other e-commerce channels. This data is provided by the online brand protection services providers, though how the value is calculated varies depending on a brand owner's preferred methodology.

3. *Offline Enforcement*—Includes the total value of goods seized in raids and enforcement actions at physical locations, such as retail stores, warehouses, distribution centers, manufacturing sites, or Customs inspection stations. Calculations may vary depending on how finished goods versus unfinished goods and components are valued, and what price is applied in the calculation (e.g., market price versus invoice price).

4. *Legal Settlements*—Includes the total value of proceeds from court-ordered damage awards and restitution received from legal actions brought against infringers. These are hard dollar awards from legal judgments, though the proceeds may not be easy to collect owing to the nature of the criminal enterprise.

Again, we stress the need to be conservative and transparent with any estimates and assumptions, get buy-in from finance and business stakeholders, and to have a formal process for ongoing validation of TPVR calculations. This lends credibility to the data and gives assurance to stakeholders that it can be used as a reasonable basis for decision making.

Why is it important? TPVR is a critical metric because it is the best estimate of total value generated from the brand protection program and it is expressed in financial terms. It also becomes the numerator in the Program ROI ratio calculation discussed below. While its composition is unique to brand protection, it can reasonably provide a basis for comparison to value and returns derived from other business operations and investments.

Patients/consumers Protected

What is it? This metric goes straight to the main purpose of brand protection for any safety-critical product category, such as pharmaceuticals, health, and personal care. It simply shows the total number of units of illicit product that have been removed from the marketplace and equates that one for one with a patient/consumer protected.[4]

There are a few ways one might consider for measuring this important goal. The easiest to justify and simplest to explain is as stated above: the total number of illicit products that have been removed from the marketplace via raids and seizures or e-commerce takedowns (assuming online inventory numbers can be reliably counted) equated one for one with a patient/consumer protected. Of course, this has to be understood as an upper bound or maximum estimate, assuming that a patient has not received multiple units of the illicit product.

Another way to consider would be to calculate the total number of patients/consumers who are using products that have a formal brand protection program in place (product protection, monitoring, etc.) and no known illicit trade incidents. You could reason that if there have been no confirmed incidents for those products, then those patients are well protected from counterfeit risk. This rationale is more supportable if a brand protection program has succeeded in cleaning up the market of counterfeit products, as indicated by regular market monitoring.

Why is it important? In the healthcare industry, protecting patients and consumers is the number one priority for brand protection departments. It is the essence of our mission. By removing potentially dangerous products from the marketplace, people most assuredly have been protected from harm. There is also a strong emotional and organizational values-based message that this metric communicates. It signals the organization's commitment to protecting its patients/consumers and ensuring that they only receive genuine, high-quality products from that company.

Sales Loss Exposure (SLE)
What is it? SLE represents the estimated sales loss due to illicit trade for a company's product portfolio in the countries where it does business. It answers the key business question of "What's the size of the problem?" The figure is an output from a quantitative statistical model that estimates country-level sales loss based on actual incident data and a variety of other economic, demographic, governance, legal, and health factors that correlate with illicit trade risk. Consistent with one of the tenets of the Total Business Solution (Wilson and Grammich, 2020), the model treats the illicit trader as an "unknown competitor," whose aim is to capture a share of the market. The share of demand attributable to illicit trade in the model represents the estimated SLE for the company. While these kinds of models are more advanced for a typical brand protection program, they are used widely in the risk management and analysis field and should be considered best practice (Hubbard, 2014).

Why is it important? Similar to TPVR, SLE provides a single, critical metric that gives business leaders/stakeholders an estimate and understanding of what is at risk from a revenue standpoint. Importantly, each sale represented in that SLE total also implies a risk to patient/consumer safety and brand reputation from receiving a counterfeit product. The delta between SLE and TPVR can be quite high, which makes a strong case for brand protection.

Incidents Trend
What is it? Incidents Trend shows actual brand attacks and is an indicator of risk. It includes the number of confirmed incidents over the reporting period and the number of reported suspect incidents that Quality was not able to confirm (usually due to lack of a product sample or other evidence). These numbers can be compared to the prior period, enabling discussion about whether incidents and risk are increasing or decreasing, and for which products.

Incident data includes reports received from all sources, including the Quality Management System, brand protection market monitoring, supply chain partners, investigators, law enforcement agencies, employees, and so on. When discussing incidents, it is important to make stakeholders aware of the percentage of reports generated by proactive market monitoring or investigations versus those reported by patients/consumers, supply chain partners, or employees (unaided). Proactive monitoring will, of course, cause positive spikes in the data trend.

Why is it important? Viewed together, estimated SLE and Incidents Trend provide a business leader with an understanding of the overall risk picture from a brand protection perspective and enable further discussion regarding risks to business objectives and what brand protection is doing about it (see Program Execution Perspective). An important point that should always be raised when discussing incidents is the fact that "one does not equal one." While sometimes there is only one confirmed incident reported, there is never only one instance of a counterfeit in the marketplace. An instance of one most definitely means more are present, as in the "tip of the iceberg" analogy. The key question then becomes, "Is the level of SLE and Incidents we're seeing acceptable to the organization, or should we be doing more?" This question prompts the important "risk appetite" conversation that brand protection professionals need to have with corporate decision makers.

Program ROI (ratio of TPVR/cost)

What is it? Program ROI as we apply it here is simply the result of TPVR divided by the total brand protection budget (investment), expressed as a percentage (e.g., 400%) or as a ratio (4:1). Rather than a profitability metric, ROI is used here as an efficiency metric. TPVR represents brand protection's best estimate of the total value of all the positive outcomes/returns generated through application of the available resources (i.e., inputs: budget, people, etc.) and execution of various activities (i.e., outputs: program elements). In other words, for every dollar invested in brand protection, X amount of TPVR can be expected. Over time and with regular investment, this data point becomes more stable and predictable.

Why is it important? Though the methodology and formula for Program ROI are simple and obviously unique to brand protection, it does provide a basis for comparison to other potential investments. It frames brand protection in the language of business and helps support decisions for resource allocation. It is somewhat limited in that it does not capture total return from all positive outcomes generated by brand protection, such as patient safety or protection of reputation, but it does provide a fair, supportable, and conservative approximation of the value and efficiency delivered by the program. Just be sure to make assumptions, methodologies, and validation clear to stakeholders, as mentioned earlier.

Program Execution Perspective

The next section of the scorecard goes a level down into the program activities that are driving and/or contributing to TPVR, Patients/Consumers Protected, and Program ROI. These are the core capabilities and programs of the brand protection function that are essential to delivering its returns and value proposition. Metrics here don't include everything the team might be doing, just the biggest contributors. In a typical business scorecard model, this section would compare to the Internal Business Process Perspective, answering the question, "What must we excel at?"

In line with a Total Business Solution approach, these metrics communicate actions related to both "controls and mechanisms for detection and response" and "proactivity and prevention" (Wilson and Grammich, 2020). They are grouped here into "Offensive Actions" and "Defensive Actions." Both types of actions include both proactive and preventive aspects, though Offensive Actions are those mainly geared toward detection and response. While we have not done so in this example, it can also be informative to include the amount and percentage of brand protection's budget allocated to each of the program areas in this section.

As a brand protection leader presents these program metrics to stakeholders, he can explain their linkage to strategy, whether or not the programs are meeting expectations, and/or if any changes need to be made in terms of resources, suppliers, or approach.

Offensive Actions: detect, disrupt, deter, and recover value

Offensive Actions consist of proactively monitoring markets and channels to detect illicit products and then subsequently acting on signals and intelligence to further investigate and ultimately enforce intellectual property rights. They're primarily offensive in the sense that the brand owner is not sitting back waiting to react to a report of a suspect product. They're actively hunting for illicit product using a risk-based and targeted strategy for their most at-risk brands.

Market Monitoring—Offline

What is it? Market Monitoring (Offline) includes market surveillance and data collection activities (e.g., surveys, test purchases, intelligence gathering) conducted for the purpose of detecting the presence and/or prevalence of illicit products in the physical marketplace, or anywhere in the supply chain network. Outputs and outcomes from market monitoring activities typically include the following key measures:

1. *Number of Brands Monitored*—Total number of at-risk brands identified and included in the monitoring program, as an indicator of scope and coverage. Regional and/or product category breakdowns can also be shown here.

2. *Product Scans*—Total number of products scanned in the field for authentication or initial evaluation purposes (depending on the technology available). Usually, trained investigators conduct these surveys using a mobile device or smartphone-enabled application. Scans by end users/consumers are also becoming more common with increasing deployment of digital product security technologies.

3. *Test Purchases*—Total number of products purchased for the purpose of conducting additional forensic analysis to determine authenticity and/or as evidence collection to initiate legal proceedings.

4. *Confirmed Illicit Product Incidents*—Total number of confirmed illicit products (counterfeit, diverted, or tampered) based on the results of product scans and test purchases (be careful to control for double-counting). Also show the percentage of confirmed illicit compared to the total investigated.

5. *Investigations Initiated*—As a key output, the total number of Product Security Investigation and Enforcement (PSI&E) cases initiated for further action as a result of market monitoring activity. Outcomes and valuation of PSI&E activities are captured in that specific section below.

Why is it important? Risk-based market monitoring in offline channels is essential for brand protection programs. Typically, but not always, market monitoring is conducted on products equipped with packaging security technologies, so that rapid authentication can be done in the field. Active market monitoring enables brand owners to "close the loop" and realize the value of their investments in security technologies. Technologies deployed without regular monitoring schemes have less value.

Market Monitoring/enforcement—Online
What is it? Market Monitoring (Online) shows the breadth and impact of illicit trade detection and disruption/enforcement activities in e-commerce channels. Typically, third-party online brand protection service (OBPS) providers conduct these programs for brand owners, including providing dashboards and reporting tools. Key metrics for these programs include the following:

1. *Number of Brands Monitored*—Total number of at-risk brands identified and included in the monitoring program, as an indicator of scope and coverage. Regional and/or product category breakdowns can also be shown here.

2. *Enforcement Compliance Rate*—A ratio indicating the compliance rate for the total number of enforcements/de-listings requested by a brand owner versus how many are successfully removed/taken down by the platform or service provider. For example, Compliance Rates for major online marketplaces are in the 85–95 percent range.

3. *Listings Removed*—Total number of listings removed, to give an idea of volume.
4. *Offline Investigations Initiated*—Total number of offline investigations initiated based on investigations and intelligence related to online sellers/ sources and their whereabouts in the physical world. If these investigations ultimately lead to Value Recovery from offline enforcement actions, those outcomes will be captured under PSI&E.
5. *Total Value Recovery (TVR)*—Estimated TVR from online enforcement actions. This may be calculated in various ways depending on the brand owner's point of view and what assumptions are made.

Why is it important? A risk-based online monitoring program is central to effective brand protection. The rapid growth of e-commerce sales and channels, further propelled by COVID-19, has been accompanied by a similarly explosive proliferation of counterfeit goods being sold online. Online is the preferred channel of counterfeiters due to its ease of access, global reach, and relative anonymity. One major e-commerce platform reported that it had "blocked over 3 billion suspected counterfeit listings from being published to their marketplace" (Department of Homeland Security, 2020). Brand owners must be vigilant in the online world to protect their patients/consumers, business, and brands.

Product Security Investigations and Enforcement (PSI&E—all sources)
What is it? PSI&E metrics capture the efficiency and effectiveness of security-led investigations and subsequent enforcement actions and outcomes. The process starts with field intelligence and/or a confirmed incident report, or multiple, related incident reports, and ends, if all goes well, with a successful raid and seizure action on a warehouse, distribution center, and/or manufacturing site. PSI&E also includes collaboration with international Customs agencies to target and enforce against cross-border flows of illicit goods. Key metrics include the following:

1. *Investigations Initiated*—Total number of investigations started (cases opened) based on suspect or confirmed illicit trade incidents. Also indicate the ratio of total suspect/confirmed incidents to cases opened (%), because not all incidents can be further actioned.
2. *Enforcement Actions (EAs)*—Total number of EAs undertaken as a result of a successful investigation. Also indicate the ratio of investigations initiated to EAs (%).
3. *Customs Notifications*—Total number of notifications received from Customs authorities and acted upon by the brand owner. When notified, the brand owner must respond within a strict time limit (24–48 hours)

and provide a determination as to whether the detained goods are suspect counterfeit. If the brand owner does not respond within the required time-frame (varies by country), then Customs will, in most cases, release the shipment.

4. *Customs Enforcement TVR*—TVR specifically related to Customs enforcement actions.
5. *TVR*—Estimated TVR from all PSI&E activities. This may be calculated in various ways depending on the brand owner's point of view and what assumptions are made.

Why is it important? Disrupting the illicit supply chain via investigation and enforcement actions, both online and offline, is one of the main goals of most (if not all) brand protection programs. As mentioned, many brand protection programs focus only on the disruption and deterrence aspect of brand protec-tion. Outcomes from PSI&E activities (raids and seizures) are easy to compute, and TVR from these actions is usually a significant contributor to TPVR.

Legal Settlements VR
What is it? Legal Settlements includes the total VR, net of expense, either from monetary damages received from civil litigation pursued by the brand owner or restitution received from criminal prosecution undertaken by the authorities.

Why is it important? The dollar amount and proportion of VR from Legal Settlements depend first on the size of the problem, of course, and second on the brand owner's legal strategy. Many brand owners choose not to invest legal resources beyond immediate enforcement actions to remove illicit products from the market. However, defending your intellectual property in court can send a strong deterrent signal to infringers, help put offenders in jail, and potentially generate significant VR for your program. Awards can be signif-icant depending on the types of products involved and the jurisdiction. For example, in early 2021, Johnson & Johnson won an award of USD $6 million against a US distributor that was selling counterfeit versions of J&J's Ethicon products.[5] Notably, in 2018, Chinese authorities significantly increased stat-utory damages for intellectual property crimes, providing brand owners with greater incentives to pursue legal action there (Huo, 2018). If leveraging the courts is part of your strategy, Legal Settlements VR is an important metric to track.

Defensive Actions: fortify and secure the supply chain
Metrics in this section of the scorecard cover activities mainly focused on prevention. These are aspects of the strategy that generally relate to proac-tively improving the organization's defense systems, increasing engagement and awareness across the organization, and making it more difficult for

infringers to violate your brands without being detected. Core activities and processes include supply chain partner audits, Customs training and recordals, and integration of brand protection best practices into stakeholder functions. Identification of at-risk products and implementation of packaging security technologies are also covered here, the latter being one of the most important preventive tactics available.

At-risk products protected

What is it? These metrics show the total number of products (usually counted as Stock Keeping Units or SKUs) that have been identified as "at-risk" in a company's portfolio. This means that, based on risk assessment and/or known brand attacks, they require additional brand protection actions to reduce and/or control illicit trade risk.

1. *At-Risk Products*—Total number of SKUs identified for additional brand protection measures.
2. *Products Secured*—Percentage of "at-risk" SKUs with recommended packaging security features in place.
3. *Products Secured and Monitored*—Percentage of "at-risk" SKUs with recommended packaging security features *and* active market monitoring in place (either online or offline, or both as per risk assessment and recommendation).

Why is it important? There are many factors that drive illicit trade risk for individual brands and products in the healthcare industry. Some products, such as the recent COVID-19 vaccines, require a high degree of protection. Other products may not require any additional security. All products in a company's portfolio should be assessed and segmented based on their risk level (e.g., Level 1, 2, 3, and 4). This section of the scorecard makes clear how many products have been deemed "at-risk" and then how many of those products actually have the recommended security feature(s) and active monitoring in place. Depending on the size of a company's portfolio, resources may not be available to protect all products, so these metrics help drive those decisions and communicate any gaps in recommended coverage. In some cases, implementation of additional security features and/or monitoring may be a work in progress, and that can be communicated here as well.

Supply chain partner audits

What is it? Audits ensure that supply chain partners (e.g., contract manufacturers and distributors) have the required controls in place for brand protection. While audits may also be conducted for internal sites, the risk is significantly higher with external partners from a brand protection standpoint, and that is the focus of the audit measures for this scorecard. The measures here show the status of the audit program for both manufacturers and distributors, the aggregated findings across each of the five areas of the audit, and the number of open corrective actions or gaps identified.

1. *Sites Assessed vs. Plan*—Total number of completed assessments versus planned assessments over the reporting period, along with percentage completed versus plan.
2. *Audit Area Scores*—The audit surveys five key areas of operation and control from a brand protection perspective. Those areas are as follows:
   (a)   Security Controls
   (b)   Operational Controls
   (c)   Human Resource Controls
   (d)   Intellectual Property Controls
   (e)   Supplier Management Controls.
   Each area is then scored according to the following scale:
   (i)   Meets Best Practice
   (ii)   Needs Improvement
   (iii) Does Not Meet Best Practice.
3. *Open Corrective Actions*—Total number of negative observations that need to be corrected by the responsible party. It is also helpful to indicate the trend for this data point compared to the prior reporting period.

Why is it important? Third-party supply chain partner relationships are essential for most brand owners and audits help ensure that those partners are complying with standards and best practices, which should be delineated in contract terms and conditions. As with audits for regulatory and Good Manufacturing Practices (GxP) requirements, brand protection audits are an important aspect of maintaining a high level of performance and compliance among supply chain partners. Establishing an audit program also improves education and awareness concerning illicit trade issues.

Customs recordals and engagement
What is it? Customs recordal enables US and international Customs authorities to monitor, detain, and/or seize goods they suspect of being counterfeit or infringing a brand owner's intellectual property rights. Brand protection programs will typically have a strategy and plan designating brands for recordation and in which jurisdictions—it's a risk-based strategy, as it's likely not necessary for all brands in all countries. Metrics include the following:

1. *Customs Recordals*—Shows ratio of total recordals completed and current versus plan. Expiration timeframes vary by country, so it's necessary to track, maintain, and regularly review recordals to stay current and effec-

tive. This data may be segmented by product and/or region depending on a brand owner's portfolio and distribution footprint.

2. *Customs Training*—Number of trainings completed versus plan (on a location basis). May also include the total number of Customs officials trained, as this will vary by location.

Why is it important? Customs authorities are important allies in the fight against illicit trade. Recording registered trademarks and demonstrating your commitment to working with Customs by providing training to help them identify genuine versus fake versions of your products can increase the likelihood that they will detain any suspect products for further investigation by you, the brand owner. Recordal also establishes key points of contact within your organization who must be notified in the event suspect products have been detained. There are strict response time limits and if Customs is not able to contact a brand owner for confirmation, then the goods are usually released. VR from successful seizure and destruction of illicit product is captured above under PSI&E.

Best practice integration
What is it? This may be one of the more difficult performance measurement areas to compile and capture in a high-level scorecard, but it's one of the more important ones. The idea is to measure the degree to which brand protection best practices (i.e., standards, processes, tactics) have been successfully deployed across the organization. Success would mean that a given process, for example, has become part of the day-to-day operations of the responsible functional area (e.g., Supply Chain). They own it and effectively manage it with support from Brand Protection, as needed.

A comprehensive organizational assessment/survey model can be used for this purpose with a "readiness score" as an output for each functional area. The assessment tool would include all the required best practices grouped by functional area, and the score would be an indication of current state of conformance with the specified requirements. Performance for each element of the survey can be measured on a five-point rating scale, such as:

(0)   Not Started/Non-existent
(1)   Ad Hoc
(2)   Repeatable
(3)   Defined
(4)   Managed
(5)   Optimized.

Aggregated and weighted scores by functional area can then be calculated and graded as: Does Not Meet Best Practice, Improvement Needed, or Meets

Best Practice. These scores can also be color coded (red, yellow, green) to aid readability and understanding. This list of functions assumes there is a dedicated Brand Protection Department that is conducting the assessment, so brand protection is not included:

(1)   Security
(2)   Law Department
(3)   Commercial
(4)   Supply Chain
(5)   Quality.

Why is it important? Assuming a brand protection team has incorporated a Total Business Solution approach into their strategy, these Best Practice Integration measures will illuminate to what degree key stakeholders across the organization are engaged and prepared from a brand protection standpoint. Only the most important functions are included at this high level, and these may differ by organization, but these functions represent about 80 percent of the unique brand protection tactics reported in the research (Wilson and Grammich, 2020).

Operating Excellence Perspective

The third and final section of the scorecard is designed to capture metrics related to important foundational aspects of effective brand protection department operations. These are indicators of operational efficiency, project management, staffing, organizational health, stakeholder (customer) engagement, and innovation, for example. These factors are also program enablers and support the sustainability of the department. While all sections of the scorecard can be tailored to fit specific strategic and organizational needs, this section is likely the most variable depending on the size of the department, its operating model, and its organizational culture. In terms of having a balanced view, these metrics are all key contributing factors to positive results under Program Execution and Total Program Measures. They are the final leg of the stool.

In comparison to the business scorecard, this section can capture both the "customer perspective" and the "innovation and learning perspective." Brand protection serves the end-user customer only indirectly—that is, the person or entity who purchases the product—so there is not likely to be a metric to report concerning the "customer" in the usual sense. If a company happens to be engaging their end users directly on brand protection issues, then that is a different story. In that case, we would add a relevant customer engagement metric to the Program Execution section. Typically, brand protection's customers are internal stakeholders, those business leaders we've been referring to throughout the chapter, so we have a metric to measure the quality of those relationships.

Budget Utilization

What is it? Budget Utilization shows whether the department is either on track, or under-/over-spent compared to plan for the period in question. This is a standard business metric, but it is especially important for brand protection teams due to the uncertainty and challenges inherent in brand protection activities.

Why is it important? Brand protection teams committed to planning and working strategically face several challenges that can potentially derail their plans:

1. *Incident Investigations and Enforcement*—For typically lean brand protection operations, the need to shift priorities and resources to an incident triage and investigation—or multiple investigations—often means having to pause or delay other, more strategic, projects and programs.
2. *Reliance on Cross-Functional Collaboration*—Getting things done in most cases means working through and with business partners in Quality, Supply Chain, Commercial, Packaging, Legal, and so on. Aligning priorities and to-do lists can sometimes be difficult and a source of delay for brand protection projects. This emphasizes the need for strategic alignment, communication, and integration with key stakeholder functions so that plans stay on track.
3. *Project Management (PM) Risks*—Some strategic projects for brand protection, such as implementation of product security technologies on packaging lines, or integrating audits across a large supply chain network, have a long timeline, many moving parts and stakeholders, and other risks to their successful implementation. Keeping them on track requires strong PM processes and skills.

By keeping a close eye on Budget Utilization, brand protection managers can regularly manage expectations with stakeholders and be prepared to re-allocate resources, if necessary, or request additional resources if unexpected costs arise.

Project Management Office (PMO)

What is it? PMO shows the status of a brand protection department's current project portfolio, sometimes called a "book of work" (BoW). These are all defined projects for the period (usually annual but sometimes multi-year) that support the team's strategy. Status indicators show how the BoW is tracking in the aggregate, compared to plan and budget. Because this is a big picture, high-level metric, project status can be broken down into three buckets: On Track, At Risk, and Off Track. Disclosure of budget and budget status for the BoW is the same as above (on track, or under-/over-spent).

Why is it important? Strategic goals and objectives are achieved through some combination of programs (ongoing effort), projects (time-bound effort), and operational effectiveness. Successful project management and execution are therefore essential for delivering on commitments, and accountability for delivery is critical. Owing to the potential derailers mentioned above and other factors, rarely do all projects within a BoW stay on track during the reporting period.

As with Budget Utilization, tracking PMO status is a basic management practice, but it is a critical one for holding team members/project managers accountable and for setting expectations with stakeholders if projects are off track or falling short of their commitments.

Stakeholder Engagement (customer)

What is it? Stakeholder Engagement includes two metrics: (1) Engagement Level and (2) Satisfaction Survey. The Engagement Level is a subjective rating that shows the strength of key internal stakeholder relationships on a five-point scale (Leading, Supportive, Neutral, Resistant, Unaware).[6] The Satisfaction Survey provides feedback from stakeholders about Brand Protection's services and collaboration. Survey questions can be tailored to organizational needs, but, as with any customer satisfaction survey, the idea is to elicit meaningful feedback to understand customer perceptions and expectations.

Why is it important? As mentioned above, Brand Protection's primary customers are internal stakeholders. Typically, these include commercial business unit leaders and enterprise-level department heads across the organization (Quality, Supply Chain, Legal, Government Affairs, etc.). Regularly engaging and collaborating with them is critical for program success.

The first step in doing this well is identifying and mapping all the key stakeholders within your organization who are/may be needed for the execution of your brand protection strategy (this is easier said than done in a large, multi-national organization). Once you have identified all the stakeholders, then you can assess the strength of those relationships and make a plan for addressing any gaps in support and collaboration.

By keeping regular tabs on the strength and quality of internal stakeholder relationships, brand protection managers will be in the best position to address any gaps that may occur due to employee turnover, shifting priorities, or any other organizational dynamics that could come into play. This metric is also useful for developing and evaluating internal brand protection communication efforts.

External partnering
What is it? These measures indicate the strength and effectiveness of a brand protection team's engagement with key external partners and the brand protection ecosystem. Metrics to highlight here include Customs training/ engagement (number of trainings versus plan), participation in industry conferences and/or consortia (actual versus planned), government affairs activity, and thought leadership initiatives. Obviously, these will vary according to your strategy, but it is important to underscore external partnering and how it factors into your program.

Why is it important? To be successful, brand protection programs need to engage and network with the community of practice and broader ecosystem. External partners not only provide essential services (investigation and enforcement, market monitoring, security technology, intelligence, etc.), they are also important as force multipliers and for learning and collaboration. The illicit trade threat landscape and risk scenarios are dynamic, as are services and solutions designed for prevention, control, and response. Staying engaged externally helps practitioners stay abreast of what's happening and also understand viable new technologies and approaches.

People/human resources
What is it? People are an organization's most important asset, as the mantra goes. Ensuring the success and sustainability of the brand protection team means hiring, motivating, and retaining great talent. Two people metrics that are probably most important at a high level for the brand protection team are:

1. *Current Staffing Level/Open Positions*—Shows the current staffing level on a percentage basis and the number of open positions, if any. For example, "80%/2 OP" (with 10 full-time equivalents assigned).
2. *Succession Planning*—Indicates how many individuals are "ready now" for mission-critical positions on the team. These positions are usually the head of the team and one or two levels down, depending on the size and scope of the organization. Individuals identified may be currently on the team, an employee within your broader organization, or even individuals outside of the organization that have been identified as strong potential candidates for a role (identified separately).

Why is it important? In terms of staffing levels, leadership needs to be aware of any open positions and their potential impact on the team's commitments to the business and its overall goals and objectives. Brand protection is a specialized discipline and, depending on the role, finding a qualified candidate may take longer than usual. Also, because brand protection is a relatively new and growing discipline, it is not uncommon to find great candidates with backgrounds in related disciplines (commercial, legal, supply chain, quality, etc.) who are interested in cross-training and learning brand protection. In these cases, the onboarding and training cycle will take longer.

In terms of succession planning, it's a critical management process from an operational continuity standpoint. Losing the department head or a key player on any team is detrimental, but not being prepared to quickly backfill a critical brand protection role can have serious implications.

As mentioned earlier in this chapter, brand protection programs are often under-staffed. Including people metrics on the scorecard provides an opportunity to talk about your team, how they're performing, and any additional resource needs you may have, now or in the future. If the metrics have told a great story up to this point, you may have improved your chances of getting more help!

Innovation
What is it? Last on the scorecard but not least, innovation is critical for brand protection teams, though this factor may be the most wide open in terms of interpretation and deciding what metrics/information to present. You may have a well-established innovation process within your company and/or team, in which case the deciding is easy. If you don't, then an innovation funnel is a common way to showcase innovation efforts. Inputs (ideas, opportunities, technologies to be reviewed) enter the top of the funnel and outputs (viable technologies, products, or processes) flow from the bottom. Targets can be assigned to each phase of the funnel, which can be represented on the scorecard.

Another way is to highlight two or three key innovation areas and show the status of any related initiatives (e.g., R&D, Design, Deploy). Data and Analytics and Digital Product Security Technologies top the innovation agenda for many brand protection teams and deserve mention. Of course, innovation covers many areas, including process improvements and ways of working more efficiently or effectively. Prioritize whatever is most important to your team's strategy, goals, and objectives from an innovation perspective.

Why is it important? Technology is one of the key drivers of the growth of illicit trade. The infringers have access to the same advanced tools and technologies for manufacturing and distribution as the legitimate enterprises do. They also innovate to attempt to break or bypass technologies and security measures designed to stop them. This one-upmanship and pressing need for brand owners to stay one step ahead makes anti-counterfeiting technology a very dynamic and innovative space. Brand protection practitioners need to stay informed, and regularly evaluate and test new technologies to understand what will provide the best combination of cost, robust security, and ease of deployment.

Innovation contributes to bigger end-game goals for brand protection, but because innovation is an upstream process, this data is more informational than actionable. However, as with other aspects of the scorecard, bringing up the topic always presents an opportunity to address resource needs with stakeholders.

Pulling it all together in practice

Brand protection—protecting people, brands, and businesses from risks related to counterfeiting and illicit trade—is a complex, multi-faceted, multi-functional, and multi-disciplinary undertaking. As Wilson and Grammich's (2020) research has shown, virtually every part of an organization can play a part in the effective implementation of a brand protection program. In theory, this makes sense and seems reasonable, but in practice, getting all the necessary parts of a business, especially a big business, engaged, aligned, coordinated, and working toward a common goal is a major and ongoing management challenge. This applies very much to any organization's primary objectives, such as revenue and profit, let alone its secondary or tertiary ones, where brand protection likely sits in the scheme of things. What's a brand protection leader to do?

The reason we raise this point is not to challenge a Total Business Solution approach to brand protection, but to emphasize how vital effective communication and change management are to making it work and getting results. Communication is truly half the battle. The process starts with articulating the case for brand protection to senior leaders and getting their support—if you don't explicitly have it already. That lights the way for cooperation from functional heads and their teams. It takes time for all the pieces to fall into place and to establish regular engagement and shared goals with all the right stakeholders. However, once those ties are established and a well-thought-out, business-aligned brand protection strategy and balanced scorecard are in place and the scorecard is regularly used as a communication tool to advance the program, that is when the Total Business Solution approach really begins to yield results for an organization and its customers.

CONCLUSION

The International Anti-Counterfeiting Coalition (IACC), which is the oldest and largest "organization devoted solely to combating product counterfeiting and piracy," celebrated its 40th anniversary in 2019. Most well-established brand protection programs in the pharmaceutical space, which we are most familiar with, came into being only ten to twenty years ago. Compared to core areas of business such as finance, accounting, law, sales, marketing, supply chain, IT, human resources, and others, brand protection is clearly the new kid at the enterprise table, joining other areas of rising corporate risk, such as cybersecurity (the big kid at the risk table!).

While relatively new, the brand protection discipline continues to rapidly mature and evolve in response to the continually escalating threats for brands and patients/consumers in the marketplace. With maturity naturally comes more understanding and agreement among practitioners about how to effectively combat the problem: what works and what doesn't. This then leads to sharing of best practices and the creation of foundational principles and standards that advance the discipline over time. Brand protection is still at an early stage on this path to standardization—we're a long way from GAAP-level[7] agreement, for example—but coming to a consensus on what we should be measuring and how we should be valuing our contributions to the success of the enterprise is certainly a keystone in the maturity model and a must for practitioners.

With that in mind, successful outcomes from the contribution of this chapter to the brand protection community would be that (1) practitioners generally agree with the approach and adopt it for their own programs, perhaps with some tweaks and customization; (2) the chapter stimulates further robust conversation, both for and against, about what we should be measuring and valuing for brand protection and how; and (3) as a result of the ensuing conversation, the community of practice arrives at a consensus on this topic and that leads to the forging of a generally accepted standard. That last one would be the best outcome of all!

NOTES

1. A cost center is a department or function within an organization that does not directly add to profit but still costs the organization money to operate (from Investopedia).
2. A profit center is a branch or division of a company that directly adds or is expected to add to the entire organization's bottom line (from Investopedia).
3. Value Recovery is a measure of *all* calculated proceeds or outcomes from brand protection activities, both soft and hard measures. It includes the value of all reasonably computable outcomes from the variety of tactics undertaken by brand protection.
4. A process needs to be defined and assumptions documented about what gets counted and why. For example, raids of warehouses and manufacturing sites usually find finished and unfinished goods and/or raw materials. A conservative approach would be to count only finished goods. Another approach would be to estimate the manufacturing capacity of the site and use that number. Whatever method you choose, define and document it so that the data is consistent.
5. Johnson & Johnson et al. v. Advanced Inventory Management, Inc. et al., 1:2020cv03471 (US District Court for the Northern District of Illinois June 15, 2020).
6. See Project Management Institute, www.pmi.org.

7.   GAAP stands for Generally Accepted Accounting Principles.

REFERENCES

Department of Homeland Security (2020). *Combating Trafficking in Counterfeit and Pirated Goods: Report to the President of the United States.* Washington, DC: Department of Homeland Security Office of Strategy, Policy, and Plans.

Hubbard, D. W. (2014). *How to Measure Anything*, 3rd Edition. Hoboken, NJ: Wiley.

Huo, A. (2018, May 24). *WTR Topics.* Retrieved from World Trademark Review: https://www.worldtrademarkreview.com/anti-counterfeiting/procedures-and -strategies-anti-counterfeiting-china-0.

Kaplan, R. S. (1996). *The Balanced Scorecard: Translating Strategy into Action.* Boston, MA: Harvard Business School Press.

Wilson, J. M., and Grammich, C. A. (2020). Brand Protection across the Enterprise: Toward a Total Business Solution. *Business Horizons, 63*(3), 363–376.

Wilson, J. M., Grammich, C. A., and Chan, F. (2016). Organizing for brand protection and responding to product counterfeit risk: An analysis of global firms. *Journal of Brand Management, 23*(3), 345–361.

10. Determining the value of brand protection programs: identifying and assessing performance metrics in brand protection

Jeremy M. Wilson, Clifford A. Grammich, B. William Demeré and Karen L. Sedatole

INTRODUCTION

Branding is critical for firms to differentiate and communicate the value of their products and services (Kotler and Pfoertsch, 2006). One of the key risks to brands is counterfeit products. Such products threaten the value of the brand by diminishing its image, placing consumers and society at risk, and undermining sales of authentic products (International Anti-Counterfeiting Coalition, 2005; US Office of the Intellectual Property Enforcement Coordinator, 2016). One recent estimate found counterfeit and pirated goods in 2016 accounted for $505 billion or 3.3 percent of world trade (Organisation for Economic Co-operation and Development and European Intellectual Property Office, 2019). Counterfeit goods touch seemingly every industry, including aircraft and automotive parts, consumer electronics, toys, footwear and apparel, jewelry and luxury goods, and pharmaceutical and personal care products (US Customs and Border Protection, 2019).

The size and scope of counterfeiting suggests a fundamental need for brand protection and, indeed, many firms devote considerable resources to it (Wilson et al., 2016). Nevertheless, while brand protection is important, its costs and value must be weighed against other potential investments, especially if resources are scarce. Brand protection programs can cost tens of millions of dollars, especially when including full litigation of cases (Berman, 2008). Consequently, those responsible for brand protection seek to demonstrate the return on investment (ROI) for brand protection activities to both justify the investment and ensure they are investing their resources most effectively. Establishing metrics and assessing the overall performance of a brand protection program and the relative effectiveness of its various activities are fundamental aspects of implementing a total business solution that is strategic, proactive, and data-driven (Wilson and Grammich, 2020).

Questions Brand Owners Ask Themselves

As noted in Chapter 1, in seeking to protect their brands from counterfeits, among the questions firms typically struggle with answering are: How big is our counterfeiting problem? How should we allocate resources to address it? How do we measure the performance of our efforts? These questions, though seemingly simple, are difficult to answer for at least three reasons. First, measurement issues plague attempts to estimate the prevalence of product counterfeiting. Second, there has been little empirical research on the effectiveness of brand protection strategies. Third, evaluating the achievement of brand protection goals, which are often considered intangible (e.g., protecting brand reputation), has stymied performance assessment.

As a result, demonstrating and communicating the need for and value of brand protection within a firm remain difficult. Some in the field have suggested common measures, such as ROI, as one way to overcome this problem. Practitioners suggest they would receive greater support from their firms if they were to use commonly understood and accepted business metrics for reporting their successes (Grammich and Wilson, 2016). In seeking to demonstrate the ROI of brand protection, practitioners must answer questions such as:

- What does ROI mean for our company? Do we seek to protect sales of our products and technologies? Convert illicit sales to legitimate ones? Warn customers of counterfeit goods? Achieve some other objective?
- Is our goal zero counterfeiting? Or is some level of counterfeiting acceptable from a cost–benefit perspective?
- What are the costs of counterfeiting? Is it lost customers? Detrimental impacts on the health and safety of customers? Damage to brand image that could lead to lost revenues?
- How do we utilize all functions of the organization to bolster brand protection, reduce the cost of counterfeiting, and prevent the erosion of brand value?
- How can we measure brand protection performance? What types of metrics are used?
- What are the strengths, weaknesses, and assumptions of each metric? How accurate are these metrics? What is missing or needing improvement in these metrics?

Purpose and Organization of the Chapter

This chapter provides baseline information about how firms measure and assess the performance of brand protection programs. Drawing upon a sample of major brand-owning corporations across multiple industries, we seek to identify the metrics that firms use to gauge the effectiveness of their efforts. In doing so, we aim to advance knowledge about a critical area of research that has not received systematic attention. We also develop lessons regarding the measurement of brand protection ROI.

Ultimately, we will examine what firms are doing to assess brand protection performance relative to what they would need to calculate ROI. As we will see, firms were most likely to have activity metrics, followed by outcome metrics, with relatively few metrics on valuation. This is not surprising given the difficulty that even public authorities have in precisely estimating the effects of counterfeiting. Nevertheless, valuation remains a critical need in measuring ROI.

We turn next to an overview of how firms implement brand protection, followed by a brief background on measuring the ROI for brand protection efforts. We then discuss our approach for identifying and analyzing metrics that firms use to assess brand protection performance and examine these metrics. We close with a discussion of our findings and their implications for research and practice.

HOW FIRMS IMPLEMENT BRAND PROTECTION

When creating a brand protection team, firms most frequently place it within their legal function, although placement in another function, across multiple functions can also occur, and some firms may even set up a stand-alone unit (Wilson et al., 2016). Such teams tend to rely more on externally focused activities, such as product seizures, than internally focused ones, such as tracking product movement. Many current practices are reactive, addressing counterfeiting incidents after they occur, rather than taking a proactive approach to preventing such incidents (Wilson and Kinghorn, 2014). Brand protection practitioners tend to perceive proactive strategies, such as consumer education and package design, to be more effective than reactive ones (Clements, 2016). At the same time, they perceive reactive strategies to be more efficient to implement and manage.

How firms approach brand protection can vary across firms and even across divisions within a firm. A primary driver of differences in brand protection approaches is what firms view as their greatest risks. For one industry, loss of sales to counterfeits may be a pressing matter. For another, quality concerns arising from the diversion of goods in the supply chain may be an urgent problem. More generally, a firm for which consumer safety must be paramount (e.g., a pharmaceutical firm) may have different needs, and metrics, than one for which revenue recovery from counterfeits is prioritized (e.g., where technology infringers can be converted to licensees). Firms may even have different valuations of product protection at different stages of the life cycle of a product (De Stefano, 2017).

The traditional ROI metric focuses narrowly on the financial (i.e., accounting-based income) effects of an investment. While it may be feasible to measure the loss of sales owing to counterfeit products, how does one compute the accounting income effect related to consumer safety? Could the traditional ROI measure be too narrow to capture all the benefits, including consumer safety and welfare, of tackling counterfeit products?

MEASUREMENT AND ITS CONTEXTS

The estimation of ROI, like other forms of efficiency analysis (Weiss, 1998), not only indicates whether a program is performing well, but can also help to identify the degree to which differing levels of a program might achieve desired ends and therefore inform program implementation (Yates, 1996). Rather than using such analyses to inform program implementation, however, brand protection professionals, like many others, may evaluate ROI retroactively to assess the cost-efficiency of their current operations. Of course, there are many measurement challenges to calculating ROI, particularly in terms of identifying and estimating the amounts of both tangible and intangible costs and benefits. It is important to recognize that such analyses may suggest if current operations are delivering a return but will not indicate if the return is the best possible.

Estimating brand protection ROI involves several steps. Among other things, it requires categorizing and cataloging costs and benefits. This step requires listing all investments, activities, and outcomes, some of which may be small or difficult to quantify. Physical and intangible costs may vary by goal or project. We consider brand protection *investments* to be the costs of brand protection staff and equipment, *activities* to be what brand protection staff do with their time and equipment, and *outcomes* to be the benefits that firms realize from brand protection activities. It also requires monetizing (attaching dollar values to) all costs and benefits; that is, it requires *valuation* of how benefits relate to costs and whether benefits exceed costs, ensuring a program realizes more benefit than it does costs.

In short, to properly assess a brand protection program, firms should have metrics related to investments, activities, outcomes, and the value of the program. We turn next to the metrics firms typically employ and how they compare to what firms might ideally use.

INTERVIEWING FIRMS ON BRAND PROTECTION

To better understand performance measurement in brand protection, we conducted a series of interviews to elicit insights from practitioners. We used these interviews to illustrate firm experiences and approaches.

Interview Participants

One of the challenges of conducting research on brand protection is the difficulty of gaining access to practitioners and data. Firms are understandably cautious in discussing the threat of counterfeits and their efforts to combat them. Given the difficulty and cost of recruiting a large, representative sample of firms willing to discuss issues around counterfeiting, we leveraged our partnerships with the brand protection community (see Wilson and Grammich, 2020; Wilson, 2017; Wilson et al., 2016; Wilson and Sullivan, 2016) to develop a small, purposive sample of ten firms.

While we were unable to conduct interviews across a large sample, the individuals we interviewed were knowledgeable and employed by firms that are leaders in brand protection. Respondents held a variety of roles in anti-counterfeiting, brand protection, product integrity, intellectual property compliance, security, and legal functions. They varied in responsibility, with titles ranging from group leader to vice president and associate general counsel. Our interviews generated a rich source of information about a critical function on which there has been little systematic research.

The ten participating firms provide goods and services in a wide variety of industries, including pharmaceuticals, medical devices, entertainment media, microelectronics, aerospace parts, apparel and footwear, jewelry and luxury goods, computer software and electronic games, consumer products, foods, and agriculture and veterinary products. They vary in size from 2,000 to 120,000 employees, with annual sales ranging from $1 billion to over $70 billion. Their number of brands ranged from 1 to more than 1,000. The size of their brand protection teams ranged from 2 to 50 employees, with the team typically positioned in the legal or security function.

Interview Approach

For each firm, we conducted an interview of the brand protection executive best able to represent the firm's brand protection activities and performance assessment. (For the few firms that elected to have a second practitioner join the interview, we aggregated the responses from both respondents to represent the firm as both agreed with all the information shared.) The format of the interview was a blend of structured and semi-structured questions. The structured questions included those on the firm's size, industry, brand protection group, and perceived success of brand protection efforts. The semi-structured questions sought details about metrics related to brand protection performance and evaluation. We conducted our interviews from February to May 2017, either in person or by phone, with at least two researchers present for each interview. Each interview lasted 60 to 120 minutes. Each interviewer took notes, which we used to code responses to the structured questions and identify themes from responses to the semi-structured questions.

Organization of Metrics

We identified and categorized all metrics reported by respondents. For *investment metrics*, we asked all respondents common questions, such as the number of personnel working in brand protection, but respondents tended not to identify additional metrics when asked more open-ended questions. We therefore focus on activity, outcome, and valuation metrics. These were gathered in response to questions such as "In what ways does your company measure brand protection performance?" and "Please identify the specific ROI metrics (quantitative and qualitative) and formulas your company uses to estimate the ROI of brand protection efforts." *Activity metrics* are measures of activities that firms conduct with the investments they make in brand protection. Examples include the number of raids, seizure actions, or takedowns. *Outcome metrics* are measures of the effectiveness of brand protection activities. Examples include the prevalence of counterfeits, the effect that counterfeits have on brand image or value, sales of counterfeits and how they affect sales of legitimate products, and market share for counterfeit and legitimate products. *Valuation metrics* are measures of the monetary value of outcomes, which, combined with the monetary value of investments, are necessary for calculating the ROI for brand protection efforts.

The categorization of metrics is subjective and sometimes difficult. To increase the validity and reliability of our categorization, two members of the research team worked collaboratively and agreed on all categorizations. Our analysis resulted in a list of metrics, which itself is an important contribution to brand protection. We also identified qualitative insights that provide context for understanding the circumstances and issues that firms face and the lessons they have learned.

HOW FIRMS VIEW THEIR OVERALL BRAND PROTECTION EFFORTS

Perceived Success

All but one of the ten firms we interviewed characterized their brand protection efforts as "successful" or "very successful." While this may reflect subjective bias among our respondents, it also may suggest these firms are leaders in brand protection and therefore good examples of how to effectively manage resources. Nevertheless, several of the firms claiming to be "successful" acknowledged they could do better, particularly if they had more resources. Even one "very successful" firm acknowledged the need to take a "very dynamic approach" and to be "constantly re-evaluating." Another said the question of success is "tricky." The respondent explained that:

> From what we're doing and what we're learning about the entire market in general and how we're growing with respect to creating programs that match the needs of our company, I'd say that we're very successful ... But when it comes to seeing the actual changes in the marketplace, in a way that you see the problem reducing, from that point of view I'd probably say that we're unsuccessful. But that has to do with the ability to get out and create enforcement activities, a lot of which is controlled by our legal team which is very risk averse. A lot of these companies are in China so there's fear of provoking the government which we've already faced tough problems with.

Importance of Demonstrating Value

Most firms in our sample indicated that demonstrating the value of brand protection activities (e.g., using ROI metrics) is highly important to them, giving it at least an 8 on a 1-to-10 scale where 10 was most important. Among those firms ranking it most important were those whose brand protection programs depend on recovering revenue. A representative from one of these firms said their program was "very self-funding ... for head count, they hold us to the fire to bring in more money." The two firms reporting that their brand protection programs depend on revenue recovery were also the only two to say that only monetary metrics were incorporated in calculating returns.

Firms placing less importance on demonstrating value noted other goals, particularly the primacy of safety. A representative of one such firm said, "We don't have overwhelming pressure to [demonstrate ROI]. The reason we don't ... is because when we stood this group up a decision was made at the executive level that this group would have longevity, would be able to operate in the interests of ... safety alone." A representative for a similar firm also placing primacy on safety asked, "How do you measure 'quality' in brand protection?

How do you measure if you're not doing something? We need to measure both the upside and the downside." In other words, brands need to know the effects both of what they are doing and of what they are not doing.

Resource Acquisition, Resource Allocation, and Performance

Half of the firms reported that metrics showing brand protection performance, whether or not in the form of an ROI, are tied to resources, ranking this at least an 8 on a 10-point scale. Among those saying their resources are not tied to their program, one said it uses its brand protection program primarily to identify problems, a second noted its management is aware what would occur if there were no brand protection program, and a third said its leadership views brand protection as an essential element of corporate practices.

In terms of focusing on proactive or reactive investments, most firms reported spending less than half of their brand protection budgets on prevention. A representative of one firm that spent half of its brand protection budget on prevention also noted that a recent acquisition would change its emphasis. Claiming that much of the emphasis on prevention or reaction stems from "cultural" issues, this representative noted that the recently acquired firm "understood the importance of having a strong brand." At the same time, this representative said that the recently acquired firm "is consumer facing," with products that are "easy to counterfeit." As a result, the parent firm was seeking "to increase total spend to be more focused on the classic aspects" of brand protection (i.e., responsive types of activities such as investigation and enforcement).

Firms may also shift their focus depending on their markets. This is evident in earlier research indicating that executives in differing nations have differing views on drivers for counterfeit trade and hence on the most fruitful tactics to combat it (Stumpf and Chaudhry, 2010). A brand protection representative in our interviews said, "Some markets are more susceptible to brand protection issues. Marketplaces with large market share will have a large risk of infringement if governing laws are not satisfactory ... In countries where English is a second language and there are weak regulations, there is also a larger risk." These views suggest the need for firms to maintain a diverse set of metrics for assessing and guiding decisions in a variety of circumstances.

METRICS FIRMS USE IN ASSESSING BRAND PROTECTION

Identification of Metrics

We asked respondents to "identify the specific ROI metrics and formulas" they use to estimate the value of their brand protection efforts. Altogether, respondents reported 52 unique metrics. Box 10.1 shows metrics by type, groupings within type, and, where relevant, individual metrics within grouping. Of the 52 metrics, only 6—typically involving customs personnel in some way, such as training or seizures—were used by at least five of the ten firms we interviewed. Most of the metrics reported are used by no more than two firms, indicating many approaches to measuring brand protection performance.

BOX 10.1   UNIQUE INDIVIDUAL METRICS IDENTIFIED BY RESPONDENTS AND THEIR CLASSIFICATION BY CATEGORY AND GROUPING

Category

> Grouping (and number of individual metrics for those with more than one metric)

Activity Measures

> Arrests
> Complaints (2: internal and external)
> Identification of products at risk
> Internal investigations of incident causes
> Internal investigations of incident occurrence
> Inventory management—tracking distributed product
> Legal (4: civil, criminal, and other law enforcement cases reported; firm legal actions)
> Manufacturer shutdown (2: capability measured by units, number of manufacturers)
> Market surveys
> Merchant credit card account terminations
> Physical inspections (5: inspections of manufacturers or suppliers, raids, retail sweeps, shop visits, trade show shutdowns)
> Response time to resolve complaints
> Seizures (4: number of civil, criminal, customs, and all other seizures)

Training sessions (8: sessions and number of personnel trained for customs, law enforcement, firm, and suppliers)

Outcome Measures

Countries—number where counterfeits discovered
Fines (2: levied by authorities, paid by offenders)
Prevalence of counterfeits
Recovery—identification of offending licensees
Returns—percent counterfeit
Seizures (3: number of units seized by customs, number of units seized by other sources, number of units destroyed)
Website (2: number of websites takedowns, number of product units in takedown)

Valuation Measures

Loss (2: due to effects on brand image, due to effects on product quality)
Recovery—restitution or revenue recovered
Returns—estimated monetary value of counterfeits based on returns
Seizures (3: value of products seized by customs, seized by others, and program cost per seized piece)
Website—value of products removed in takedown

As Box 10.1 indicates, most of the metrics we found were activity metrics. Valuation metrics were least common. We identified only eight such metrics used by the brand protection professionals we interviewed. The emphasis on activity metrics, as we discuss further below, stems from respondents finding it easier to measure what they do than to measure the results of their efforts.

Metrics Use and Perceived Performance

We did not find a relationship between the number of metrics a firm uses and the perceived level of success of brand protection efforts. For example, among the firms claiming to be "very successful" in brand protection, none reported using more than 10 metrics, while of those claiming only to be "successful," none reported using fewer than 15. Nevertheless, we remind the reader that our small sample makes generalization difficult.

Different Uses of Metrics

We did find variation in how firms use metrics, even the same metric. One example of this is the number of complaints firms reported receiving. Some professionals noted that higher numbers of complaints are a problem, because they indicate a greater extent of the counterfeit problem. One participant, however, considered higher numbers of complaints to be an indication of program success. This individual explained, "We know we're doing well internally when we have our designated points of contact in each country sending us potential counterfeit complaints, because that means they know we exist … [I]f we're not getting complaints through the proper channels, that's an indication we're not creating enough visibility for our program." Greater numbers of complaints provided intelligence on a problem that this professional assumed would always persist and that might always be underestimated.

Brand protection teams may also differ in the metrics they use based on the problems they address. A participant who reported using only two metrics noted his team is "more geared toward counterfeiting. It would be different for gray market or diverted products," for which this firm's legal function is responsible. This team, however, focuses on "counterfeiting, [which] is a direct threat to consumers. Gray market is often due to our own doing." Similarly, another professional told us, "Prevention is mostly done by our legal counsel, who takes care of all the trademark and copyright registrations … We do support the efforts of the IACC [International Anti-Counterfeiting Coalition] and other groups that are involved in customer education, but … we're not spending much resources there."

Activities and metrics may also change depending on market presence and product maturity. One respondent told us:

> Some very inexpensive actions can be very effective. Even if you don't manufacture in a particular country, you still have to register your trademarks … Spending and focus changes with the maturity of the brand protection group. It's very different in the beginning, with initial actions such as registering with customs. In our first four months, we just focused on 12 countries. More mature brand protection groups are digging deeper.

QUALITATIVE INSIGHTS ON MEASURING BRAND PROTECTION

Metric Variation by Firm

Our interviews yielded several qualitative insights on measuring brand protection efforts. Foremost among these is that the sophistication of measures that firms use in assessing brand protection performance may vary by firm needs.

For example, one executive, while noting a requirement to present a quarterly estimate of ROI, added that the choice of metrics to present "depends on the audience. If we're presenting to Quality, then ROI doesn't matter. They're typically not interested in ROI. They're more interested in what is being done to protect customers." Another noted, "We'll tailor it to the audience. We have a system that allows us to export our data and someone who's dedicated to working on those reports, so we have the flexibility to put metrics together pretty quickly." A third said, "Depending on who our audience is, we pick and choose the metrics. All our stakeholders do not speak the same language, so we have to speak in their language." One brand protection professional for a firm with multiple consumer brands provided "one sheet [of metrics] to everyone [so that] I'm sending out a consistent message," but also giving each of the firm's brands "the opportunity to set up a meeting or call me ... if they have questions or they want some additional follow up."

Challenge on Industry Benchmarks

Our interviews suggested that the development of industry benchmarks might be challenged by firm-specific values and unique uses of metrics. Our respondents often discussed what was important to their firm, and the metrics they discussed flowed from that. As a result, different companies might view the same metric in different ways. One example of this is the number of complaints. As noted earlier, some firms asserted that higher numbers of complaints are a problem, because they indicate a greater extent of the counterfeiting problem. Others consider this to be evidence of success, because it indicates program visibility and provides valuable intelligence.

Use of Valuation Metrics

Valuation helps firms understand the relationship between the costs and benefits of their brand protection programs. Yet firms reported few valuation metrics. This may in part have been due to the difficulty of placing a value on counterfeit products. A brand protection professional for a firm with multiple brands claimed, "There's about 15 ways to compute the value of counterfeit products. If I choose one, somebody will come at me with one of the other 14. So I put more emphasis on the number of units." Valuation may also depend on how a brand owner views its markets. As the respondent for multiple brands further noted:

> There is a finite demand for a product in the marketplace ... And every customer that buys a counterfeit is now out of the marketplace. Th[eir] demand has been satisfied. Now you temper that with the fact that some people say, "I'll never spend

that much on [our product]." Well, they weren't our customer in the first place, so you didn't lose anything.

Similarly, another executive noted her firm does not use valuation metrics to measure its brand protection performance, "because they have to be rock solid and they aren't," particularly for the purposes of determining a rate of conversion to sales of legitimate product. At the same time at this firm, "Most of the executive team cares that counterfeiters are being locked up and seizures are taking place." Hence, the brand protection team focuses on gathering metrics such as raw counts of program activities.

DIFFERENCES BY INDUSTRY GROUPING

Though our small sample limits generalization, there are some differences that future research may wish to explore. Among these are differences by industry. Previous research (Wilcock and Boys, 2014) has suggested that firms in different industries may find different approaches to be effective, which is consistent with our findings.

Industry Groupings

We classify the ten firms we interviewed into three broad groupings: (1) microelectronics and computer products (three firms), (2) food, agricultural, and pharmaceutical products (four firms), and (3) apparel, luxury, and consumer products (three firms). Brand protection teams in food, agricultural, and pharmaceutical products tended to be larger, each having at least 20 members on their team, with only one of the six teams outside this industry grouping having more than 15 members.

Size and Focus of Brand Protection Teams

Larger brand protection teams may be able to consider more metrics and perform deeper analyses of metrics. As Table 10.1 shows, firms in food, agricultural, and pharmaceutical products reported the greatest number of metrics. They also reported the greatest number of valuation metrics. Indeed, while we found only eight valuation metrics used across all firms, those in food, agricultural, and pharmaceutical products reported using seven of them. Such firms also reported using more activity metrics than firms in other groupings did.

Firms in microelectronics and computer products reported using the most outcome metrics, but the fewest valuation metrics. This was somewhat surprising given that both firms in our sample that reported unequivocally emphasiz-

Table 10.1   Types of metrics by industry grouping

Type of Metric	Number of Metrics	Total Metrics Used by Firms in …		
		Microelectronics and Computer Products (3 firms)	Food, Agricultural, and Pharmaceutical Products (4 firms)	Apparel, Luxury, and Consumer Products (3 firms)
Activity	33	18	29	16
Outcome	11	10	8	4
Valuation	8	4	7	5
TOTAL	52	32	44	25

Note: Some metrics are used in multiple industry categories, so the number of metrics is not the sum of metrics across industries.

ing monetary metrics in their ROI calculations were in this grouping. Apparel, luxury, and consumer product firms reported using the fewest overall metrics.

Unanswered Questions

Our research suggests several questions for further exploration. In particular, are larger teams able to implement and assess more metrics? Does the nature of food, agricultural, and pharmaceutical products, where counterfeit products may pose greater immediate harm to consumers, mean that firms in these industries must focus on different types of metrics? Or does the nature of these products mean firms in these industries must have larger teams?

BEYOND MONETARY CALCULATIONS OF PROGRAM BENEFITS

Brand protection is becoming increasingly important as firms recognize the value of the brand and its reputation as well as the risk that counterfeits pose. Yet obtaining more resources is an ongoing challenge for brand protection programs. Firms seek to better understand whether their efforts produce meaningful results. Our interviews reveal that C-suite executives expect performance metrics, with several tying resources to them. Just as firms grapple with assessing the magnitude of counterfeiting, measurement challenges complicate the estimation of returns from brand protection investments.

Current Measurement Focus

We found that even among a small number of firms there is a wide variety of brand protection metrics. In many ways, however, the number of metrics tracked is less important than what the metrics assess and how accurately they do so. We found that firms tend to concentrate their assessment on activities rather than results or the ultimate success of their efforts. This is largely because measuring activities is easier than measuring and valuing their effects. This inhibits the way firms characterize their performance. It leads firms to operationalize the value of their productivity (e.g., numbers of takedowns) as opposed to their success (e.g., monetary value of protection to brand image).

Future Measurement Approaches

Future directions in measuring the value and performance of brand protection efforts depend on what firms seek. If they truly wish to calculate a monetary ROI for brand protection, then they need to improve their data and measurement systems, particularly to develop better outcome and valuation metrics and move beyond identifying activities as measures of achievement. They would need to construct data systems that allow staff across functions to report the necessary information. For example, a firm could create an enterprise-wide electronic portal where individuals from relevant functions across the firm could report information that the brand protection program deems critical. A firm might also attempt to incorporate new metrics into existing data systems, and to integrate data platforms across functions. Lessons for moving in this direction may be drawn from efforts to measure ROI in other business functions, such as marketing, human capital, research and development, and information technology.

Alternatively, firms can consider the value of brand protection more broadly, and the broader value that brand protection brings to a firm. This would mean reconceptualizing brand protection from a narrow financial return to a broader value proposition, such as protecting the consumer and society, improving brand integrity and value, enhancing communication and coordination across functions, and exercising corporate social responsibility. This also suggests the need for different, broader metrics to assess brand protection efforts. In practice, these would vary by industry and firm, but some metrics might include the prevalence of counterfeits in the marketplace, the rate at which consumers suffer injuries from counterfeits, the number of functions across the enterprise that are coordinated to facilitate brand protection, and the contribution to brand reputation and value.

Firms can also consider a hybrid approach. Such an approach would track a group of metrics over time to indicate how brand protection challenges and performance are changing, as well as set broad performance goals (e.g., thresholds or benchmarks). This is what many executives appear to do—indeed, one told us "part of the[ir] reporting strategy is to show how things used to be"—but we suggest they do so with an explicit understanding that this approach approximates performance thought to be associated with success and does not explicitly represent a monetary ROI. The use and interpretation of metrics is also important as changes in metrics over time can indicate either improvements (e.g., fewer identified counterfeits due to more effective strategies) or additional challenges (e.g., fewer identified counterfeits due to changes in tactics by counterfeiters). Regardless of the approach taken, firms need to carefully consider the metrics that would best support their assessment of brand protection and the data needed for these metrics.

CONCLUSIONS AND FUTURE DIRECTIONS

Research Approach

Our study has the strengths and weaknesses of similarly conducted research. Our small, purposive sample may not represent all firms, particularly the vast majority that are smaller than the smallest in our sample. Nevertheless, it allowed us to target specific individuals with strong experience representing firms with mature brand protection groups. The small scale of the study even limited the number of individuals we could interview within a single firm, but it allowed us to identify individuals with extensive experience in brand protection and anti-counterfeiting issues.

Given the limited scope of this work, future research should further examine our insights using larger, representative samples of firms. This could identify additional metrics as well as the extent to which metrics are used and better gauge variation in metrics by industry. Such an examination could also assess whether our qualitative lessons manifest themselves across a larger variety of firms.

Measuring Investments

Additional research might also consider investment metrics further. Our analysis elicited information most heavily focused on the productivity and accomplishments of brand protection teams. There has been little research about investments in brand protection efforts from a measurement or cost perspective. Future inquiry could provide insight into the investments that firms make to prevent and detect counterfeiting and how they measure such investments.

Measurement Methods and Focus

Research that develops and applies new and existing measurement methods to brand protection is much needed. We found that firms tend to track what they can most easily measure (i.e., their activities or what they do), while at the same time recognizing the limitations of those metrics and seeking ways to improve them. This suggests they have an interest in improving how they measure their activities and performance but need help doing so. Firms may wish to develop metrics for gauging the impact of their brand protection programs on brand image, counterfeit prevalence, consumer safety, and sales. Once firms identify these effects, they can turn to methods for monetizing the results. Identifying the impact of brand protection on brand image, counterfeit prevalence, consumer safety, and sales can highlight the value that brand protection brings to the firm, but only through monetizing the results can firms actually calculate a monetary ROI.

Organizational Context

Just as it is helpful to know what firms are doing and to consider alternatives for thinking about the value of brand protection, it is critical to assess how these issues play out in practice. Detailed case studies that illustrate what firms do and why they do it would increase our understanding of current practices and help shape the development of future ones. Additionally, and perhaps more difficult, there would be considerable value in examining actual firm data on brand protection investments and performance. Such data would provide valuable insights into the efficiency and effectiveness of brand protection activities, further contributing to firms' understanding of how to prevent and detect counterfeiting, and thus promoting strong brand value.

Establishing New Performance Appraisal Systems

Brand protection programs need a mechanism to assess their investment and productivity that allows them to gauge their performance. New performance appraisal systems (e.g., those formed as part of a new brand protection program or where no assessment indicators exist) should provide a means to evaluate (1) the overall success of the brand protection program and (2) the substantive and relative effectiveness of specific activities. This helps decision makers determine how best to allocate future resources to maximize performance and efficiency. The analysis of metrics and approaches in this chapter indicates there is no best way to do this. However, it does suggest that firms should seek to develop performance measurement approaches for brand protection that are consistent with their corporate ethos and values, allow them to distinguish various elements of their program performance (e.g., isolate costs and differentiate between activities and outcomes), incorporate multiple measures of each element to allow triangulation of true levels, and, importantly, permit systematic collection that can gauge progress over time.

Advancing Existing Performance Appraisal Systems

While some performance appraisal systems are more comprehensive and rigorous than others, the findings presented in this chapter suggest several ways brand protection programs could improve their existing ability to assess performance. First, program leaders should identify the various audiences to which they must (and those they should) share details on brand protection performance, and the information and metrics each of these stakeholder groups wish to examine. To provide necessary context, brand protection staff may need to educate other parts of the firm about the importance of protecting the brand, the roles and activities of the brand protection function, and current measurement challenges. Key to these conversations is determining the basis on which the brand protection function should be judged (e.g., through the lens of a narrower financial ROI or a broader value that is brought to the firm). Ultimately, the kinds of information desired by and most influential to the general counsel, the chief financial officer, and the chief security officer, for example, may be very different.

Given measurement challenges and the need for multiple types of reporting, brand protection professionals should employ multiple metrics (and build appropriate infrastructure for collecting data) on each item of interest that they can compile over time. These metrics should further distinguish between and accurately measure investment, activities, and outcomes, and the interplay of this information (i.e., valuation) to assess overall performance. Insight from this chapter suggests brand protection professionals would benefit by prioritizing the development of metrics and approaches for estimating the outcomes of brand protection activities and approaches for valuing their productivity relative to their investment. These are areas of performance appraisal where the field appears to suffer from significant measurement shortcomings.

Total Business Solution

The importance of performance assessment to the implementation of a total business solution to brand protection is undeniable. The comprehensive delineation and accurate measurement of the brand protection function and its accomplishments, which effective performance appraisal systems provide, support data-driven decision making and a culture of continuous innovation and learning. They also help to illuminate the roles of various parts of the firm, and to assess the relative success of the actions they take (be it for detection, reaction, or prevention), thereby helping the firm be more proactive and strategic. This chapter inextricably links performance assessment to the total business solution, yet, in so doing, illustrates the difficulties of implementing both in practice. Methodological issues significantly hamper their advancement, particularly as they relate to metrics, measurement methodologies, and data integrity, but other challenges are evident as well. Different interpretations of metrics and "how to know a high-performing brand protection program when you see one" suggest broad benchmarks for defining success are less valuable than each firm determining for itself what "doing well" looks like. Given the importance of performance assessment to the acquisition and allocation of resources, and to the implementation of a total business solution, firms are well-advised to continually develop and improve their performance systems. Importantly, the systems should be tailored to meet the unique circumstances and needs of the firm.

REFERENCES

Berman, B. (2008). Strategies to detect and reduce counterfeiting activity. *Business Horizons*, *51*(3), 191–199.
Clements, W. N. (2016). Examining and evaluating the effect of brand protection strategies on product counterfeiting. PhD dissertation, Northcentral University, Prescott Valley, AZ.
De Stefano, M. (2017). Managing multi-brand brand protection programs. *The Brand Protection Professional*, *2*(1), 22–23. Retrieved from http://joom.ag/nwTW/p22.
Grammich, C. A., and Wilson, J. M. (2016). The 2015 A-CAPP Center Brand Protection Strategy Summit: learning from partnerships. East Lansing, MI: MSU A-CAPP Center. Retrieved from http://a-capp.msu.edu/wp-content/uploads/2018/05/PAPER-SERIES-2015-A-CAPP-Center-Brand-Protection-Strategy-Summit_-Learning-From-Partnerships.pdf.
International Anti-Counterfeiting Coalition. (2005). The negative consequences of international intellectual property theft: economic harm, threats to the public health and safety, and links to organized crime and terrorist organizations. White Paper. Retrieved from http://cdm16064.contentdm.oclc.org/cdm/ref/collection/p266901coll4/id/3379.
Kotler, P., and Pfoertsch, W. (2006). *B2B Brand Management*. Berlin: Springer Science & Business Media.
Organisation for Economic Co-operation and Development and European Intellectual Property Office (2019). *Trends in Trade in Counterfeit and Pirated Goods: Mapping the Economic Impact*. Paris: OECD Publishing. Retrieved from https://www.oecd.org/governance/risk/trends-in-trade-in-counterfeit-and-pirated-goods-g2g9f533-en.htm.
Stumpf, S. A., and Chaudhry, P. (2010). Country matters: executives weigh in on the causes and counter measures of counterfeit trade. *Business Horizons*, *53*(3), 305–314.
US Customs and Border Protection (2019). *Intellectual Property Rights: Fiscal Year 2018 Seizure Statistics*. Retrieved from https://www.cbp.gov/sites/default/files/assets/documents/2019-Aug/IPR_Annual-Report-FY-2018.pdf.
US Office of the Intellectual Property Enforcement Coordinator (2016). *Supporting Innovation, Creativity, and Enterprise: Charting a Path Ahead, U.S. Joint Strategic Plan on Intellectual Property Enforcement, FY 2017–2019*. Retrieved from https://

www.whitehouse.gov/sites/whitehouse.gov/files/omb/IPEC/2016jointstrategicplan. pdf.

Weiss, C. H. (1998). *Evaluation: Methods for Studying Programs and Policies*. Upper Saddle River, NJ: Prentice Hall.

Wilcock, A. E., and Boys, K. A. (2014). Reduce product counterfeiting: an integrated approach. *Business Horizons*, *57*(2), 279–288.

Wilson, J. M. (2017). The future of brand protection: responding to the global risk. *Journal of Brand Management*, *24*(3), 271–283.

Wilson, J. M., and Grammich, C. (2020). Brand protection across the enterprise: toward a total-business solution. *Business Horizons*, *63*(3), 363–376.

Wilson, J. M., Grammich, C., and Chan, F. (2016). Organizing for brand protection and responding to product counterfeit risk: an analysis of global firms. *Journal of Brand Management*, *23*(3), 345–361.

Wilson, J. M., and Kinghorn, R. (2014). Brand protection as a total business solution. East Lansing, MI: Michigan State University Center for Anti-Counterfeiting and Product Protection. Retrieved from http://a-capp.msu.edu/?p=22008.

Wilson, J. M., and Sullivan, B. (2016). Brand owner approaches to assessing the risk of product counterfeiting. *Journal of Brand Management*, *23*(3), 327–344.

Yates, B. T. (1996). *Analyzing Costs, Procedures, Processes, and Outcomes in Human Services*. Thousand Oaks, CA: Sage Publishing.

PART V

The total business solution in practice

11. Brand protection: creating an enforcement framework for action

Warren MacInnis

INTRODUCTION

Most rights holders realize that product counterfeiting is a complex problem and combating it effectively can be difficult. Companies face numerous challenges at many levels and there are no simple answers for dealing with this type of criminal activity. Advances in technology, manufacturing processes, communications, and eCommerce platforms are changing the way companies do business and how consumers purchase products. As beneficial as eCommerce is for business sales outreach to the world, it also introduces new avenues for the criminal element to extend their reach too.

In this ever-changing world, intellectual property has become inextricably linked with the long-term success of companies, and protecting these important assets has become more important than ever. Criminals who deal in counterfeit products do so to gain profit from the popular and well-known brands of others. Counterfeiters unlawfully profit from the value that is attached to the goodwill, reputation, and guarantee of legitimate brands. These illegal activities equate to unfair and, in most cases, unseen competition.

From a competitive perspective, while counterfeiting incidents may seem minor on a case-by-case basis, the widespread commission of these crimes with impunity could be potentially devastating to a rights holder's reputation. Even relatively small-scale violations of counterfeiting, if allowed to occur openly and without sanctions, can lead others to believe that such conduct is tolerated. A comprehensive approach and a zero-tolerance attitude toward counterfeiting activities can help protect a company from the risks associated with these crimes.

Counterfeiters are essentially hidden competitors to legitimate business and do not need to invest in research, follow laws, play by any rules, stand by their products, respect national borders, or care who gets hurt. Counterfeiters are in business to create wealth for themselves. They will focus on areas which have the greatest profit potential and the least amount of resistance or risk.

Counterfeiters do not discriminate between brands or product types and, for the most part, they will manufacture and distribute anything that generates profits regardless of the consequences to others. On the other side of the equation, legitimate businesses need to invest in research and development, manufacture their products safely, follow regulations, respect borders, compete fairly in the open marketplace, and guarantee and stand by their products. This inequity creates an unlevel playing field for legitimate businesses, provides unfair competition, and can endanger the health and safety of consumers.

To level the playing field and assist with reducing unfair competition, rights holders should focus some of their efforts toward minimizing or eliminating the counterfeiter's opportunities, increase the counterfeiter's business risks, and implement solutions that effectively shut down their illegal operations. The "cat and mouse game" between rights holders and counterfeiters is continuously evolving, but rights holders can get one step ahead by implementing proactive and innovative strategies.

Most rights holders that invest in brand protection programs are certainly committed and engaged in their own individual battles against counterfeiters. But commitment and engagement, while absolutely necessary, are not sufficient to effectively protect their intellectual property and/or brand on their own. Given this complexity, it should come as no surprise that it is not possible to create a "a one-size-fits-all" solution for all rights holders. While product counterfeiting is complex in nature and difficult to overcome, counterfeiters, despite being criminals, do face some similar challenges to those that legitimate businesses face. They need to manufacture, advertise, sell, and ship their illegal products. The goal of the counterfeiter is to conduct their business without being exposed. But they do face risks and their weakness can be exploited through proactive, effective, and aggressive actions taken by rights holders.

To effectively protect intellectual property and brand image from well-versed nefarious actors with global outreach, brand protection departments should direct their resources and efforts to the right actions taken at the right time in alignment with the right strategies. Even with the litany of challenges faced by rights holders, there are best practices and proven tactics that can be deployed to mitigate the risks associated with product counterfeiting. As the old saying goes, "to learn from one's own experience is wise but to learn from others' is genius."

BRAND PROTECTION STRATEGY

Before an effective brand protection strategy can be developed, a rights holder must clearly understand the specific challenges they face with product counterfeiting. While the vast majority of industries will face common issues with these types of crimes, a unique and tailored approach should be developed that can be integrated into a total business solution across all relevant business functions. As with any other company department, a brand protection function will not have access to unlimited resources. Because the magnitude of harm caused by counterfeiting can be so great and because the likelihood of it occurring is so high, rights holders should invest strategically in their brand protection programs. Brand protection departments should create strategies, develop operational objectives, and implement solutions that are as effective and targeted as possible to deal with their own individual challenges.

Any enforcement function should choose a proactive methodology in order to get ahead of the counterfeiters. A reactive approach to these crimes is not as effective as a proactive approach. A reactive approach to anti-counterfeiting may work in the short term for increasing seizure numbers or generating positive statistics, but it will never sustain success over the long term. If implemented effectively, proactive measures can help reduce or even prevent incidents of counterfeiting from occurring. Rights holders need to be aggressive in their enforcement activities and invest wisely in their programs if they truly wish to make an impact in the fight against counterfeiting.

ENFORCEMENT CASE STUDY

This case study will focus on several enforcement components for brand protection programs. An effective enforcement strategy is critically important, forms a strong foundation for anti-counterfeiting efforts, and can constitute an integral part of any total business solution. The following recommendations can be used as a guide for the design, implementation, and operation of an effective enforcement function and can be applicable for new brand protection programs or can help strengthen existing programs.

Depending on individual company needs, a rights holder can incorporate their specific requirements into their own unique enforcement framework, which will help them create a customized solution. While individual rights holders will have different priorities, the main objectives of any enforcement strategy should be to identify, disrupt, and ultimately dismantle counterfeiting operations. Part of the enforcement strategy should also focus efforts on holding offenders accountable for their actions through administrative, civil, or criminal remedies. An effective enforcement function should target counterfeiting activities throughout all levels of the stream of commerce, including manufacturing, shipping routes, distribution channels, eCommerce platforms, and traditional retail outlets.

While the requirements of individual rights holders will differ, it is recommended that an effective enforcement function should, at minimum, include investigative, intelligence and analysis, case management, and product authentication capabilities. Operated effectively and efficiently, these enforcement components can form strong pillars for any brand protection program. Of course, the number of components added to any brand protection program will rely heavily upon available resources and corporate support.

INVESTIGATIONS

One of the most critical components of any enforcement function is that of investigations. In order to identify counterfeiting operations, submit complaints to law enforcement agencies, and hold criminals accountable for their illegal actions, rights holders must have the capabilities to effectively manage investigations. An investigation can simply be defined as a thorough and systematic process used to gather evidence and determine the facts of an incident. When a complaint is received or an incident uncovered, the job of a brand protection manager or investigator is to look at the facts at hand and ascertain if there is enough information to open and pursue an investigation. Once the decision has been made to open an investigation, the next step is to gather the facts and compile evidence. The evidence, once carefully examined, will help determine how the case should be handled and whether the allegations are substantiated or disproven. Both inculpatory evidence (evidence that indicates an offense has been committed) and exculpatory evidence (evidence that shows an offense has not been committed) must be considered prior to determining the final direction or outcome of an investigation.

Before any investigation can be undertaken, an effective complaint intake process should be put in place. Rights holders will receive complaints and information about counterfeiting incidents from a wide variety of sources, including law enforcement, employees, retailers, consumers, distributors, or licensees. In order to receive these complaints a method or process should be established to record and assess the information. There are several methods to set up an intake system within your program to receive complaints. Rights holders can use anti-counterfeiting email addresses, web site complaint forms, phone numbers, or other methods to receive and document complaints or incidents. Intake of complaints should be shared between a few brand protection team members to ensure complaints are not missed during periods of vacation or through an employee moving on. All relevant information should be gathered, documented, and saved, with the full details and circumstances of the complaint being outlined. When captured and assessed effectively, these original complaints will form the basis of opening a full-scale investigation.

When investigating a counterfeiting incident, a brand protection manager can help make the process more effective by answering the six big questions of who, what, when, where, why, and how. Whenever an incident happens or a complaint is received, these questions should be answered before any type of law enforcement referral or enforcement action is undertaken. Without a complete understanding of the facts and evidence of the case it will be very difficult to pursue any type of enforcement action. If the six big questions are fully answered and the evidence is sufficient to prove the allegations then it will be much easier for a rights holder to pursue administrative, civil, or criminal remedies. It is also important that brand protection managers or investigators have a good understanding of the offenses that are being investigated and of the intellectual property law in the particular country involved. Additionally, they should have a good understanding of the evidentiary requirements to prove the necessary elements of the offenses, have an in-depth knowledge of the investigative process, and have the ability to effectively collect, document, analyze, and preserve evidence.

In addition to the six big questions, there are three other questions that should be considered during the course of the investigative process. The answers to these questions will help a brand protection manager or investigator determine the facts and assess the evidence of the case. These three questions can also help focus attention, and support effective note taking, report writing, and the presentation of evidence at any judicial proceeding.

What Do I Know?

One of the primary requirements of any investigation is to collect information from all sources and accurately document the facts of the case in chronological order as they are gathered. Everything that has been learned over the course of the investigation should be systematically and accurately recorded. This will help the brand protection manager or investigator analyze the facts and the evidence relating to the case, which in turn will help determine the appropriate course of action moving forward.

How Do I Know It?

A secondary requirement of the investigative process is to ensure that any source of information or evidence is properly identified and documented in the case file. Was the information or evidence gathered through an initial complaint, a witness interview, a database search, public records, test purchases, or an open source? It is important to clearly and accurately identify all sources of information and evidence that was gathered during the investigation.

Why Does It Matter?

In order to build an effective case for administrative, civil, or criminal actions, a brand protection manager should clearly show how the facts of the case link to the offenses that are under investigation. In most situations, the facts/evidence of an investigation will be obvious to the investigator because they are the ones who have direct knowledge of the information that was gathered. However, others who become involved with the investigation during the later stages will not have an in-depth knowledge of the case. As such, it is helpful to reference in their reports where the relevant facts and evidence come together, to help others understand these important and sometimes critical connections.

The ability to effectively investigate infringement activities should be the cornerstone of any brand protection program. Without a strong investigative component to an enforcement function, most rights holders will not be completely successful in their anti-counterfeiting efforts. During any investigation, it is highly recommended to act as if every matter will be going to trial and continue to do so throughout the entire investigative process.

INTELLIGENCE AND ANALYSIS

Effective intelligence gathering and analysis capabilities are important to any brand protection program and can provide real value by clearly identifying and targeting counterfeiting operations, prioritizing investigative efforts, focusing limited resources on repeat or serious offenders, and helping rights holders increase their overall effectiveness and efficiency. By harnessing information and leveraging data, a brand protection manager or investigator can make well-informed tactical and strategic anti-counterfeiting decisions that can positively impact their programs. Intelligence-led investigations are the key to targeting investigative efforts and will help guide the collection, analysis, and use of information that will ultimately minimize waste and maximize positive results. Deployment of effective intelligence and analytics capabilities will greatly assist brand protection managers or investigators in identify illegal activities, the suspects behind the operations, the scope of their operations, their weaknesses, and their intentions. Intelligence gathering and analysis capabilities, if used effectively, can be a huge asset to brand protection programs.

CASE MANAGEMENT SYSTEM

Another key component for an effective enforcement program is a case management system or database. While many brand protection managers or investigators track and manage cases from their various desktop applications or spreadsheets, a case management system should be considered an essential requirement for every rights holder. During the course of an investigation a large amount of data is collected such as suspect information, investigative notes, emails, photographs, witness statements, test purchases, and related detailed information. If a rights holder cannot fund a full-scale system, then internal company support should be garnered to identify existing or more cost-effective internal tools.

A case management system provides a systematic and organized approach for the collection of data, provides a secure method for documenting the entire investigative process, allows for the collation and analysis of information that can be turned into useable intelligence, and ultimately preserves data for future requirements during any legal proceedings.

The case management system, at minimum, should have the capabilities to capture, store, preserve, and retrieve data. Some cases do not go to court for many years and as an investigator it is impossible to remember all aspects or details of an investigation. The ability to hold all investigative information in one secure electronic case file is very beneficial. It will help with the presentation of case materials to law enforcement agencies, support the successful prosecution of suspects at legal proceedings, and allow brand protection managers or investigators to manage the workflow of their cases while allowing easy access to all investigative data.

PRODUCT AUTHENTICATION

Product authentication is another key area of any brand protection program. It is imperative that rights holders are able to readily identify counterfeit products and can articulate the differences between an unauthorized version and a legitimate one. This is particularly important during the course of a judicial proceeding where the brand protection manager or investigator will need to present evidence of the infringement activity. Ultimately, brand protection programs are about securing intellectual property, and in most cases this translates to trademark protection. Counterfeiters go to great lengths to copy popular products, and they try to mimic the legitimate item as closely as possible.

In order to successfully investigate and hold counterfeiters accountable for their illegal actions, rights holders should ensure they invest in product and packaging anti-counterfeiting technology, provide law enforcement with product identification training and valid sample materials, as well as put in place a systematic process that will enable them to easily and quickly identify counterfeit products with 100 percent accuracy. Product authentication is a core requirement for any enforcement program and should be included as an integral part of any anti-counterfeiting strategy.

CONCLUSION

As a rights holder you are not in the business of brand protection. You are in the business of producing and selling products or services to meet customer needs and market demands. However, as a rights holder you should realize that to be as effective as possible in today's environment, brand protection needs to be integrated as part of your total business planning. Because brand protection is at best a secondary objective for most rights holders, it is important that the position and priority of brand protection in the overall corporate strategy be crystal clear.

At its core, product counterfeiting is an economic crime, but, like a pebble dropped into a calm pool of water, it can produce ripple effects that go far beyond direct economic harm to rights holders. While it is true that many anti-counterfeiting requirements are unique, it is also true that there are certain foundational brand protection best practices and tools that are applicable to most, if not all, counterfeiting challenges. The first step in the brand protection journey for a rights holder is to acknowledge that the counterfeiting risk applies specifically to them and their company. The next step is to realize that counterfeiting is no longer someone else's problem, and that there are essentially only two categories of rights holder: those who are already a victim of product counterfeiting and those that will become a victim.

A proactive approach is the key to effective brand protection. Rights holders should be watching their company dashboards for any signs of counterfeiting attacks. Before risks emerge, processes should be put in place that can be integrated within a total business solution framework that will address the threat. There are classic warning signs of counterfeiting attacks, such as loss of market share, customer product complaints, an increase in warranty claims, and calls from enforcement agencies questioning the authenticity of products.

Make no mistake: counterfeiting is an opportunistic crime, and if a rights holder can successfully identify their unique situation and the basic characteristics of their challenges, they are well on their way to finding solutions. Brand protection programs should be tailored to the specific requirements of the rights holder, with a focus on addressing identified counterfeiting risk areas. Well-thought-out strategies and clearly defined objectives that are supported by senior management are critical for brand protection programs. Like wisely chosen insurance, an effective brand protection program is the best way to protect against counterfeiting attacks.

If your company is not under full attack yet, that is good. Now is the time to be proactive and get your risks defined and begin to build an effective brand protection program. But if your company is currently under attack by counterfeiters, you should move quickly to implement solutions that will protect your intellectual property. Regardless of any "how-to" approach or framework undertaken for the design and implementation of a brand protection program, rights holders should recognize they are not alone in this battle. There is support through other rights holders, anti-counterfeiting associations, strategic and tactical partnerships, service providers, technology firms, and law enforcement agencies. By leaning on and leveraging best practices or proven solutions you will be well on your way to developing and implementing an effective brand protection program.

12. Product integrity for patient safety: a Pfizer case study[1]

Chanterelle Sung

INTRODUCTION

Counterfeit medicines, and efforts to combat them, have been a reality for many years. The current external environment and the realities of the COVID-19 pandemic are causing more people to seek medical treatments online, potentially increasing the demand and supply of counterfeits in the market. This growing trend requires renewed focus and innovative approaches in the war on criminal networks that seek to exploit vulnerable populations by producing, selling, and profiting from fake medicines and vaccines.

In an effort to address the growing need for innovative strategies to protect patients by mitigating the counterfeit risk, earlier chapters of this book set forth a variety of operational principles for establishing an enterprise-wide intellectual property strategy: 1) identify the criminal infringer as the unseen competitor; 2) emphasize prevention, proactivity, and strategy; 3) use performance metrics and data analysis to assess, quantify, and mitigate risk; 4) highlight the value of internal and external controls and mechanisms for detecting and responding to infringements; 5) create a culture of continuous improvement and learning; and 6) promote a holistic approach that integrates brand protection into all parts of the company. This chapter demonstrates, through the perspective of Pfizer's product integrity program, how a "total business solution" strategy that incorporates many of these principles can be implemented in practice, and how it might offer effective solutions in the war against counterfeit medicines.

THE COUNTERFEIT MEDICINES RISK LANDSCAPE

Pfizer continuously self-assesses and evaluates the effectiveness of its product integrity program. To generate the greatest positive impact to patients and the public, we monitor the evolving external environment, assess the nature and scope of the counterfeit risk, and enhance our risk mitigation strategies and techniques in coordination with the internal enterprise. The risk, as we assess it today, suggests several evolving threats that will require collaboration from both public and private entities to implement the most effective mitigation strategies.

Counterfeit prescription medicines are a global threat, but most of the data referenced herein is from US organizations because of strict US oversight. We are concerned that patients and healthcare providers are increasingly exposed to sources outside the traditional supply chain for medicine. Data shows that most online sellers of prescription medicines to the United States are not following regulatory requirements and guidelines. Research over the last several years, recently reaffirmed in an October 2019 report by the National Association of Boards of Pharmacy (NABP), has consistently shown that 95–96 percent of websites selling prescription medicines to US patients are operating out of compliance with US state and federal laws and/or patient safety and pharmacy practice standards. Nearly 90 percent did not require a valid prescription and 86 percent appeared to have affiliations with rogue networks of internet drug sales sites.

When patients purchase medicines from unlicensed sources, they are at risk of buying counterfeit and substandard medicines from fraudulent sellers that put patients' health and safety at risk. For example, Pfizer's Forensics Lab evaluates test-purchase samples, a number of which have revealed products with no active ingredients, unsafe amounts of active ingredients, expired active ingredients, or even toxic additives. These samples were purchased online by Pfizer, in the same way an unsuspecting buyer would have purchased and received them.

Conversations around counterfeit medicines have long focused on medicines for pain and erectile dysfunction, but we are increasingly seeing counterfeits across other therapeutic areas, including medicines for life-threatening health conditions. During a crisis, fraudulent sellers prey on fears and target the most vulnerable patients, an example being the offering of illegitimate vaccines during the current global COVID-19 pandemic. According to Homeland Security Investigations of the US Department of Homeland Security, since the start of the COVID-19 pandemic, law enforcement agencies have seen a significant increase in criminals attempting to capitalize on and profit from fear and anxiety about the virus, including through illicit online sales and illegal importation of counterfeit pharmaceuticals, medical equipment, and products claiming to be treatment options.[2] The brazen attempts to exploit patients seeking COVID-19 treatment, coupled with the growth and convenience of online shopping for medicines, shows that all therapeutic areas are at risk. When financial pressures mount, as they have during the pandemic for many, people look for ways to reduce expenses and may fall victim to the offers of criminal counterfeiters through the online sales of illicit medicines.

PFIZER'S "PRODUCT INTEGRITY FOR PATIENT SAFETY" PROGRAM

Considering this evolving risk landscape, protecting the health and safety of patients and the public is of utmost importance, and the foundation of Pfizer's purpose and work. Our product integrity program is comprehensive in nature and, as described more fully below, is an example of the "total business solution" strategy at work.

Pfizer's product integrity function is based primarily within the Pfizer Global Security team, which works enterprise-wide, cross-functionally, and cross-regionally with other business units to help protect patients from counterfeit medicines. The program consists of two primary workstreams: one focused on reducing the public's demand for counterfeits through education, awareness, and advocacy initiatives; the other focused on reducing the supply of counterfeits through proactive enforcement measures, in which we conduct investigations that are referred to law enforcement and customs agencies for interdiction, investigation, arrest, and prosecution. At the core of this program is a data-driven risk mitigation strategy that seeks to optimize the value and impact of Pfizer's efforts for patient health and safety.

Reducing Demand: Education, Awareness, and Advocacy

Pfizer believes that the public and private sectors have an opportunity to work together to enhance awareness, reduce demand, and address the ongoing risk of counterfeit medicines before it becomes a bigger threat. For this reason, Pfizer has spent years working internally and with industry partners to develop a strong education, awareness, and advocacy program that targets patients, the public, policymakers, law enforcement and healthcare professionals (HCPs). We leverage cross-enterprise functions such as Global Security, Compliance, Corporate Affairs, Legal, and the core business units to provide anti-counterfeiting training, and disseminate educational materials and key messages, including print and digital media, to our stakeholders. Our goal is to educate, raise awareness, and ultimately reduce counterfeit medicine demand.

Patients and the public
The public is increasingly exposed to sources outside the traditional supply chain for medicine via spam email, search engine results, social media, and even radio advertisements. Patients and healthcare providers are increasingly using online, as opposed to traditional brick and mortar, pharmacies to purchase their medicines. There is, therefore, an urgent need to educate consumers about the counterfeit risk.

Pfizer conveys through its outreach that it understands the convenience of online and mail-order pharmacies for patients to access their medicines and wants them to have confidence that they are obtaining authentic medicines, as prescribed by their physicians. To this end, Pfizer has developed education and awareness materials to help patients understand that when ordering prescriptions online, it is critically important to verify the authenticity of the pharmacy providing the medicines. Through Pfizer's public website, as well as through media outlets, trainings, and speaking engagements at conferences and other forums, we educate stakeholders to become aware that all legitimate online pharmacies are registered, and that before ordering any prescription, US patients should be sure the pharmacy is accredited by the NABP. They should also be aware that even if the online pharmacy's website shows the VIPPS (Verified Internet Pharmacy Practice Sites) accreditation seal, there is still a risk that the seal may be counterfeited, and the online pharmacy may be illegitimate. We tell our patients that the safest way to ensure that an online pharmacy is legitimate is to enter the actual online pharmacy website address and verify its authenticity at https://www.safe.pharmacy or via the NABP's list of accredited online pharmacies. Patients should also check to see if there is a licensed pharmacist available through the website who can answer questions about how to take the medication. If a patient suspects a Pfizer medicine is counterfeit, we ask that they contact Pfizer to report the incident.

Policymakers
From a government advocacy standpoint, we emphasize that legitimate medicines are the result of rigorous regulatory review and oversight. Pfizer has found it valuable to maintain a voice and presence in the realm of policy and legislation. In the United States, for instance, we regularly participate in anti-counterfeiting briefings and speaking engagements with state and federal legislatures to encourage collaboration between public and private sectors in order to reduce the supply and demand of counterfeit medicines, increase law enforcement resources directed toward these efforts, and maintain the security of our supply chain.

Pfizer maintains active memberships with various product integrity associations around the world, through which we share data and intelligence, support investigations, and provide input on key policymaking decisions. For example, Pfizer is an active and leading member of the Pharmaceutical Security Institute (PSI), a non-profit organization established in 2002 dedicated to protecting public health, sharing information on the counterfeiting of pharmaceuticals, and initiating enforcement actions through appropriate authorities. Through this global association, we share data and intelligence with manufacturers as well as with law enforcement and legislative officials around the world to support product integrity investigations and policies that seek to ensure safe and secure supply chains. We continue to work with policymakers and community and industry leaders to keep our supply chain secure, and to ensure the public has the information they need to purchase legitimate medicines.

Law enforcement

For many years, our Global Security team has dedicated significant resources toward educating and training law enforcement and customs officials around the world about the counterfeit medicine threat and how to mitigate this threat through proactive investigations and enforcement. Our efforts have resulted in partnerships and anti-counterfeiting trainings with law enforcement officials in 164 countries to help them prevent counterfeit medicines from reaching patients.

Healthcare professionals

Pfizer also engages with HCPs as they interact directly with patients and are key stakeholders in our education and awareness efforts. The cross-functional partnerships that the Global Security team has developed across the Pfizer enterprise with the business units and the medical safety teams have enhanced our anti-counterfeiting training and awareness program and enabled us to reach more patients. Due to their trusted relationships with patients, we work with HCPs to help ensure their patients know how to confirm if a website or online pharmacy is licensed and how to recognize a real medicine from a counterfeit.

As one example of these efforts, in 2018, Global Security partnered with the Pfizer group responsible for preparing medical information for HCPs to develop a training module to educate HCPs on the dangers of counterfeit medicines. Topics included the definition of counterfeit medicines; the conditions in which counterfeits are manufactured; the negative impacts of counterfeit medicines; technologies used to detect counterfeit medicines; how companies are helping global anti-counterfeiting efforts; strategies and recommendations for pharmacies; how to identify counterfeit medicines; and how to report suspicious medicines. In the first year that this anti-counterfeiting module was launched, Pfizer conducted four training sessions for over 800 HCPs globally, including for the Americas, Africa, Europe, the Middle East, and Asia. As a result, these HCPs are now better equipped to help protect the patients they serve.

Reducing Supply: Proactive Enforcement

Counterfeiting medicines is attractive to criminals because it is very lucrative and often hard to identify, track, and prosecute as it involves multiple countries and layers of the supply chain. We proactively work with law enforcement to remove counterfeits from the supply chain and to educate them by sharing data about counterfeit medicines in their communities.

In particular, we gather and centralize data and intelligence relating to counterfeiters and their criminal networks and monitor illicit online pharmacies on the internet—both the open indexed web and the darknet, which is an increasingly important marketplace for counterfeiters. Additionally, we have long committed resources to conducting investigations and referrals to law enforcement and customs officials to help identify and arrest counterfeiters. Ultimately, successful intelligence sharing can lead to investigations and prosecutions, and can result in the seizure of large quantities of counterfeit medicines. This in turn removes counterfeits from the supply chain, thereby preventing them from reaching patients and stopping the criminals from continuing their illegal production, distribution, and sales. For this reason, Pfizer believes it is extremely beneficial to develop long-term partnerships with police, customs officials, and prosecutors around the world so that they are aware of the counterfeit medicine threat and its harm to patient health and safety; are trained on how to identify counterfeit versions of specific products; and are well equipped to investigate referrals and requests for law enforcement action.

In May 2020, Pfizer joined a public–private partnership with the National Intellectual Property Rights Coordination Center (IPRC) and companies including Amazon, Alibaba, 3M, and others to fight against COVID-19 related fraud. Due to the pandemic, the US government has prioritized its efforts toward pandemic-related fraud and counterfeiting to protect citizens in desperate need. At the same time, Pfizer has expanded the counterfeit search from products in its portfolio to all potential counterfeit COVID-19 related products.

A sampling of metrics demonstrates the impact and necessity of our proactive enforcement efforts. Globally, between 2004 and 2020, Pfizer helped to prevent at least 300 million doses of counterfeit Pfizer products from reaching patients (see Table 12.1) while also demonstrating that counterfeit medicines pose a threat to people around the world.

Data-Driven Risk Mitigation Strategy

One of the more innovative operational principles of the total business solution approach to brand protection calls for the use of performance metrics and data analyses to assess and mitigate risk. Consistent with this approach, Pfizer places increasing emphasis on data-driven risk mitigation to make strategic decisions that optimize the value and impact of its anti-counterfeiting efforts for patient health and safety. Global Security tracks and records data relating to various enforcement, educational, and advocacy activities, such as doses of counterfeit Pfizer product seized, illicit manufacturing plants dismantled,

Table 12.1   Total number of doses (in millions) of counterfeit Pfizer products seized

Period	Amount seized (millions of doses)
2004–2020	At least: 300
2016	7.3
2017	12.4
2018	12.3
2019	19.2
2020	40.8

Note: Metrics include Upjohn products.

illicit online pharmacies dismantled, and anti-counterfeiting trainings conducted. These data sets represent valuable information that can enhance the way we conduct our investigations, as well as provide useful indicators for how we can more efficiently and effectively allocate our resources. Therefore, as a foundational step, we implemented a data quality assurance program to help ensure the timeliness, completeness, accuracy, and reliability of data inputted into our systems and platforms. This enables us to use our data sets to measure risk, outcomes, and effectiveness through an identified set of metrics, as described below.

Visualization of risk priorities through dashboards and matrices
Global Security's data-driven product integrity strategy seeks to more closely align and integrate with that of the business units that manage the brands of medicines. This approach rests on the notion that effective brand protection requires a total business solution—the budget and resources of Global Security should be considered in concert with the Pfizer commercial units' ownership of their products' security. Commercial performance data that can be visualized over time to reveal changes, patterns, or trends are key to integrating the responsibility for this work across all relevant functions of the enterprise.

Data visualization tools, dashboards, and risk matrices seek to assess the risk for Pfizer's products for proactive mitigation and potential prioritization. For example, we examine key product integrity risk and performance indicators relating to counterfeiting. We also take into consideration additional enterprise information and inputs to consider holistic factors, to positively impact our patient-centric goals for anti-counterfeiting. Aligning product integrity risk mitigation efforts with product development efforts early in the product lifecycle enables us to work with the core business units to implement proactive and preventative anti-counterfeiting measures for new products, ideally before the product is ever counterfeited. Ultimately, this approach helps to demonstrate the value that product integrity efforts bring to the enterprise to enable fit-for-purpose proactive efforts throughout the product lifecycle, inform resource allocation, and drive proactive risk mitigation for counterfeiting.

Self-assessment through data analytics and performance modeling
Global Security is exploring proactive and innovative ways to use its data to self-assess the effectiveness of its anti-counterfeiting program, as part of continuous improvements to maintain a cutting-edge product integrity program. Global Security aims to go beyond tracking metrics such as numbers of investigations, seizures of counterfeit product, arrests of counterfeiters, and law enforcement trainings. While quantity of prevention activities and efforts is certainly one way to measure the success of a given program, it is more meaningful to be able to measure the effectiveness and impact of those activities. To this end, Global Security has explored using data science to determine whether there is a correlation between certain anti-counterfeiting activities and outcomes. For example, to what extent do those investigations, seizures, arrests, and trainings help deter the demand for counterfeit medicines? To what extent do they influence the demand for legitimate medicines? To what extent do those trainings result in more educated, skilled, and motivated law enforcement agents so that they in turn investigate and prosecute more cases, and more effectively seize counterfeit medicine so that less of it remains in the illegitimate supply chain for patients to purchase? Understanding the impact of our efforts is critical to communicating our value to internal and external stakeholders, including patients.

Global Security partnered with Dr. Jeremy Wilson of Michigan State University to lay a foundation to assess the performance of Pfizer's product integrity program. Given the complexity of specifying and estimating a formal, comprehensive performance model and working with incomplete data sets, the goals of analysis were exploratory in nature. One goal was to build a pilot data model illustrating the relationship among available data sets, for example global seizures, raids, and arrests relating to counterfeit medicines; global anti-counterfeiting trainings conducted for law enforcement officials; and legitimate prescriptions issued of a given medicine. Our aim was to illustrate how such a model or analysis might work so that we can encourage its future use and development. Another goal was to identify challenges in constructing and estimating a model and to think about how to overcome these challenges.

Ultimately, the available data permitted the development and assessment of a pilot model for assessing Pfizer's product integrity performance and drawing correlations between data sets, albeit with various limitations. The data offered metrics on actions, outputs, and outcomes, as well as some control variables. This effort illustrated the complexity of assessing the relationships among product integrity activity, outputs, and outcome metrics. The data limitations in the existing samples of data preclude us from being able to rely on the models for substantive decision making in the initial, pilot phase. We aim to collect additional data and metrics to permit more sophisticated analyses that can better model, isolate, test, and estimate the relationships among product integrity activities, outputs, and outcomes.

Overall, this innovative outcomes-focused initiative helped to demonstrate the value of our efforts and encouraged us to think differently about how best to allocate resources, making decisions more data-driven and strategic. It also required and underscored the importance of working with other functions across the enterprise in a total business solution approach to brand protection.

* * *

While Pfizer's product integrity program is only one of many such cross-industry programs, it can hopefully provide academics and practitioners in this realm with a living, breathing example of the "total business solution" strategy to brand protection. In this way, Pfizer is proactively working across the enterprise and with external stakeholders in the public and private sectors to reduce the supply and demand of counterfeit medicines. This is just one illustration of how a pharmaceutical company, whose patient-centric mission is to deliver Breakthroughs That Change Patients' Lives™, can combat the ever-present global counterfeit medicines threat.

NOTES

1.   The author would like to thank Lev Kubiak, Neil Campbell, Sergio Marquez, Amy Callanan, Mary Alice Hiatt, MaryAnn Rekuc, Lindsay Havern, Sally Beatty, and Jeremy Wilson for their comments and assistance in the development of this case study.
2.   National Intellectual Property Rights Center (n.d.). HSI Announces Partnership in Fight against COVID-19 Fraud. https://www.iprcenter.gov/news/hsi-announces -partnership-in-fight-against-covid-19-fraud.

13. Calculating brand protection impact

John Carriero

In developing brand protection programs, I have found that among the first things which executives want to know is the impact the program is having. How much money are we gaining, or saving, by having a brand protection program? How can we calculate that? What do these values tell us about how our program is working, and what we need to change?

Still other questions have risen over time that we have sought to address. Where, for example, can we best apply prevention, proactivity, and strategy to our efforts? What internal controls and mechanisms would work best for us?

In this chapter, I discuss how over the course of my career I have calculated and quantified a Brand Protection Impact (BPI). Executives will want to see an impact from a new brand protection program, but also need to understand that the returns on their program will not be immediate. The BPI offers a means to demonstrate the impact a program is having, as well as its change over time.

While the bulk of this chapter is on the BPI, I also discuss how non-quantitative programs can improve brand protection, as well as how initiatives such as smart tag technology can benefit multiple functions within an organization. Altogether, these initiatives highlight several elements of the total business solution to brand protection which I have found applicable in the course of my career for different manufacturers and rights holders.

BRAND PROTECTION IMPACT

To quantify the BPI, we generate or estimate numbers for each of five components. These are:

1. Units seized through *ground enforcement* work.
2. Units seized through *factory raids*.
3. *Marketplace and auction site enforcement* (including social media and mobile).
4. *Websites/domain enforcement*.
5. *Restitution*/Settlement funds/Supplier (factory) penalties.

1.   Ground Enforcement

For our ground enforcement component, we simply calculate units recovered through our cease-and-desist programs and combine that with units seized during actions with customs and other law enforcement, namely market raids, shop raids, warehouse raids, traffic stops, and customs seizures. We confirm the quantities and follow each case through to destruction. We apply an Average Unit Retail (AUR) of $40 per unit. This is a blended value reflecting the average cost of items that are seized. For example, if half the items seized have a retail price of $60 and half have a retail price of $20, then the average blended value for calculations will be, as here, $40. This can change over time as the composition of seizures changes. It can also become more sophisticated as you develop better means to track specific items seized. The point is to have an accepted, accessible, and understandable figure for your calculations.

2.   Factory Raids

We calculate the BPI of a factory raid differently from that of shop or warehouse raids. While the minimum value of a shop or warehouse raid is the value of products seized there, we believe raiding a factory has a greater impact because factories can produce thousands of products and continue producing counterfeits unless we take action. It is our job to give factories the incentive to stop the manufacturing of counterfeit products bearing our trademarks. The best way we have found to do this is to raid and remove all products while also seeking to remove any equipment used to make counterfeit product.

To estimate the impact of factory raids, we multiply the number of units of product seized by six. While this is a somewhat arbitrary number, we believe this provides a conservative estimate for several reasons. Multiplying by six assumes that the factory would produce the number of counterfeit units on-hand every other month for an entire year. Realistically, we have found a factory is likely to produce this quantity on a weekly basis. It is widely known that factories regularly move finished product from their factory location to avoid detection by the authorities and avoid large fines as well as potential criminal charges. By estimating a conservative annual production and using that to calculate the value of a factory raid, we believe we acknowledge at least the minimum impact of factory raids with a conservative value that can be applied across factory settings. By being conservative in our estimates throughout, we provide estimates that even program skeptics can accept, while also managing expectations for future program performance.

3.   Marketplace and Auction Site Enforcement

Marketplace and auction enforcement data allow us to accurately calculate the number of auctions and dollar values of the auctions we successfully shut down on most marketplace platforms around the world. Marketplace auction sites include sites such as Amazon and Alibaba, where third parties may sell products at a specified price. Auction sites include sites such as eBay, where third parties may seek to auction items or sell them at a specified price.

We do not calculate the blocked sales as "seized items" because they are not seized and remain with the sellers. Indeed, a seller seeking to market a counterfeit item on one site may, if blocked, seek to market it on a different site. The only real solution to such infringing sellers is to go from an online to an offline investigation, identifying and raiding the infringers and their operations.

Nevertheless, we do calculate the blocked sales associated with those sites, using this value to identify and quantify the financial impact of these actions in our BPI calculations. Specifically, we include the list price of an item for a blocked listing in our BPI calculations. A listing that we shut down for a counterfeit pair of shoes selling for $100, for example, would count as one listing shutdown and have a BPI of $100. One hundred such actions would have a BPI of $10,000 (though values will vary by specific items listed).

Though infringers may seek to sell their items elsewhere if their listing is shut down, the elimination of any illegal auction or marketplace listing provides the opportunity for the sale of authentic items by our brand and our legitimate partners. We continually scrub and crawl hundreds of related sites, changing those we monitor as counterfeiting activity shifts by region and platform. We find platforms in every region of the world, helping us identify our presence around the world as well as increased opportunities for legitimate sales.

With the increased popularity of social media and mobile apps, we are seeing an increase in the advertising and sale of counterfeit products on social media platforms. We face a different set of obstacles when investigating these cases. Most social media sales are conducted within "Invite Only" private groups. These private sales are similar to in-home "purse parties," with sales arranged among an extended group of friends and purchases available only to those receiving an invitation. Investigations of social media platform sales are complicated and time-consuming. We calculate success from these investigations through the number of recovered items, which we may obtain through a well-prepared cease-and-desist letter or with the assistance of the local authorities.

Social media ads may also lead consumers to various websites associated with direct garment printers, who may produce items such as t-shirts, hoodies, coffee mugs, and mobile phone covers while infringing and misusing logos and trademarks of reputable brands. Websites associated with direct garment printers all display legal language attesting to respecting intellectual property but use this same language to indemnify themselves by claiming the selling or campaign creator is ultimately responsible. Owners of these websites also fail to monitor the activity on their websites and continue to gain proceeds and profit from these sales.

4.   Websites/Domain Enforcement

We similarly take a conservative approach to calculating the impact of our program for website and domain enforcement. While none of our work guarantees sales, it creates the opportunity for our business to sell authentic products to consumers who are searching for them. There are a few different categories of websites or domains that we encounter. These are copycat websites, bargain hunter websites, and generic websites. Our work in addressing these websites has been affected in recent years by the *General Data Protection Regulation* (GDPR) of the European Union (EU). Counterfeiters have exploited the GDPR, which regulates data protection and privacy in the EU, to hide behind privacy walls while fully taking advantage of unsuspecting consumers.

Copycat websites
Copycat websites look and feel like the authentic site. They use copyrighted images and marketing to fool consumers into believing the site is associated with the brand. You may see some variation of the brand's trademark or brand name in the domain name. Often they use the exact same legal language, "about us" information, and contact information as the authentic website. Consumers ordering from such sites may receive counterfeit products of the brand, they may receive counterfeit products from other brands, or they may receive no products. Those who receive counterfeit products or no products may contact the legitimate brand only to learn their order number or invoice details are not valid. This causes much frustration for both the consumer and the customer service team of the brand. We believe most if not all the consumers shopping on these sites were actually looking for the legitimate products. So, we work extra hard to identify and eliminate these copycat websites.

Bargain hunter websites
Bargain hunter websites usually sell a variety of brands at highly discounted prices. You may also see original prices inflated, only to be crossed out with claims of huge discounts. These sites usually offer free worldwide shipping, claim colors or styles may vary due to in-stock quantities, and offer payment options in many different currencies. The offers are usually too good to be true, and the websites are usually loaded with typos and grammatical errors.

The trained investigator or brand protection professional can quickly identify which website template is being used for a bargain hunter website, sometimes by the free-form contact-us page, and even by the logos being used and by other information from the shipping services. Most of the bargain hunter websites have moved away from providing an actual e-mail address, because the same customer service e-mail address could show the connection among multiple sites. Yet by searching specific templates, brand protection personnel can identify related sites, each with their own operator but each also possibly fronting for a centralized counterfeit operation that fulfills orders that are made through these different sites.

Over the years we have been able to learn more through various sources, including by accompanying journalists and reviewing customer-complaint forms, about purchasers of items from different counterfeit sites. While those who use copycat sites are the most deceived, we believe a fair number of shoppers on bargain hunter sites were hoping to get bargains but still wanting to believe the items could be from original factories, or that the items were excess or liquidation. That is, these shoppers, in contrast to many that shop at generic websites, wanted to believe in some way that their purchases were legitimate.

Generic websites
Generic websites often have obscure names, show up after several pages of an internet search, or are only found through direct links. My experience over the years indicates that such sites are usually shopped by those who not only want a bargain but don't actually care if the item is real or fake. Rather, such customers want something that has the desired logo and "looks" like the item they want. You will often see language claiming that products are AAA+, replicas, or made in the same factories as the originals. There are thousands of these sites, and they use prefabricated templates which are later customized for counterfeiting purposes. Such templates may be replicated across hundreds of generic websites with names like "Billy's Bargains" or "Joe's Shop" (notional, not actual, examples). We suspect that there are several criminal organizations creating, selling, and managing large numbers of websites associated with the prefabricated templates. This practice continues to grow along with standard e-commerce businesses. There are many quality web service teams and individuals actively pursuing these bad actors. For us, we know this practice exists and has a significant impact on our brand, as well as many other brands we see being peddled on many of the same sites. Still, as we discuss below, we doubt the impact of such websites is as great as that for copycat websites or even bargain hunter websites. This is because we assume customers using these websites have little to no interest in legitimate product.

General guidance on calculations from cyber enforcement

There are several special considerations brand protection professionals may wish to make in calculating the impact of online enforcement. Some brands may calculate the value of every domain being shut down by calculating the number of products being offered on the site. Others have sophisticated IT support which can objectively calculate the impact of site shutdowns by comparing the Search Engine Optimization (SEO), Moz and Alexa scores, derived from online tools available to any user and which give an estimate of traffic for a site and how it compares to others, for each site seized. Still others may seek to calculate how long the site has been actively selling counterfeits and causing additional brand damage.

Our estimates for the impact of cyber enforcement depend on the type of enforcement action we take. We conduct three levels of domain takedown, each briefly described below:

1. Removal of Copyrighted Images Only. These sites are legally selling authentic products but are using our copyrighted images. We take action to have these copyrighted images removed and have the website use its own images.
2. Standard Domain Takedown. The domain is closed with assistance from the host provider. This basically breaks the web link, meaning the website is inoperable and cannot be accessed.
3. Domain Takedown and Recovery. We conduct a domain takedown and request transfer of the ownership of the domain to us. The domain is transferred and redirected to our official e-commerce website. Often there is time remaining on the website contract, which we receive to track orders placed through the website—and which we may also extend once the domain registration expires.

Level 2 and 3 takedowns provide additional options to better calculate the value for each domain. For example, a brand may choose to provide an informative landing page when a seized domain is accessed. This landing page can educate consumers on the damage caused by counterfeiting networks and provide the ability to access the brand's authentic website by clicking a link. Brands can track this redirection, and any sales resulting from such redirected traffic. This tracking provides an actual dollar value and insight into consumer behavior. Either the consumer was looking for authentic merchandise and ultimately makes a purchase, or the customer doesn't convert to a sale and leaves the site in search of something else.

We believe copycat websites pose a greater risk to our brand than the bargain hunter or generic websites. Copycat websites cause frustration and confusion for would-be consumers who may be hoping to experience our brand for the first time. The use by copycat websites of our trademarks, trade names, brand names, and associated product names, as well as of our copyrighted images and similar marketing techniques, allows such websites to look most like us, and hence they represent the greatest risk to legitimate sales of our product. A sincere customer who inadvertently buys counterfeits of our product from a copycat site may decide to never buy our brand.

Bargain hunter sites also tend to use our marketing or product images, but they also use those of other brands and typically look and feel less professional. Generic websites look and feel suspect. They could and should be avoided by your average consumer but are regularly shopped by those with little or no concern about receiving counterfeits or replica products. Put another way, sincere customers may be less likely to shop at and feel truly deceived by such websites.

Ultimately, BPI calculations might consider different tiers of values for each website. For example, we might value copycat sites at $12,000 each, bargain sites at $6,000 each, and generic sites at $1,200 each. One might also derive these values from findings in seizing domains from squatters and pirates. These values may also reflect costs associated with acquiring similar domains.

Nevertheless, in calculating the BPI of website domain seizures, we take a conservative approach and assume a single website seizure has a BPI of $1,200. This reflects not only what we have seen in seizing domains, but also our observation that a website would each month sell approximately $100 of counterfeit goods wrongly bearing our logos, representing $1,200 in forgone sales of legitimate products in a year. Again, we believe this to be an underestimate, but it does provide a standard dollar value that can be applied. Additional considerations in calculating the BPI of a seized website domain might include how long the website was active prior to detection and disabling. Over time, you may develop more elaborate standardized estimates that can be used to evaluate your work alongside that of your trusted peers.

5.   Restitution

The final calculation in estimating BPI is restitution. In simple terms, restitution consists of monies recovered from infringers through settlements. Restitution may represent monies that infringers are ordered to and actually do pay us for infringing upon our intellectual property rights. Restitution may also result from penalties levied on factories in breach of an agreement to provide a specified amount of genuine product, where excess product has been produced that then enters the market through illicit channels. Infringements may have different meaning for different companies and their purposes. Some companies may see brand protection as a profit center and seek to recoup through infringements what has been lost to infringers. More typically, companies may seek restitution to deter infringers from committing future violations. Oftentimes the restitution received is reinvested into the company's brand protection program. The amount given in the BPI calculation below for monies from infringements is a notional number and meant as a reminder to the reader to include restitution in any BPI calculations. Sometimes restitution can include non-monetary actions, such as public acknowledgment of the infringement and commitment not to infringe again. Such non-financial restitution can be valuable as well.

Calculating the Brand Protection Impact

Ideally, our BPI calculations should show our impact in not only removing and stopping the flow of counterfeit products, but also in creating the opportunity for sales of authentic product. Every counterfeit product we remove from the stream of commerce and every illicit website we remove from the internet provides the opportunity for our sales team and our legitimate partners to regain market share from the counterfeiters. We intentionally take a conservative approach in our calculations. We aim to provide data and analysis that would be generally accepted by most skeptics. Our conservative approach may understate the impact of our work, but our calculations still show a significant impact.

One indicator of our conservative approach is that we do not consider items such as seized labels, trims, zippers, marketing, and packaging in our calculations. While such items are significant in production, we do not include these at present. We count only finished goods when calculating our BPI, although we do track unfinished goods, labels, packaging, and other trims for identification and investigative purposes.

Because we believe the most dangerous counterfeit threats to us are from those seeking to best imitate our marketing, we use an AUR for the dollar value of seized products. Product seizures may come from customs interdictions, law enforcement raids, and our own cease-and-desist program. In our factory raids, we also search for sales records, purchase history, and supplier records to identify other key targets in the counterfeiter's network. Sales records in particular may help us put together a more complete picture of a specific target's potential impact. If a counterfeiter's partners are allowed to continue their illicit behavior, then they may still produce hundreds of thousands of products annually. Once we have taken actions against a counterfeiter and any of its partners that we can identify, we find financial and criminal penalties to be the best deterrent.

Table 13.1   Notional BPI calculations

Component	Units	BPI per unit	Component BPI
Ground enforcement	90,000 units of product	$40	$3,600,000
Factory raid	20,000 units seized multiplied by six to reflect conservative annual production (120,000 in total)	$40	$4,800,000
Marketplace or auction sales blocked	24,000 listings blocked	$100, based on actual selling price	$2,400,000
Websites seized	750 sites seized	$1,200 for each site, as indicated above	$900,000
Restitution	Notional value listed, which also represents the minimum annual value seen in our work		$50,000
TOTAL			$11,750,000

Having gathered a year's worth of data for our operations, we calculate BPI as the sum of the following values.

1.   Ground Enforcement Seizure Impact = # of Units × Average Unit Retail
2.   Factory Raid Impact = # of Units × Average Unit Retail × 6
3.   Marketplace and Auction Listings Blocked = $ Value of Blocked Sales
4.   Website Enforcement Value = # of Domains Shut Down × $1,200
5.   Restitution = $ Recovered Settlement Dollars.

For example, if in one year there were 90,000 units seized in ground enforcement, 20,000 units seized during factory raids, 24,000 marketplace and auction listings blocked, 750 websites seized, and restitution payments made of $50,000, then our BPI for the year would be as shown in Table 13.1 (presented for illustrative purposes only).

Different brands may find that different values are relevant to their work. And you may be able to refine your estimates, and the analyses that can be made with them, over time. My point here is that this provides one basic way to make a conservative estimate of the impact of your work, which can be adapted elsewhere as you first set out to demonstrate the value of your work.

NON-QUANTITATIVE PROGRAMS WITH POSITIVE IMPACT

In addition to quantifying your BPI, you should also highlight other programs whose impact it is difficult to quantify but which can be essential to protecting your brand. For example, Awareness Training is a key program to address.

Conducting brand protection training for law enforcement can directly affect the number of cases that law enforcement officials report.

We host law enforcement trainings to familiarize new law enforcement teams with our products and standard operations. Our trainings are not intended to make individual officers experts on our brand, but we do aim to provide officers the tools they need to identify infringements, along with information on whom they should contact when they see concerning situations. We train thousands of officers around the world annually, and every year we have seen an increase in law enforcement actions that protect our brands. We offer trainings in key ports around the globe. We recognize that even if officers we trained this year do not have a case for us, they may encounter future cases that our training helped them identify and develop, which in turn will increase our demonstrated BPI.

Brand protection workers may seek different ways to offer training—and may always be on the lookout for new training or outreach opportunities. One strategy I have followed is to continually provide trainings at the ten leading ports in each of three different global regions (the Americas; Europe and the Middle East; and Africa, Asia, and the Pacific). This provides 30 ports to target worldwide. At some of these trade centers, my colleagues and I have been invited back repeatedly to discuss our products and ways they may be counterfeited. Others have been more resistant, but we continually approach these, especially those in regions where we believe counterfeits of our goods are increasing.

Changing events may also provide new opportunities. For example, the COVID-19 pandemic, while greatly restricting in-person trainings, opened new opportunities for virtual trainings. Such trainings could be delivered relatively easily in areas where they had not been conducted before. Participants could participate at their desktop without their employers needing to arrange on-site facilities for our sessions. Recasting training sessions as information sessions to introduce your brand and its issues may also help you gain access to reluctant law enforcement officials.

Factory audits also provide a positive impact, but we have not calculated or associated direct monetary value to them. Among the benefits of factory audits are better control over production facilities and enhanced protection of our trade secrets and product development. We also have direct involvement with the destruction of excess product, quality fallout, and left-over materials. Our involvement provides guidance on improved controls for our product supply chain. For example, we attempt to control product diversion to ensure we are not directly competing with ourselves. Some brands have monetary penalty clauses in master sourcing agreements as well as licensing and distributor agreements. Some choose to impose financial penalties when audits reveal policy violations. Such penalties can easily be included as restitution recovered in BPI calculations.

SMART TAG TECHNOLOGY

The total business solution suggests that multiple functions across the organization can play a role in brand protection. Smart technology such as radio frequency identification (RFID) and near field communication (NFC) labels, which wirelessly transmit information about each item in inventory and tracks its disposition, are examples of how one solution can benefit several teams in brand protection and provide an immediate return on the investment. Smart tags can help Sourcing, Quality Assurance, Asset Protection, Logistics, Retail, and Marketing functions, among others, both perform their own work and that of brand protection. The following examples demonstrate this cross-function potential.

Within factories, smart tag technology can be used not only to monitor inventory but also to track sensitive, high-value, or special edition items throughout the production and storage process. Sample rooms or innovation centers can be wired to set off an alarm if products bearing these tags are removed. Factories can also use this technology when storing excess or substandard products prior to destruction. They can also track the products until they are shipped, enabling shippers to match the purchase order with packaged product before it leaves the factory.

The tags can allow teams to identify shipment losses or shortages in a timely fashion. If companies can implement inventory checks in-transit, they can then also better identify points of loss and opportunities to repair their supply chain. Smart technology may allow brands to track their products on transport routes taken by trucking companies to the ports, the boats or planes on which they are shipped, or products on the routes to and from distribution houses. Having better control of inventories that are accurate assists many teams. Planners with accurate on-hand numbers of products in each phase of the supply chain can better forecast product demand and distribution.

In retail locations, smart tagged products can be automatically received into inventory when the shipping boxes enter the stockroom through the shipping or receiving door. Stores can also identify and differentiate product on the sales floor from products remaining in the stockroom. The smart tags can also be integrated with stores' Electronic Article Systems, which may eliminate the need for hard security sensor tags and their associated costs. This enables store teams to easily conduct a partial or complete store inventory as often as is required without the need to prepare and pay for a professional inventory vendor. Asset Protection Teams and store management can quickly identify and respond to stores needing extra attention due to poor inventory results.

Smart tags can aid investigations involving goods that are lost in transit, diverted, or stolen. Accurate information could help identify products for law enforcement. For lost or stolen goods that are returned to retail locations, a smart tag system can inform personnel that the products were "never received into inventory" or that personnel should "hold goods for law enforcement investigations." Smart tags provide many options to better control inventory by utilizing track-and-trace abilities.

Smart tags can help brands track disposed goods to ensure they do not re-enter their inventory. For example, many companies donate goods to charitable causes, but unfortunately some of these goods end up in unintended places. Companies can use track-and-trace features to confirm their donations are reaching the intended parties.

Smart tags can assist marketing and sales teams. Many companies provide samples for sales representatives, for "influencers," and for customer wear tests. Smart tags can help track and trace these sensitive products and ensure they are being used as intended. The tags can also enhance in-store marketing campaigns, encourage increased consumer engagement, and enable the use of new technologies such as smart mirrors (fitting mirrors where customers trying products may also get information about related products), self-help kiosks, handheld sales points, and advanced loyalty programs.

Quality assurance and Compliance teams, with the help of smart tracking technology, can conduct recalls much more easily from our supply chain and from consumers worldwide. Smart tag technology can help these teams identify where products were shipped and stored and where the returns will be coming from. These teams can identify regional collection points to make the recall easier.

In short, brands adapting new technologies for myriad purposes may often find such technologies not only help specific functions perform their primary tasks but also help protect their products from counterfeits, diversion, and other activities that infringe on their intellectual property. Often in my work, I did not request a specific piece of smart technology, but I learned how to use existing technologies for brand protection. Similarly, demonstrating the value of your technology for other business purposes can help engage other functions in supporting mutually beneficial technologies—and ultimately enhance your brand protection efforts.

SUMMARY

My final advice is simple: choose a program that meshes with your company's mission and trust the process. The key is to start slow, execute your plan in measured steps, and try to think beyond the present moment by building one-year, three-year, and five-year plans. Innovate whenever you have the opportunity, collaborate with internal teams to identify mutually beneficial programs, and surround yourself with brilliant minds willing to commit the energy needed to see your program grow and succeed.

The specific examples that I have identified in this chapter can help you build a program that is effective, and whose effectiveness you can readily demonstrate. For example, BPI calculation can launch you toward performance metrics and using data and analysis to assess and mitigate risks. Identifying and calculating the impact of some of its individual components, such as copycat websites, can help you better understand the unseen competitor to your own products. Program features that are not as easily quantified, such as trainings, can help you create a culture of continuous improvement and inspire your partners to embrace learning in identifying ways to protect your brand. New technologies such as smart tags can help you highlight the value of internal and external controls and mechanisms for detecting and responding to infringements. It can also, by involving multiple functions, promote a holistic approach to brand protection that integrates and coordinates all parts of the business.

Ultimately, we believe the success of our program is not much different from that of other successful programs. We designed a thoughtful strategy that complemented the vision, mission, and values of our company and we stayed the course. We remained patient and consistent and believed in our strategy, our programs, and our partners. We remained closely connected to the business and were able to identify times when we needed to adapt or adjust our plans as the business required. But throughout everything we continue to maintain our focus.

14. The never-ending brand protection conundrum

Vivian Vassallo

The movie *Catch Me If You Can* comes to mind every time I am asked about my work in brand protection. The story of how an aspiring conman impersonated professionals in multiple fields, and how the law enforcement official pursuing him crosses oceans and must learn the intricacies of multiple settings, has its parallels in brand protection.

Similarly, I have found work in brand protection to involve identifying offenders in different guises and settings. Few of us chose this career explicitly. Rather, it found us as, in other positions, we were asked to investigate issues such as a grey market complaint or an untraceable return merchandise authorization, or a more serious occurrence involving injury from an ultimately counterfeit product. But our common experience has been one of developing a new art of brand protection. My professional experiences across my career have helped me understand brand protection as an art: the need to find a balanced team for this work, the importance of always looking for new connections, and the importance of where the brand protection function resides within the corporation.

THE ART OF BRAND PROTECTION

In calling brand protection an art, I mean to emphasize that there is no single set of rules that will yield all the goals your organization should pursue. Some results may be readily apparent and desirable, but others, including indirect results such as deterrence, lessons learned in protecting your brand, and other process improvements, can be equally valuable.

Artists may have many common skills, but they are not all skills one typically learns or trains for professionally. Artists may view their work as a puzzle and need to be able to step back from the puzzle at times and see what pieces are missing. Artists who start working on a painting or sculpture may, as they paint or mold their work, see something that they need to incorporate.

Like artists, brand protection professionals may never be satisfied with their work. They will always see something more that can be done. But they realize that success can be found in any win you can get, no matter how small, and that brand protection can be a set of battles in an ongoing war. As artists may be influenced by different styles, so brand protection practitioners may learn from each other. Brand protection practitioners may find, in addition to all the tools they have for analyzing, monitoring, tracking, tracing, targeting, and training law enforcement, one of the most valuable resources they can develop involves the sharing of best practices, regardless of industry. Learning what others are doing is not only useful but can even be therapeutic in a space where you may often take two steps forward and one back.

ASSEMBLING THE RIGHT TEAM

Of course, while colleagues in other firms may be able to share lessons and some best practices with you, the biggest contributor to your success will be your colleagues within a firm.

In short, you will need different artists. It can be difficult to find talent with the right combination of skills to join an effort where passion, a deep sense of justice, a good sense of humor, and, when needed, nerves of steel are all essential.

I have found it does not matter if new members have a background in brand or intellectual property protection. What is more important is interest in the work, in digging for clues, in analyzing what is found, and in being continually curious about it. Brand protection practitioners need to be interested in finding facts and new solutions. They must not get discouraged when a puzzle is not making sense.

Above all, they need to be team players. In hiring, brand protection managers need to stay away from those who want to "own" the findings, who do not "play well with others." I have never been involved in a brand protection case that I could have solved all by myself. You always need somebody else to think of something else.

Although, as I say above, a background in brand protection is not strictly necessary, it has been good to see academia becoming involved in this space in the last few years. It is now possible to get a broader level of education focusing on various aspects of intellectual property crime. Students or interested professionals exploring and learning more about this field find it is an option for a meaningful career.

POSITIONING THE BRAND PROTECTION PROGRAM

Beyond assembling the right team, the key to success for protecting your brand is to ensure it is not treated as just another program of the legal, global security, or supply chain functions. It should be everyone's problem to address. The key to a successful program lies in how well the corporation understands the problem in order to address it properly. It is not until your Board of Directors, your chief executive officer (CEO), chief financial officer, and the heads of your sales and business units openly recognize the problem and agree to a coordinated plan including resources that you have a true, functional corporate program.

It does not matter where the program begins, but it does matter where it ultimately resides. Most companies will start their brand protection program where they first detect a problem with intellectual property infringements. Such programs may develop organically, as someone somewhere in the organization identifies a problem with intellectual property infringements and seeks to address it. This is acceptable and to be expected.

Ultimately, however, the program should rest with a centralized organization within the company that has direct access to the highest levels of corporate leadership. Without such centralization and a high-level advocate, the brand protection program will come to reflect the interests of the function where it resides, and not of the firm as a whole. If, for example, a brand protection program originates and remains within the finance function, then there may be more emphasis in the program on the return on investment than on prevention and enforcement. Recovering financially what you have lost is important, but you need to consider other goals, such as sending messages that you will make efforts to protect your brand.

By sitting in a central organization, at the highest level, your program can have an executive sponsor or access to a member of the executive team that reports to the CEO. Your program has to have visibility. Everybody needs to know that a brand protection organization exists in your company, and that it has support at every level and in all business units. That is when you can have a successful, meaningful program, not when it is embedded in another, derivative function. Something like the legal group can be ideal—a neutral party whose job it is to protect the corporation no matter what, and which seeks enforcement. But the highest goal is to be visible to the front office.

In searching for a champion, search for a high-ranking executive whose interest is piqued by this work. Seek someone who is wondering what is happening with brand protection, what are the reasons for problems surrounding it, and how brand protection failures can lead to other problems.

CHOOSING THE ENFORCEMENT BALANCE

Though having a visible, centralized brand protection program with high levels of support can help you avoid conflicts with the interests of specific functions, some conflicts of interest will remain and need to be addressed. Your company may have legitimate concerns about the effectiveness of a particular action.

In some jurisdictions, it may not make sense to pursue infringement problems far. It could take years to get to court there, in return for only modest penalties, punishment, or retribution. In some jurisdictions, it may not make sense to commit many resources to a case, although perhaps you will still want to demonstrate that you will pursue infringers there.

Other conflicts can be harder to address. In some cases, you may find customers of legitimate goods "playing both sides" in procuring both legitimate goods from you and goods bearing your name from other channels. If you find a legitimate customer of yours is infringing on your rights as well, then you may need to ask if enforcement will cause a rupture in the relationship. Converting customers to legitimate product raises similar questions of how to make your company whole again following past violations. The company may seek ways to address the relationship with infringers beyond enforcement. The point is that even when ideally positioned a brand protection team may have to address conflicts of interest, so make sure you know who your customer is.

EXPECTING THE UNEXPECTED

It is tempting to build processes to streamline how we handle incidents. Relying too much on process, however, can cause you to miss the outlier. Do not get me wrong, we do need processes, but we need to ensure we don't just rely on them.

As one example, I note a case we had been building against a culprit in Asia. We were about to send the case to outside counsel for enforcement, when we got a call out of the blue that this perpetrator was operating in another region closer to the United States and importing goods through a port in the southeastern United States. I stress that we had not known this perpetrator was operating in that region, and we had not identified this perpetrator through our usual processes. But once we learned this perpetrator was operating in a region that was more open to our enforcement actions, as well as in a US port, we shifted plans. We knew we could do something then that had more teeth.

This is also where data and analysis can be your best ally. I later discuss another example where our data and analysis ultimately found the tentacles of an operation for a long-time perpetrator—and helped us curtail that culprit's operations.

CLEAN YOUR OWN HOUSE AND REAP THE BENEFITS

Often, brand protection programs can benefit by first cleaning their own house. As an example of this, I note that we once received a complaint from a customer feeling they were not getting enough market traction because of an unauthorized party that was selling our product and undercutting our prices. We were able to procure some of the products and traced the chain of events. My first thought was that this was either a counterfeit product or a channel issue. It was the latter.

In this case, the serial number revealed the product was genuine and sold to a legitimate channel as part of a promotion from the prior year. I personally have always disliked channel promotions. In my view, such incentives—buy Y and get X free, buy Z and you get Y rebate—also provide the wrong incentives to potential perpetrators. No matter the terms and conditions you think you have in place to ensure a level playing field, the opportunity to game the system is always there.

In this case a channel partner in collusion with a greedy and unscrupulous salesperson concocted a bogus Enterprise User in order to receive the substantial discount. More specifically, they forged documents from a legitimate customer to create a sale of products the legitimate customer did not want, but which were ultimately channeled and paid elsewhere, circumventing our normal processes for screening customers.

On the surface, this may seem inconsequential, because the company still made a sale. But this can affect the integrity of the supply chain and result in dissatisfied partners.

This points to other lessons that brand protection teams ought to apply, such as knowing who your customer is and conducting judicious random checks to verify products end up where they were intended to go in the first place. This may even mean verifying that a company exists. Verifying websites alone is not sufficient, because websites can be created very easily. In one case, we were able to determine that the website for a new customer was created just two weeks prior to the customer wanting to develop a business relationship with us.

You may want to leverage other resources of your company in such efforts. For example, you may ask your field personnel to verify the physical addresses of new potential partners. Sometimes they will find that it is a legitimate site, but sometimes they will see that it appears to be only an office fronting for another operation.

You may particularly want to visit manufacturers who wish to work with you. If your prospective partner protests that it is too far away to visit, that should be a warning sign—and should make you more determined to visit.

In short, there is no one "magic" trick in investigating potential partners. Rather, the secret lies in conducting thorough research and due diligence, especially into corporate registrations.

"CATCH ME IF YOU CAN": INVESTIGATING A PERPETRATOR OVER TIME AND ACROSS CONTINENTS

Investigating grey market sales, that is, sales made outside authorized channels, as well as sales that commingle legitimate and other product, may seem like a piece of cake once you have experienced a more sophisticated operation. As an illustration, I note the case of a customer who had stopped paying for our products while still using and commercializing our inherent technology. Because this company was headquartered in China, enforcement efforts were challenging. But given the size of what looked like a large operation, we decided to investigate further. At the time, our brand protection team was still small, so we had to rely on other functions such as finance, sales, operations, and legal to help us learn how this entity was still able to manufacture products with our intellectual property.

We reached out to the company directly to discuss the matter at hand. Somehow, I naïvely thought that a face-to-face dialogue could lead to common ground. Unfortunately, the end result of the visit was clear defiance from the infringer, who claimed that the owner was well-established in Chinese politics and the company had so much power that it did not need to comply with any of its contractual obligations. His attitude was essentially, "catch me if you can."

Given the continued complaints from other paying customers, who were frustrated by seeing lower-priced products flooding the marketplace, we worked with other functions in our company to find every possible bit of information we could on this perpetrator.

Our first break actually came somewhat indirectly from the perpetrator himself. He got very emboldened and created a company in the United States that hired known, reputable leaders who were executives at other corporations. The executives, with the best of intentions and with no previous knowledge of the founder's questionable history, contacted us to explore a business partnership. Given this break, and our ability to connect findings from it and our own internal information, we identified several other problematic customers with whom we were still doing business and that were all related to the same individual. We had a weekly internal synchronization call where we learned from Operations about the new applicant. Finance shared the status of the additional problematic customers who were not paying for our supplies. And our compliance team began looking at the information, cross-referencing phone numbers, last names, addresses, product models, and market data.

We were able to terminate the contracts with most of the additional entities connected to our large perpetrator in China. The others eventually disappeared once we began working with big retailers and customs authorities, notifying them of the illicit use of our brand.

We spent considerable time looking at the consolidated sales channels and ports of entry for the overarching entity. We informed significant retailers of this entity's unauthorized product sales. We also provided US Customs and Border Protection enough product information to ensure proper identification of unauthorized products connected to this entity and entering the United States.

This case kept us busy for almost four years and took us all the way to South Africa to find another of the perpetrator's fully functional factories. Our data and analysis and ability to identify connections outside our usual processes led us to the South Africa factory, which had family connections to the original perpetrator that we had previously overlooked.

Fortunately, once retailers were educated and brought up to speed on problems with products from this entity, we began to see a significant decrease of this entity's products on retailers' shelves. The South Africa factory also ended operations. While I cannot be sure that we were completely successful, we did learn invaluable lessons from this case that we could apply to others.

APPLYING A TOTAL BUSINESS SOLUTION

Protecting your intellectual property requires a company-wide effort. We have had a long learning curve, but we have seen improvements in having all key functional groups educated and participating in the day-to-day enforcement efforts from their own domains. While the counterfeiting problem will continue to exist, we have become better equipped to handle it, and continue to learn and improve.

Our efforts have involved each principle of the total business solution in some way. These principles should be part of employee orientation trainings as well as part of processes for sales and marketing, finance, product development, supply chain, and legal departments in fighting product counterfeiting. The principles can help build processes to flag entities or internal gaps that could cause future problems. The most important ingredient in adopting a total business solution for brand protection is your executive team. Your program needs to be sponsored at the highest level of the corporation, either by your CEO or by a senior leader with access to the CEO. The tone should come from the top.

PART VI

Tenets of the total business solution

15. Implementation of a total business solution for brand protection: core principles in theory and practice

Jeremy M. Wilson

The total business solution represents a comprehensive and thoughtful way for firms to consider brand infringements and to formulate and implement an effective approach to mitigate risks associated with them. Throughout this volume we have learned a great deal about the nuances of this philosophy and framework, considering essential brand protection program elements, perspectives on risk assessment and response, approaches to resource allocation and performance assessment, and even examples of field implementation of the total business solution. Echoed among the contributions are references to ideas and activities that help illuminate the basic tenets of the total business solution. The purpose of this chapter is to briefly revisit and summarize some of these examples to more fully operationalize and illuminate the interconnectedness of the basic tenets, each of which I will discuss in turn.

IDENTIFY THE INFRINGER AS THE UNSEEN COMPETITOR

The total business solution posits that firms need to recognize the existence and importance of brand infringements and consider the infringer as it would other competitors. This means firms should systematically examine infringers just as they would other competitors. Several contributors spoke about this process. Setting the stage, Chaudhry and Reiners (Chapter 4), Demeré, Sedatole, and I (Chapter 8), and MacInnis (Chapter 11) discussed the nature and growth of infringement risk, which present features demanding acknowledgment and attention by firms. Chaudhry and Reiners explained that illicit trade is quickly growing across all countries in Europe, even where sophisticated approaches to resist it have been implemented. This has been fueled by the rapid evolution of technology, globalization, and the development of e-commerce and frictionless supply chains. Firms may be unaware of consumer concerns regarding product authentication and the negative consequences of illicit trade.

Consumers increasingly find it difficult to confirm their purchases are genuine. Illicit trade, especially when it passes through legitimate retail and online channels, undermines consumer confidence in legitimate goods. Demeré, Sedatole, and I noted that deceptive counterfeits also result in costs associated with lost sales, warranties, and brand image. Yet even purchases of nondeceptive counterfeits have long-term consequences for the intellectual property owner. MacInnis (Chapter 11) highlighted the hidden and opportunistic nature of counterfeiters that enable them to work against firms and maximize profit without regard to product safety or performance considerations. These advantages create an unlevel playing field that has detrimental consequences for both the firm and the consumer. MacInnis suggested the first step in protecting the brand is for the firm to acknowledge its susceptibility to infringement.

Grammich and I picked up on this notion (Chapter 2) in presenting the six elements of a total business solution program model. The first step is problem recognition. This includes defining and setting policy for the problem, obtaining approval to take action on it, and setting responsibility for addressing it. Recognition goes beyond simply noting the problem exists: it requires a response that sees the infringer as the unseen competitor.

Senior leadership committing to this form of action is critical. Sean O'Hearen made this point in both his chapters. In Chapter 3, he explained that the total business solution is consistent with industry standards. Leadership and commitment in setting policy regarding risk is core to the risk management guidelines of the International Organization for Standardization (ISO). He warned this must come before risk assessment, just as Grammich and I did in laying out the total business solution program model. In Chapter 9, he further argued the importance of senior leadership buy-in. This is essential in facilitating cooperation from other parts of the firm, implementing a thoughtful brand protection strategy, and instituting a balanced scorecard for gauging performance. This process, starting with recognition of the problem and the unseen competitor, is key to promoting brand protection.

Silk, Thomas, Paintsil, and I considered the process for facilitating the support of senior leadership (Chapter 7). We highlighted the utility of communicating internally about the risks of counterfeiting and the value of brand protection programs through a communication strategy that includes all parts of the organization. Firms can call upon their skilled communications professionals and their "informational power" to help integrate the brand protection message throughout the organizational culture. More specifically, we indicated the importance of creating awareness around the risks of unauthorized competitors and the reasons to thwart them. This can help persuade others to prioritize brand protection within their own roles. Beyond persuading leadership, internal communications can leverage other forms of power in communicating the expert knowledge, rewards, and potential punishments of a brand protection strategy supported by leading organizational figures. Brand protection professionals can partner with communications staff to persuade others in relevant functions to play their part in mitigating infringement, further establishing organizational culture around brand protection. Similarly, O'Hearen (Chapter 3) found that communication on brand protection is important for external stakeholders as well.

Of course, a communication process around the risk of unseen competitors is not enough. It must be informed by key dimensions, including a formal risk management plan. O'Hearen (Chapter 3) stressed the importance of understanding how the counterfeiter thinks and operates as well as how the firm may counteract the counterfeiter's methods, motivations, and modes of attack. This calls for a systematic risk management plan. Vassallo (Chapter 14) extended this notion to business customers who could essentially become illicit actors as well. Firms need to learn about the authenticity of business partners and verify that they handle intellectual property appropriately. Other resources of the firm, such as field personnel who can make physical checks of products and locations, can help do this.

PRIORITIZE PREVENTION, PROACTIVITY, AND STRATEGY

The total business solution posits that firms should build their brand protection around a cohesive, proactive strategy that emphasizes the reduction of infringement opportunity and thereby prevents incidents from occurring. MacInnis (Chapter 11) commented on the necessary but limited nature of reactive approaches, arguing for strategy that is more forward looking. Moreover, there are many ways in which practitioners advise firms should be proactive. Grammich and I (Chapter 5) reported that many of the most important practitioner-suggested actions that firms can take to protect the brand are proactive. These include communicating and coordinating with key stakeholders and educating the public and law enforcement. Breaking out of the typical reactionary stance to be more proactive, O'Hearen wrote (Chapter 3), requires firms to adopt a risk management mindset. Such a mindset prioritizes the goals of creating and protecting value as well as of providing decision makers with insight about risks that could affect the enterprise.

Strategy Development

The contributors touched on strategy development in many unique ways. Grammich and I (Chapter 2) raised the importance of both strategy development and implementation to build brand protection programs. Firms need to consider strategy development from fixed structural and dynamic procedural dimensions. Structural dimensions include the size, location, expertise, and supporting infrastructure of the brand protection team. These all influence the capacity of the program. The procedural dimensions include the various activities and initiatives the program implements to address brand risk. Both are critical elements in developing a proactive strategy.

Vassallo (Chapter 14) also discussed the importance of building in mechanisms to indicate when not to take an action. There are instances when it may not make sense to pursue infringement problems, such as in jurisdictions where pursuing litigation would be a lengthy process and the expected penalties would be minor. Strategy must balance the cost of inaction against taking an aggressive stance to deter other would-be infringers.

Supply and Demand

Other discussion centered on supply and demand in developing anti-counterfeit strategy. Chaudhry and Reiners (Chapter 4) focused on demand, outlining the importance of fully understanding the reasons consumers purchase illicit goods in guiding a strategy to reduce demand. Considering both the level of complicity and motivations is key to this process. Grammich and I (Chapter 6) found researchers are more likely than practitioners to suggest tactics that focus on both supply and demand. For example, researchers suggested demand for counterfeits may be reduced by minimizing price differentials between genuine and counterfeit products, and by addressing consumer, cultural, product, and institutional characteristics that may affect the purchase of counterfeit products. By contrast, supply-side tactics that may curb counterfeiting include increasing production of high-demand products, and focusing on preparation and shipment of goods at their place of manufacture, transport of goods, freight forwarding, and the operation of handling and storage facilities and terminals. Of course, as Grammich and I (Chapter 2) also noted, both supply and demand are related to opportunity. Proactive efforts should seek to reduce opportunities for counterfeiting as much as possible. Such efforts can succeed through the implementation of situational crime prevention techniques, such as by increasing the difficulty and risks of counterfeiting.

Investment and Costs

As noted by MacInnis (Chapter 11), the probability and scale of the negative consequences associated with counterfeiting necessitate that firms invest strategically in their brand protection programs. Demeré, Sedatole, and I (Chapter 8) examined this issue by exploring the intersection of brand protection cost and strategy, using a cost of quality framework to do so. Firms can use such a framework rather than a strict return-on-investment criterion to allocate brand protection resources across time and place. By understanding the types, relationships, and characteristics of costs, firms can formulate a cost-effective proactive strategy that prevents brand infringement. There are trade-offs between different costs, and some costs have iterative effects that provide benefits into the future or help contribute to the effectiveness of other investments. Investment in prevention and appraisal should reduce failure costs to the point where there may be diminishing returns to preventing quality problems. This means firms should choose a strategic goal of minimizing the total costs of failure, prevention, and appraisal. Such costs will vary by industry and firm. Understanding the relationships between cost categories can help firms better understand the value of their investments and create strategy that has the highest probability of success.

Communication

Silk, Thomas, Paintsil, and I (Chapter 7) considered strategy not through the lens of cost but through the lens of communication. We surmised that strategy development and implementation is a function of power. Practitioners limit themselves, however, if they believe their influence is only based on their position, which is common in organizations. Rather, their influence in seeking change is also associated with their ability to persuade. Hence, effective communication is paramount to brand protection strategy.

Sung's case study of Pfizer (Chapter 12) illustrates the key role of communication in developing strategy, facilitating public–private partnerships, and coordinating with the larger enterprise. Pfizer believes that the public and private sectors can work together to enhance awareness, reduce demand, and mitigate counterfeit risk. Indeed, Pfizer has done this by working internally with core business units and functions such as global security, compliance, corporate affairs, and legal as well as externally with industry partners, to develop a strong education, awareness, and advocacy program that targets patients, the public, policymakers, law enforcement, and healthcare professionals.

External Efforts

Several chapters in this volume described firms working externally to embody a proactive approach. Grammich and I (Chapter 6) discussed the value of public policy tactics for preventing counterfeit product. By working with public authorities to identify and remove counterfeit product, firms can help minimize opportunities for counterfeiters. Education and awareness activities can help establishing a proactive response, as Demeré, Sedatole, and I found (Chapter 8). Consumer education about the dangers of counterfeits and benefits of authentic products as well as training of law enforcement and customs officials can facilitate a proactive stance. Grammich and I (Chapter 2) focused on specific external stakeholders with which firms can partner to execute their strategy as well as leverage their support and resources. Such partners may include law enforcement, academics, regulatory institutions, industry associations, and even other firms, but certainly many more exist. External partners can bring unique skills, expertise, and support on which a firm's brand protection strategy can capitalize. As MacInnis aptly noted (Chapter 11), firms should recognize they are not alone in protecting their brands—there is support through a wide range of partners. Relying on them and leveraging best practices is a great way to bolster brand protection strategy.

Enforcement

Enforcement is typically considered a reactive response to brand infringement. Nevertheless, as Grammich and I demonstrated (Chapter 6), enforcement tactics may also support the prevention and control elements of a total business solution. Both practitioners and researchers identify a need for monitoring and deterring counterfeiters in their potential marketplaces. They both also suggest conducting and documenting test buys and other internal means for monitoring the problem and litigating against infringers. These traditionally reactive actions can support a proactive strategy to the extent that they help firms identify and learn about infringement as well as deter future infringers. As MacInnis (Chapter 11) noted, violations of counterfeiting, if allowed to continue without intervention, can lead others to believe that such conduct is tolerated, thereby contributing to more counterfeiting.

Linkage to Tenets

Contributors touched on how the development of a proactive strategy is linked to other tenets of the total business solution. Grammich and I highlighted examples of the interconnected nature of the tenets in many ways. In Chapter 2, where we presented a total business solution program model, we explained that the development of strategy should rely on risk analysis and performance metrics whereas the implementation of strategy should draw upon internal and external controls for detecting and responding to infringements. More generally, we discussed the value of a holistic and enterprise-wide approach to brand protection strategy in Chapters 5 and 6. Together, these chapters suggested having a layered approach to brand protection strategy that rallies the vast and varied functions of the enterprise for a unified response. O'Hearen (Chapter 9) likewise linked strategy to other tenets, particularly in using performance metrics as part of a balanced scorecard to gauge progress in achieving strategic goals and objectives. Metrics help the brand protection team align its mission with that of the enterprise and communicate its success in doing so.

INTEGRATE CONTROLS AND MECHANISMS FOR DETECTING AND RESPONDING TO INFRINGEMENTS

Controls serve as signals to indicate something may be wrong. They help identify the risk of potential infringements. They can also provide guidance for standardized, pre-planned responses to incidents when they occur. Contributors in this volume spoke highly of their value. For example, Carriero (Chapter 13) noted that executives care about internal controls and mechanisms and want to know which can work best for them. Grammich and I (Chapter 2) found that firms could benefit from leveraging controls as an ongoing source of intelligence for problems. As such, controls can inform risk assessment, response, and even performance measurement.

There are many types of controls that can be instrumental to brand protection. Among them are:

- Consumer complaints (Chapters 2 and 11)
- Contract clauses (Chapter 2)
- Intelligence (Chapter 12)
- Law enforcement inquiries (Chapter 11)
- Market share (Chapter 11)
- Online activity (Chapter 12)
- Physical security of locations and transportation (Chapter 2)
- Real-time inventory data throughout supply chain (Chapter 13)
- Sales (Chapter 2)
- Supplier management/partner audits (Chapters 2 and 9)
- Warranty claims (Chapters 2 and 11).

While not exhaustive, this list highlights the breadth of mechanisms available and the importance of working across the enterprise in the implementation and management of them. Procurement, quality assurance, security, sales, and supply chain are just some of the functions that can collect and share information with the brand protection program about possible infringements.

Grammich and I extended this comprehensive theme in Chapters 2 and 6. We highlighted some different ways of considering the placement of controls. One way is, as noted, for functions across the enterprise to help protect the brand, and to consider how each function can create and make use of brand infringement controls. Another way to organize controls is through the various elements of the supply chain, seeking insight at each tier. Still another way is to differentiate between internal and external controls. Internal controls are those the firm directly implements; external controls are those for which the firm must rely on others, such as distributors, retailers, and law enforcement, to implement. Above all, firms must embed controls in their culture.

Contributors discussed less the utility of standardized responses to problems, but Grammich and I (Chapter 5) noted their importance. We reported that 31 brand protection experts identified 86 tactics associated with establishing firm policy and process and commented on them 100 times in our sample. This demonstrates the importance of policy and standard operating procedures in building brand protection programs. Future research should explore this more fully.

MAXIMIZE DATA, METRICS, AND ANALYSIS TO ASSESS AND MITIGATE RISK AND GAUGE PERFORMANCE

The importance of evidence, measurement, and analysis in building effective brand protection programs cannot be overstated. They essentially fuel all the other tenets of the total business solution by illuminating problems, informing responses, and assessing success. This is supported by the fact that analysis in support of brand protection is associated with no fewer than 27 functions across the entire enterprise (Chapter 5). Contributors to this volume highlighted many important aspects of this tenet, explaining its importance, outlining risk elements and approaches, delineating performance frameworks, and discussing the nuances of metrics. I summarize elements of these discussions in the paragraphs that follow.

Importance of Analysis and Metrics

The chapters in this volume illustrated the importance of analysis and metrics from different perspectives. O'Hearen (Chapters 3 and 9) explained that risk assessment is the central mechanism for promoting cross-functional and value chain relationships in the pursuit of a proactive and integrative brand protection strategy. This is because it creates general awareness and understanding, establishes priorities, informs activities, and affects resource allocation. The output of such analysis should provide decision makers with an understanding of the likelihood and potential consequences of particular risks relative to business objectives. This is instrumental to "right-sizing" investment in the brand protection risk. Risk assessment is an ongoing and dynamic process that supports understanding of the enemy's opportunity structures and capabilities relative to the firm's own strengths and weaknesses. This process is critical because it informs risk management, which prioritizes the protection of firm value, such as brand equity, business reputation, revenue, and market share, and consumer health, safety, and trust. Each business will determine what level of risk it finds acceptable. The role of brand protection is to clearly present the risk, and options to mitigate it, to inform that decision. A brand protection scorecard can support this decision-making process and help gauge and communicate progress in addressing the risk.

Complementing risk analysis is performance assessment and metrics. Grammich and I (Chapter 2) drew attention to its importance for determining how well the brand protection program is meeting its goals, and whether it is adding value to the enterprise, noting that it also enables a culture of continuous improvement and learning. Ongoing modification of plans, based on continuous measurement of risk and progress, is necessary for preventing and responding to brand infringement crises. Grammich, Demeré, Sedatole, and I (Chapter 10) similarly noted the importance of metrics. Firms routinely want to know if their brand protection efforts are achieving meaningful results. As a result, C-suite executives expect performance metrics, and often allocate resources based upon them. Given measurement challenges, firms should capture multiple metrics over time on each item of interest. These can help advance proactive brand protection strategy.

Risk Assessment and Approaches

Several chapters presented approaches to risk assessment. Grammich and I (Chapters 5 and 6), for example, pointed out areas on which risk analysis might focus. These include product markets, physical and virtual marketplaces, product returns, and excess product, all of which are areas where counterfeiters may try to infiltrate. Firms can also gain an understanding of counterfeiters by examining errors counterfeiters make (e.g., in packaging details), counterfeit products, country-specific elements of risk, stages of product production, and planning for products not yet even in the market. Effectively addressing the diversity of counterfeiting risk requires enlisting the support of and coordinating business leaders and many firm functions, such as research and development, legal, security, manufacturing, marketing, sales, packaging, and quality assurance.

Grammich and I (Chapter 2) offered a framework for examining these various forms of risk by focusing on specific and likely threats, vulnerabilities, and consequences. Independently identifying and estimating these elements can illustrate where they intersect and the risk is greatest. The outcome of this analysis informs proactive strategy and efficient resource allocation to prevent the most dangerous infringements.

Demeré, Sedatole, and I (Chapter 8) complemented this framework in discussing brand protection investments. The cost of quality framework offers a unique perspective on risk analysis for brand protection. It can assist managers in employing and organizing performance metrics and data analysis to assess and mitigate risk. This approach helps overcome challenges in measuring counterfeit prevalence by understanding the long-term effects of different forms of cost and how they interact to advance resource allocation and metric development.

Chaudhry and Reiners (Chapter 4) focused on a specific element of risk—consumer motivations. Understanding consumer motivations in the purchase of illicit products can help craft approaches to addressing illicit trade. Though price matters, so too do other influences. Consumers are often aware of the implications of illicit trade. Hence, brand protection practitioners should help enable consumers to authenticate products. This is especially important as online commerce grows.

There are still other ways to consider and approach risk, as O'Hearen noted (Chapter 3). Brand protection programs can learn much about risk assessment via collaboration with other units, such as cybersecurity, that routinely assess risk. There may also be advantages to integrating brand protection into an existing enterprise risk management framework.

Performance Frameworks

There are many ways to assess the performance of brand protection programs. This volume introduced some useful approaches. From a broad perspective, O'Hearen (Chapter 9) offered a strategic scorecard approach to performance measurement. A scorecard can move performance assessment beyond financial measures and consider other important aspects such as those pertaining to the customer, internal processes, and innovation and learning. The measures chosen for a brand protection scorecard should be linked to a firm's goals and properly vetted so that only key performance indicators are incorporated. This broad approach would foster clarity and alignment among managers and staff, thereby leading to improved organizational performance and goal achievement.

Carriero (Chapter 13) introduced a more focused framework, offering a useful way for calculating the impact of a brand protection program. Responding to the reality that executives always want to know the impact that the brand protection program is having (even new programs), what it is saving, and how it can be improved, he laid out a formula that estimates impact as a function of units seized, online enforcement, and restitution. In doing so, he acknowledged the importance of recognizing the impact of activities that are difficult to measure. A prime example here is law enforcement awareness training. Such an activity is essential to brand protection because it directly affects the number of cases that law enforcement officials report, not just in the year of training but beyond. This follow-on effect is difficult to assess but still important to consider. Other important activities might be equally difficult to measure. Vassallo (Chapter 14), in contending that brand protection is an art, similarly illustrated the importance of some activities that are difficult to measure. There is no single set of rules for pursuing goals and measuring achievement—some results are direct whereas others are indirect. For this reason, firms should not rely exclusively on process as it could result in missing the outlier—such as the achievement that could not be measured.

Metrics

Metrics are useful but tricky. They help estimate costs, risk, productivity, impact, and value/return on investment, thereby informing critical decisions about strategy and resource allocation. They also pose challenges in terms of reliability, validity, precision, measurement error, and diverting attention from important concepts that are difficult to measure. Grammich, Demeré, Sedatole, and I (Chapter 10) offered several important lessons regarding metrics and their use:

- Firms should develop and interpret performance metrics frameworks based on their own values and perspectives, as there is no one best way to measure performance and deploy metrics.
- Metrics should allow firms to distinguish between various elements of their program performance, including investments/costs, activities, outcomes/ impacts, and value/return on investment.
- Firms should incorporate multiple measures for each concept of interest to allow triangulation of true levels, and, importantly, permit systematic collection that can gauge progress over time.
- Adopting commonly understood and accepted business metrics can help brand protection programs acquire greater support from the firm.
- Metrics may change depending on market presence, product maturity, and firm needs.
- Firms should make greater efforts to develop and compile metrics that gauge the impact of brand protection programs, including metrics on brand image, counterfeit prevalence, consumer safety, and sales.
- Firms should also measure the effects of what they are not doing.
- Firms should use metrics to gauge the effectiveness of activities as well as the larger brand protection program.

Grammich and I (Chapter 2) further noted the importance of using metrics to assess the implementation of program activities. This is necessary because there are often obstacles in rolling out strategies and it is not possible to know whether effects can be attributed to program elements unless it is first known that the activities were implemented properly. Information on implementation fidelity, extent, and variation can help diagnose problems in performance and optimize program effects. Metrics should include all aspects of brand protection. Data collection will continue to evolve as firms identify and manage the data they need.

Sung (Chapter 12) provided insight on how metrics are used in practice. Pfizer increasingly relies on data-driven approaches to assess risk, inform mitigation, and evaluate effectiveness relative to patient health and safety. Global Security monitors metrics associated with enforcement, educational, and advocacy activities. Such metrics include counterfeit Pfizer product seized, illicit manufacturing plants dismantled, illicit online pharmacies shut down, and anti-counterfeiting trainings conducted. This information is key for improving investigations and illuminating ways to improve resource allocation. In fact, these metrics are so important that Pfizer instituted a data quality assurance program to help ensure the timeliness, completeness, accuracy, and reliability of the data used for decision making.

FORMULATE AND EXECUTE A HOLISTIC APPROACH THAT INTEGRATES AND COORDINATES ALL PARTS OF THE FIRM FOR BRAND PROTECTION

This volume has addressed in many ways the need for a comprehensive, integrative approach to combating brand infringements, how it can work in practice, and the benefits of its implementation. Below I summarize its discussion on these points.

Comprehensive Components

Grammich and I (Chapters 5 and 6) presented a broad perspective on this in distilling brand protection tactics into a dozen broad categories that can be implemented across 35 specific firm functions. We thereby demonstrated that maximizing brand protection requires a multifaceted approach for rallying and coordinating virtually all organizational players to implement and conduct diverse activities across all levels and product life cycles. We illustrated what firms can do to protect the brand and the role for each function in that mission. The many options available to prevent and respond to brand infringements represent an opportunity to develop a layered strategy that is thoughtful, holistic, and proactive. An enterprise-wide approach would have obvious implications for the development and administration of a formal brand protection program. A brand protection program should not necessarily lead all brand protection efforts. Rather, a firm should think carefully about which types of activities the program could most effectively spearhead and which it could most effectively coordinate, leaving actual implementation to other firm partners. This inter-disciplinary posture is important for addressing the multifaceted risk of brand infringements. It counters the typical siloed approach taken by many firms that concentrates all effort in a single unit with little connection to others. In fact, we extended this notion in Chapter 2, where we explained that a holistic and proactive approach goes beyond coordinating internal stakeholders and requires enlisting the support of external partners as well.

Executive Support

As in many organizational initiatives, executive support is key to developing and successfully implementing a holistic, proactive strategy. Contributors demonstrated this in different ways. Vassallo (Chapter 14) spoke of the impor-tance of ensuring brand protection is viewed as everyone's (as opposed to a program's) problem to address. Success here is a function of how well senior leaders, such as the board of directors, chief executive officer, chief financial officer, and heads of sales and business units, acknowledge and commit to a coordinated plan that is properly resourced. Sales, marketing, finance, supply chain, legal, and other departments are important components of a brand infringement strategy, especially in identifying and responding to problems, but the most important element is the sponsorship of and tone on brand pro-tection that emanate from the highest level of the corporation. Grammich and I (Chapter 5) also discussed the importance of messaging and resourcing from senior leadership. We also noted the importance of tone and ensuring everyone sees brand protection as their job, highlighting the importance of senior leaders in developing a culture of brand protection and promoting the belief that the firm's most valuable asset is its intellectual property.

Silk, Thomas, Paintsil, and I (Chapter 7) acknowledged the importance of senior leadership support and address how to acquire it. Programs not located within high levels of the hierarchy, or at least supported by such levels, have less power to influence change. In such situations, brand protection programs should consider how else they might access other sources of power. Persuasive communication is a key strategy for those pursuing greater organizational support.

Culture and Communication

There are aspects of culture and communication that go beyond executive leadership in building brand protection programs. Grammich and I (Chapter 5) drew on the reporting of brand protection tactics by practitioners to establish the importance of communication and coordination with multiple stakeholders inside and outside the firm. Highlighting the value of a holistic approach, we referenced experts noting the value of embedding brand protection in the culture of the firm, networking around best practices, engaging in benchmarking, and exploring innovative brand protection solutions, all of which are predicated on effective communication. Silk, Thomas, Paintsil, and I (Chapter 7) explored several of these concepts further, focusing more on internal aspects of how culture and communication relate to a comprehensive strategy. Because culture affects how staff perceive brand infringement, prioritizing brand protection requires engendering a firm culture where attitudes, norms, and expectations about brand risk and protection are visible and accepted within all levels and parts of the firm. A persuasive internal communications strategy, coupled with tactics to gain compliance, can help ensure brand protection stays at the forefront of each functional unit and facilitate any necessary organizational change. Such a strategy can help influence knowledge, attitudes, intentions, norms, and subsequent behavior that promotes a culture of brand protection across the enterprise. A clear and shared vision for brand protection that is communicated through strategic planning is a necessary part of this process. Individuals leading brand protection efforts must consider and communicate how different firm functions can uniquely and synergistically contribute to this vision.

Strategy

A broad, enterprise-wide perspective is foundational to a total business solution approach, as O'Hearen and Sung illustrated in different ways. In Chapter 3, O'Hearen found that taking a broader perspective of the entire value chain rather than a more narrow focus on the supply chain facilitates a more holistic approach to brand protection. In Chapter 9, he offered the balanced scorecard to link metrics to strategy. By comprehensively tracking key performance indicators, the balanced scorecard simultaneously and efficiently illustrates risk, performance, cross-functional collaboration, and the integration of best practices. In this way, the balanced scorecard is a tool for promoting a comprehensive strategy.

In her case study of Pfizer, Sung (Chapter 12) offered a view of a holistic, strategic approach as implemented in practice. Pfizer's product integrity function is based within its Global Security team but works enterprise-wide, cross-functionally, and cross-regionally with other business units. A useful way to envision a comprehensive brand protection strategy is to differentiate it into primary component parts. For Pfizer, that means focusing on reducing counterfeit demand and supply. Informed by a data-driven approach to risk mitigation, Pfizer reduces demand through education, awareness, and advocacy initiatives, and reduces supply through proactive enforcement measures. Importantly, Pfizer's focus on risk and outcomes encourages it to think innovatively about using data to inform decision making and resource allocation. Its focus punctuates the value of collaborating with other functions across the enterprise.

Tactics

While O'Hearen and Sung spoke of broader aspects of holistic strategy, Grammich and I (Chapter 5) discussed more specific elements that contribute to a comprehensive approach to brand protection. We outlined how individual firm functions can and should implement multiple forms of tactics. For example, in addition to enforcement, the security function can play a role in influencing public policy through networking with law enforcement and other government agencies and by suggesting modifications to existing policies. Additionally, security can provide resources by hiring investigators, working with human resources to identify the best candidates.

We also noted how multiple functions can play a role in advancing specific tactic categories. For example, product protection tactics can be implemented by means of packaging via tamper-proof packaging, preventing re-use of packaging, and deploying track-and-trace or other packaging technology. Likewise, engineering, manufacturing, quality assurance, research and development, supply chain, and warehousing and distribution can all ensure brand protection is prominently considered in product design, disposal of excess production, and product obsolescence. Yet another example is communication and coordination tactics, which can differ by function as well as phase of response to counterfeiting incidents. Sales can communicate internal information on discovered incidents. Security can provide communication both on incidents and on how best to network with other private organizations to investigate incidents. Marketing can communicate the dangers of counterfeit products and develop other messaging for brand protection in efforts to prevent brand protection incidents. Media and public relations can prepare communications plans for counterfeiting incidents and communicate successes that have been made in the fight against product counterfeiting. The brand protection function itself can implement many tactics, though among its most important roles is rallying the support of other functions in promoting protection of the brand.

Learning

Organizational learning facilitates a holistic approach to brand protection. A total business solution calls upon brand protection programs to reach out across the firm and beyond to learn from the experience of others. Silk, Thomas, Paintsil, and I (Chapter 7) expounded upon this in our discussion of the learning organization. Shared vision and systems thinking are fundamental aspects of learning organizations. Establishing a shared vision requires brand protection leaders to carefully consider how different firm functions contribute to brand protection goals. Systems thinking demands those in other units look beyond their functional roles to see how their own actions, and inactions, affect brand protection strategy. Grammich and I (Chapter 6) also found this sentiment reflected in tactics reported by brand protection practitioners. They indicated that resource-based tactics, such as protecting a product throughout its life cycle and addressing the needs of products in different environments, help integrate all parts of the firm in a shared brand protection strategy. Practitioners advised that all functions are necessary to provide continuous support. Brand protection teams that draw upon the resources and expertise available across a firm will be best positioned to mitigate brand infringements.

Vassallo (Chapter 14) provided an effective illustration of how this can work in the field. She showcased an infringement incident concerning a large operation where enforcement efforts were challenging. To learn how this entity could operate, she drew upon the resources and expertise of finance, sales, operations, compliance, and legal functions. This led to discovering additional problematic customers tied to the lead infringer. Weekly synchronization calls with representatives of other functions provided a wealth of information that helped shape and support a response. Her team was able to terminate the contracts with most of the entities associated with the lead infringer, and the others disappeared, along with the illicit products associated with the lead infringer, as the enforcement strategy rolled out.

External Benefits

While the brand protection program can learn from other firm functions, Carriero (Chapter 13) illustrated how other firm functions can learn from brand protection efforts. He outlined how smart technology, such as radio frequency identification and near field communication labels, can benefit not only brand protection but also sales, sourcing, quality assurance, asset protection, logistics, retail, marketing, and still other functions. Smart tags can assist marketing and sales teams, he suggested, by tracking and tracing sensitive products firms provide to sales representatives, to "influencers," and for customer wear tests. Use of the tags can also enhance in-store marketing campaigns and consumer engagement. Altogether, new technologies can provide synergistic benefits for brand protection as well as the larger enterprise.

CREATE AND PROMOTE A CULTURE OF CONTINUOUS IMPROVEMENT

A fundamental premise of the total business solution is that firms must continually learn, innovate, and evolve. This is necessary to keep up with, if not stay ahead of, infringers, and to seek ways of becoming more effective and efficient. Contributors touched on this principle in several ways.

Ongoing Learning

Grammich and I (Chapter 2) noted a circular process of learning–action/change–learning, which needs to be embedded in firm culture. Innovation that results from such a process needs to include shorter-term actions to account for the emergence of new threats as well as longer-term shifts in program structure as threats evolve and change the risk landscape. This continuous improvement cycle is not only aspirational but necessary. Learning from experience also promotes a comprehensive approach that integrates all parts of the firm and informs all other aspects of a total business solution program model. In short, ongoing assessment and adopting a learning organization stance helps brand protection programs garner support and offer a means to improve the program over time.

Silk, Thomas, Paintsil, and I (Chapter 7) expanded on this notion, referencing the basic building blocks necessary for supporting a learning organization. Shared vision, systems thinking, mental models, personal mastery, and team learning help create an organizational culture that emphasizes proactivity, integration, and innovation. Persuasive communication is a critical component of these processes.

Expanding Focus

This comprehensive approach to learning can coincide with a broad perspective of the value that brand protection brings to the firm, as Grammich, Demeré, Sedatole, and I discussed (Chapter 10). Several firm representatives who claimed to have successful brand protection programs conceded they could do better, with one arguing that brand protection programs need a dynamic approach that is constantly re-evaluated. One example of evolution is the way in which firms define the contributions of brand protection. Many consider financial return on investment to be the key criterion, but this is often difficult to measure. One way forward is to reconceptualize brand protection in terms of the larger value proposition it offers. This includes its ability to protect the consumer and society, improve brand integrity and value, enhance communication and coordination across functions, and exercise corporate social responsibility. Firms need to learn how brand protection can best influence these broader outcomes, which also requires they develop equally broad metrics to facilitate an assessment of progress.

Supporting Frameworks

The cost of quality framework (Chapter 8) and balanced scorecard (Chapter 9) are complementary frameworks for helping firms learn from their own data. The cost of quality framework represents a resource allocation model that requires firms to continuously learn about different approaches for addressing infringements and their costs and short-term, long-term, and interactive utility. Demeré, Sedatole, and I (Chapter 8) detailed how this information can be combined with information about the costs of infringement to develop a strategy that results in the lowest overall cost to the firm. This framework is a direct example of how continuous learning can help firms navigate the dynamic nature of infringement and alternative responses to it, thereby producing an evidence-based, proactive strategy that is sensitive to the relationship between current costs and future outcomes. The balanced scorecard as offered by O'Hearen (Chapter 9) focuses more on traditional aspects of gauging program performance, but in a broad and systematic way. The formulation of a set of well-conceived performance metrics can educate firms about their achievements and struggles, helping them to diagnose where implementation problems may be occurring and to identify better ways to contribute to enterprise goals.

Specific Approaches

While much of the discussion centered on larger learning approaches, other discourse shed additional light on creating a culture of continuous improvement by identifying more specific or narrow ways that help firms learn and innovate. Vassallo (Chapter 14) wrote that brand protection professionals, like artists, will always see something more that can be done and can continually learn from each other. One of the most valuable resources available to firms is the brand protection community itself and its openness to share best practices. Cultivating relationships and sharing and receiving information from peers are critical and efficient ways for practitioners to learn. Grammich and I (Chapter 6) noted other specific ways for firms to continuously learn. These include gathering additional information from customers, providing briefings and regular communications to firm functions, and networking. In addition, we found that researchers raised the utility of assessing complaints. Together, these tactics center on learning by way of intelligence gathering, education, and awareness.

Learning in Practice

Sung's case study of Pfizer (Chapter 12) illustrated how elements of broad frameworks and specific activities converge in practice. Pfizer continuously self-assesses and evaluates the effectiveness of its product integrity program. It monitors the evolving external environment, assesses the nature and scope of the counterfeit risk, and coordinates across the enterprise to enhance its risk mitigation strategies. Its Global Security function explores creative and new ways to leverage its data. To go beyond measuring productivity to assess impact, Pfizer has explored using data science to statistically associate anti-counterfeiting activities with firm outcomes. This kind of information is paramount to communicating the value of product integrity to internal and external stakeholders. Learning and continuous improvement is fundamental to Global Security's total business solution approach to achieving its goals.

THE INTERCONNECTED NATURE OF THE TENETS

In this chapter, I attempted to highlight many aspects of the total business solution by referencing discussions and details offered by the contributors. These have included arguments in support of the tenets as well as features, nuances, components, implementation examples, successes, and challenges as offered by practitioners and scholars. The total business solution represents a useful philosophy and framework for establishing and advancing brand protection programs. Firms can operationalize it in countless ways to best address their risks, needs, and goals. While the discussion in this chapter centered on articulating aspects of each tenet, an obvious observation worth highlighting is their interconnected nature. For instance:

- A proactive strategy requires engaging all parts of the firm.
- Controls help gauge risk and monitor performance.
- Risk analysis helps the firm learn about the unseen competitor and informs strategy.
- Data and analysis are necessary for assessment, learning, and innovation, which inform all other tenets.
- Learning grounds and informs all other elements.

This suggests that investments in any one tenet are not static or fixed but are dynamic and multiplicative. These principles build on and influence each other so that improvements and capacity development in one can lead to advances in another with iterative and cumulative effects over time. This is encouraging news for firms building or bolstering brand protection programs. As demonstrated in this volume, the total business solution offers a flexible, mutually reinforcing pathway, supported by research and field experience, for firms to protect their brands.

Index

prioritization of prevention,
proactivity and strategy
7, 15, 42, 250–54
total business solution model 9–10,
21–32
assessment 23, 31–2
performance measurement 22–3,
30–31, 257–8
see also brand protection
impact (BPI);
performance metrics;
scorecard
problem recognition 22, 23–5, 249
risk assessment, *see* risk assessment
strategy development 22, 23, 25,
27–9, 250–51
strategy implementation 22, 23, 30
total program perspective 164, 168–72
total program value recovery (TPVR)
168, 169–70, 171, 172
total tactics 81–4, 96–9
integration of tactics and functions
86–91
see also tactics
total value recovery (TVR) 175, 176
track-and-trace technologies 21, 108,
119–20, 238
trademarks 108, 117
training
law enforcement 107, 113, 179,
235–6, 257–8
tactics 107, 113
Tsang, A. H. C. 110
Tzu, Sun 37

unauthorized distributor 56
unexpected, preparedness for the 243
unique tactics 81–4, 96–9, 124–5, 132
integration of tactics and functions
91–5
see also tactics

United States (US) 63, 219, 221–2
Customs and Border Protection 4,
188
Department of Homeland Security
(DHS) 219
Office of Strategy, Policy and
Plans 128
unofficial retail outlets 65–7, 68

valuation metrics 190, 191, 193, 197,
202, 205
use of 199–200
value of brand protection 13, 188–207,
264–5
importance of demonstrating 194–5
see also performance metrics
value chain 38–9, 47, 56
risk assessment 47, 50–55
vertically integrating supply chains 78
victimless crime 70–71
Viot, C. 113
vulnerability of product counterfeiting
26, 27, 28

Wang, Y. 119
warning signs of counterfeiting attacks
216
Watkins, K. 8–9
websites enforcement 107, 114–15, 227,
230–33, 235
Wilcock, A. E. 112, 113
Wilcox, K. 109–10
Wilson, J. M. 6, 28–9, 41, 47, 49, 50, 55,
114, 115, 116, 123, 129, 131–2,
133, 135–6, 185, 225
Wimmer, H. 115
Wong, K. H. M. 119

Yoo, B. 117
Yoon, V. Y. 115

Printed and bound by CPI Group (UK) Ltd, Croydon, CR0 4YY

16/04/2025

14658488-0004